Zulus & Egyptians

W. C. F. MOLYNEUX

Zulus & Egyptians
A British Officer's Experiences During the Zulu
War, 1879 and the Egyptian War, 1882

ILLUSTRATED

Campaigning in South Africa and Egypt
W. C. F. Molyneux

The Battle of Tel-el-Kebir
James Grant

LEONAUR

Zulus & Egyptians
A British Officer's Experiences During the Zulu War, 1879 and the Egyptian War, 1882
Campaigning in South Africa and Egypt
by W. C. F. Molyneux
The Battle of Tèl-el-Kebir
By James Grant

ILLUSTRATED

FIRST EDITION

Leonaur is an imprint of Oakpast Ltd
Copyright in this form © 2021 Oakpast Ltd

ISBN: 978-1-915234-28-5 (hardcover)
ISBN: 978-1-915234-29-2 (softcover)

http://www.leonaur.com

Publisher's Notes

The views expressed in this book are not necessarily
those of the publisher.

Contents

CHAPTER 1

A Hereditary Profession

It is a great thing for a boy to know from his earliest days that he must follow the profession of his forefathers. From the mere conversation of his parents and their friends he seems to learn intuitively all about it. He knows the terms, the aims, the code of honour, and the aspirations of his kin and their cloth. The family portraits, the old swords, the old flint-lock pistol in the hall, the medals, and the records of how they were won, are to a boy most sacred things: he feels bound in honour to be worthy of those who went before him; he is sure that if he fails in his examination his life is as good as done; and he will strain every nerve to pass, for he knows that the life will be congenial to him, and that his success will be a source of pride to his relations. Is it much wonder, then, that two of the descendants of the following race should have decided, time out of mind, that they could never be anything but soldiers?

Our father was a soldier, of whom Sir John Keane (afterwards Lord Keane of Ghuznee), commanding in the West Indies, wrote to Lord Worcester on September 6th, 1824:

> His regiment best shows his qualifications as an officer, for in my life I never saw a corps so near perfection.

This corps was the old 77th Foot, and my father was its adjutant.

Our uncle was a sailor first, who served five years as midshipman in H.M.S. *Plantagenet*, was engaged in the attack on the French fleet by Admiral Cornwallis on August 21st, 1805, assisted at the landing of the army in Portugal in August, 1808, and at its re-embarkation during and after the Battle of Corunna on January 17th and 18th, 1809. He was then transferred to H.M.S. *Sabrina*, and accompanied the expedition to Walcheren in July, 1809, served in the squadron of gunboats in the Scheldt covering the disembarkation of the army, and at the bombardment and capture of the fortresses of Ter Vere, Ramakins, and Flushing.

He landed with a division of sailors on the island of South Beveland; was present at the taking of Fort Batz, and on duty there during the repulse of several attacks made by the French and Dutch flotilla on it; was in frequent gunboat actions covering the retreat of the army on its evacuation of the islands in December, 1809, and, in consequence of fever contracted on this occasion, was invalided and discharged by an order from the Admiralty soon after landing in England in 1810.

He next obtained a commission in the army, and joined the 4th Foot in the Peninsula in 1811, was promoted lieutenant into the 77th Foot in 1812, was engaged at Ciudad Rodrigo and Badajos, at the operations on the Bidassoa and Adour, the affairs at St. Jean de Luz and the Mayor's House at Bidart, and at the investment and surrender of Bayonne; and finally, was sent home in charge of the wounded and invalids of the Fifth Division in August, 1814.

I will conclude his record by adding that he was adjutant of the 77th before our father; that he was the author of the *Explanation of the XIX. Manoeuvres*, 1819, issued prior to Dundas's Drill-Book of 1825; that he received the decoration of the Royal Hanoverian Guelphic Order, and the war medal with a clasp for Badajos in 1848, thirty-four years after the work was done (thanks to the exertions of Charles, fifth Duke of Richmond, but for whom he and his comrades would never have had a medal at all); and that he died a lieutenant-general. Medals and decorations were not very liberally bestowed in those days; it was only in 1856, after our alliance with the Turks, the French, and the Sardinians in the Crimea, that they began to be plentiful in our country.

Our grandfather joined the 6th Foot as ensign in 1786, served in North America from 1787 to 1793, and on the outbreak of the French Revolution joined Sir Charles Grey's expedition against the French West India Islands in 1794. At the conclusion of that short and most successful campaign he returned home, served subsequently in the Irish Rebellion of 1798, and, like his son, died a lieutenant-general.

For the rest I will merely say that those I have mentioned handed down traditions of a famous soldier high in the confidence of William, Duke of Normandy; of another who was knighted for his services in 1286 in Gascony; of a third who was with Edward the Third at the taking of Calais in 1347, and got a *fleur-de-lis* added to his shield; of a fourth who was knighted by the Black Prince on the field of Navaret in 1367, and afterwards buried in Canterbury Cathedral; of a fifth who distinguished himself at Agincourt in 1415; of a sixth slain at the Battle of Bloreheath in 1459; of a seventh who was knighted on Flodden Field in 1513 and given a tiger *passant proper* on a crown *or* for his crest; and of many others who served their sovereigns loyally and well in many capacities.

All these records, then, made us two boys mad to go to the wars; and it seems that others of our line were affected in the same way, for about twenty relations followed the drum or went to sea. Young blood is hot, or, if not, the youngster is not likely to be of much use; and, records or no records, there will never be a dearth of candidates for the combatant branches of the army and navy, however severe examinations be made, or however hard officers be worked or used. But "our praises are our wages." When the officer is done with, he is retired with scant courtesy. The army has spoiled his taste for milder occupations; he has gambled for one or more bits of ribbon with his life; what excitement remains that has not been discounted?

So, when he is retired against his will, he vows that the army and navy are no professions nowadays. It is well then, that young blood is hot; that it looks not beyond the present, choosing only the best and most successful of its race as examples; that it overlooks the one who was not successful, the other who was retired for no fault of his own in the prime of life; for by such hot-headed ones was the Empire built up, and their chief desire is to help to make it greater.

★★★★★★★★★★★★

After a due course of training—first at a private school near Evesham, then at Cheltenham, and finally at Sandhurst—I was, on December 23rd, 1864, gazetted ensign in the 22nd Foot, my brother Tom following me to the same regiment nine months later.

I was at home at the time I was gazetted, and my half-brother, then a brevet-major in the 69th, was there also on leave. I got hold of his army-list, looked for the 22nd, and saw *Cheshire* after the number, and Meeanee, Scinde, Hyderabad at the head. "Why on earth don't they put me to the Gloucestershire Regiment, and not to this one which does not seem to have done much?" I said.

"Because they gazetted you to the first regiment that had a vacancy. The County regiment has nothing to do with the county; I don't suppose there is a single Gloucestershire man among the officers of the 28th or 61st; nor a Cheshire man in the 22nd; you will probably never be quartered in Cheshire at all. I am a 'South Lincolnshire' man, and I have never been in the county in my life. Besides, you need not grumble at being appointed to old Charley Napier's regiment. Have you never heard what he said when he gave them new colours? I have got the account somewhere upstairs; I will go and fetch it." Down he came. "Listen to this," he said;

'That brave regiment which won the Battle of Meeanee, the regiment which stood by the King of England at Dettingen, stood by the celebrated Lord Peterborough at Barcelona, and into the arms of whose grenadiers the immortal Wolfe fell on the Heights of Abraham—well may I exult in the command of such a regiment.'

"Is not that good enough for you?"

"Why are not Dettingen and Quebec on the colours?"

"Because they were fought over a hundred years ago: that has been the rule as regards keeping the names there; but the 22nd lost all their records in Scinde in 1843, when their baggage was looted by the Beloochees. In those days, regiments did not keep a duplicate copy at home, and they would have some trouble to prove their services prior to that year; but everybody in the service knows all about it. The lace on their tunics is oak-leaf pattern, and at inspections they wear oak-leaf in their shakos. This was given to them by George the Second at Dettingen for being 'firm as their native oak.' Do you want any more history?"

"Is Sir John Pennefather, who is the colonel of the regiment, the general we used to see at Aldershot?" I asked.

"Yes; he and Pym Harding, the lieutenant-colonel of the first battalion, are both Meeanee men. You have not heard of that fight, so I will tell you that Napier, with the 22nd and some native corps, altogether under three thousand strong, attacked and routed over twenty thousand of the Hyderabad *Ameers*; and, according to some wag, sent home a laconic despatch, '*Peccavi* (I have Scinde).' Yes, the 22nd is good and smart enough for any man; buff facings help their smartness; I think you are in luck."

The older soldier was right. I found the officers like a band of brothers, the slow promotion proving how well they got on together, and how loath they were to leave the old corps.

In after years, I searched to try and make up the lost records. The official account at the War Office, compiled six years after the papers were lost in Scinde, allows that the corps was raised by the Duke of Norfolk at Chester in 1689 at the accession of King William and Mary. It gives the regiment credit for fighting at Carrickfergus, the Boyne,

Ballymore, Athlone, Aghrim, Galway, Gibraltar, Louisburg, Quebec, Montreal, Dominica, Martinique (1762), Grenada, St. Lucia (1762), St. Vincent, Moro Castle (Havannah), Bunkers Hill, Flat Bush, Brooklyn, New York, Fort Washington, Rhode Island, Newport, Quaker's Hill, Martinique (1794), St. Lucia (1794), Guadaloupe, St. Domingo, Barrabatta (Province of Cuttack), Deeg, Bhurtpore, Mauritius, Imaunghur, Meeanee, Hyderabad, Forts Panulla, Pownghur, Monuhurr and Monsentosh; but it does not give it credit for Barcelona nor for Dettingen; and when on May 4th, 1882, the old battles of over a century ago were replaced on the regimental colours, the Cheshire were not allowed to have established their right even to Dettingen, though in that very decade their long-borne acorn and oak leaf were sanctioned as a badge for their new territorial uniform.

I joined my regiment at Parkhurst in the Isle of Wight, where the Fifth Depot Battalion was located. After being passed for parade, and having completed the musketry-course, I found life lively enough; but in the summer I received orders to join my battalion at the Mauritius, whither it had been sent six months previously from Malta. Of Mauritius I have many pleasant recollections, but I must get on to the proper purpose of my book, and it must suffice to say that after two years, in August, 1867, the battalion was at home again.

Then followed a period of regimental duty in country-quarters: Newcastle, where we really felt ourselves at home, so many of our men being Tynesiders; Sheffield, dirty and dull; Manchester, dirty also but less dull, and as hospitable as Sheffield was the reverse; and finally, Aldershot, where the soldier is at any rate never allowed to be idle. A period of musketry-instruction at Hythe, and some colliery riots near Barnsley, were the chief breaks in the somewhat uniform course of these years, till in February, 1872, I joined the Staff College, of which Colonel (not yet Sir Edward) Hamley was then *commandant*.

This was the time of Mr. Gladstone's first administration, when Mr. Cardwell, his Secretary of State for War, was engaged in putting the queen's army in order; a Reign of Terror, as it has been aptly described, for the British soldier, who lived from day to day in a fever of apprehension as to what was going to happen to him next. It began in 1870, and for years all branches of the army were in a state of angry excitement, for every corps and department was either reformed, reorganised, remodelled, or renamed. But this is all ancient history now. For good or ill the work has been done; for which, others are as competent to judge as I am.

11

In 1874, after two busy and pleasant years, I passed out of the Staff College, just in time for the summer drills at Aldershot. Colonel Thesiger (now Lord Chelmsford) had been appointed to command an infantry brigade at them, and I was fortunate enough to receive the offer of acting as his *aide-de-camp*. It was only for a month, but it gained me the friendship of the best and kindest-hearted man I have ever known, a right good soldier, and the most perfect of gentlemen.

This was indeed a fortunate month for me, for two years later, when Colonel Thesiger received the command of the First Infantry Brigade at Aldershot, he offered to take me with him as his permanent *aide-de-camp*. I had then been employed for two years in the Intelligence Department, first as an outdoor worker in Cumberland and Westmoreland, and latterly at Adair House. My chief did not approve of the change. "Anyone can be an *aide-de-camp*," he said: "but anyone can't get employed here."

"I know that," was my answer; "but I have not had uniform on for two years, and I never seem to see a soldier, except from the top of the Horse Guards at the Queen's birthday parade. I only do clerk's work: I've no chance of getting my company and a permanent post here; and the regiment is always asking to have me back for duty in Ireland."

"Well, he said, "I'm very sorry to lose you now, but I suppose you must go; remember it's your own choice."

It was my own choice, and never have I found occasion to regret it.

At Aldershot I first met Colonel Evelyn Wood, then Assistant-Quartermaster-General. An *aide-de-camp* has nothing to do except to obey his own chief and generally be, as Lord Wolseley puts it, "*affability combined with reticence.*" They tell indeed a story of a certain *aide-de-camp* who, being shouted at by an exalted personage to do something on a field-day, saluted and replied, "I beg your pardon, Sir, but I only take orders through my own general." Now Colonel Wood knew this as well as anyone, but he had the knack of getting us idle ones to agree to do all sorts of things for the good of the division. He would get one to be secretary to the cricket-club, another to the ball-committees, another to the pigeon-shooting club, and so on.

He asked me to take charge of the officers' library, and willing enough I was to do it. A fortnight afterwards it was—"Take the men's garrison library too; the two ought to be run by one man;" and again I acquiesced. After some months it was: "Your brother (who, I should say, was now *aide-de-camp* to the general commanding the Third Brigade) has got the ball-committees; don't you think you ought to have something in the entertainment line? There's the Woolmer game-preserving association vacant."

"I don't mind that; it's rather in my line," I answered; and accordingly, I found myself ordering pheasants' eggs, buying bantams for setting, and outraging the game-laws by trying to snare superfluous black-cock.

Next came—"My dear fellow, I want you to be secretary to the Officers' Children's School; the hut is not far from yours and there is not much to do."

"No," I said, " I draw the line there. Give it to some married man; those governesses and youngsters would be too much for me." For a week I held out, but was cajoled into it at last, and bitterly did I rue the day!

At the end of that summer (1877) our brigade-major's period of staff-service was up, and my general was casting round for a successor. There happened at this time to be employed as an instructor of youth at Sandhurst Cadet College, one of the most knowledgeable men that lives in Her Majesty's Service. Originally adjutant of the 54th, and having served during the Indian Mutiny, Captain M. W. E. Gosset had been president of the mess at the Staff College the first year I was there, and was now, as he called it, an usher, longing to get back to soldiering again.

Now my general had always told me that he looked upon an *aide-de-camp* as an assistant staff-officer, not a man to order dinner and to carry shawls; and it struck me that two bachelors who knew and liked each other would divide the work in the office between them, and that I should therefore learn more of it than I had yet been doing, besides benefiting an old friend and a good man. Accordingly, I suggested his name to my chief. "Write and ask him to come over to lunch here, any day that suits him," was the answer; and on October 1st Captain Gosset was gazetted Brigade-Major of the First Brigade.

Introductions have, I believe, the reputation of being always dull, and mine is, probably, no better than the rest. Before making an end of it therefore, and getting on to my campaigning, I will try to enliven it with the account of a little episode which occurred at a royal review about this time. It must be premised that some corps are fond of regimental animals corresponding with certain distinctions that they have gained. The 4th Foot, for example, would like to have (I do not know that they ever have had) a tame lion, the 6th an antelope, the 14th, 17th, and several other regiments a tiger, the 23rd and 41st a goat, the

Royal Dragoons, Scots Greys, and 14th Hussars an eagle, the 19th Hussars an elephant, and so on.

From time to time some of these animals have been kept as barrack-pets; but the only regiment that is authorised to bring one on parade is the 23rd Royal Welsh Fusiliers, which Her Majesty has always kept supplied with a goat from her herd at Windsor. Now a certain three-figured corps once formed part of a certain brigade at Aldershot, and when parading for this review thought it a fine thing to smuggle a tame old goat among the band, which arrived unperceived by the staff on the passing line.

At these ceremonies the commander-in-chief is next to the royal carriage; the divisional commander having saluted and passed, places himself on the right of the commander-in-chief with his chief staff-officer next him and as each brigade passes its brigadier places himself in line also on the right of the staff-officer, so as to form, as it were, a chain of responsibility. When the brigaded bands came along, a small drummer-boy was observed struggling with the now enraged goat, which entirely declined to march straight.

"What is that?" inquired Her Majesty, studying the field-state to try and find the Welsh Fusiliers in it.

"What's that, Sir Thomas?" said His Royal Highness.

"What's that?" said Steele to his staff-officer.

"What's that, general?" said the staff-officer to the brigadier. He did not know, but a happy thought struck him. "Indian sheep of Indian Regiment, he said, and back it went along the chain of responsibility. "Indian sheep, Sir Thomas"—"Indian sheep, your Royal Highness"—"Indian sheep, Your Majesty." Then a brow clouded and a head was shaken. We knew not what was said, but in muffled tones from mouth to mouth went this command from His Royal Highness:

"Never let me hear of that —— thing being seen on parade again. I'll see the commanding officer after parade."

The goat was overpowered, led struggling to Cocked Hat Wood, and there tied to a tree; but the commanding officer of that regiment had a worse time than the goat.

One more anecdote of these early days and I have done with my time of peace. The first autumn manoeuvres in which I was engaged were attended by many foreign officers at the invitation of the War Office. What we thought of some of them, and some of them of us, may be judged from the following notes. The representative of one power had a carriage provided for him; he would not mount a horse after the first attempt. On one day the great soldier Blumenthal was questioned by the commander of one side: "What would you do with your artillery if you were me, general?"

He answered: "I should send for the officer commanding the artillery and tell him what I was going to do with the infantry."

At the end of another day's work Blumenthal was asked if he would like to see anything else. "I should like to see cavalry and horse-artillery manoeuvre," he said.

"Tell the 9th Lancers and that battery of horse-artillery to do something smart," said the Englishman to his *aide-de-camp*. The result was that the lancers did the pursuing practice with two squadrons, and two in support, right across Hankley Down, one of the most trappy places to ride over I know, and not a man went down; while the horse-gunner wheeled his battery in line and went at a gallop straight at a big bank with a ditch on each side, got over without an accident, halted, and sent to ask if the German general wanted to see any more "manoeuvring." I know they all agreed that our horse-artillery was the best in the world.

Most thought that our troops could march past better than those of any other nation; but I fancy some thought we were behind all the nations of Europe in tactics. Perhaps they were not wrong; but we have fought before this on the Continent against troops using different systems, and have not come so very badly out of it. Physique may have had something to do with our luck then; now we are great in theory and poor in personnel. However, physique is no better than a *cuirass* in stopping modern rifle-bullets, and the things that win battles nowadays are discipline first and good shooting next.

CHAPTER 2

On Active Service

In January, 1878, General Thesiger was offered and accepted the command of the forces at the Cape of Good Hope. He took Major Crealock, who was Deputy-Assistant-Adjutant-General at Aldershot, as his military secretary, and offered to take Captain Gosset and myself with him as *aides-de-camp*. Of course, we jumped at the offer, for the Galeka War had broken out, and it looked as if our chance had come.

The general only heard of his appointment on the 24th of January, and we had to sail on the 31st.

I believe it was Lord Clyde who said that two hours was enough notice for a soldier, and a bit of soap and a toothbrush sufficient kit. That may be all very well for a bachelor in lodgings in London; for my own part I found a week uncommonly short time for all that had to be done. I know the sacrifice of money would have been heavier had not my brother arranged to sell my goods for me and remit the proceeds to the Cape. Nevertheless, I was not sorry to get a telegram from my groom one day when I was up in London in these plain and business-like words: "Sir, the mare is sold and I have the money." However, everything and everybody were ready by the 29th; and on the 31st we embarked from Southampton on the Union Steamship Company's *American*, off at last on what every soldier longs for, active service.

There were drafts on board, some two hundred men for various regiments quartered at the Cape; and it will hardly be believed that, either because the Cape was considered so healthy or the prospect of war with Russia so imminent, they seemed to have picked out the little children for these drafts, their musketry-returns showing that over one halt had not been through even a recruit's course of musketry.

Now the Russo-Turkish war lasted from April 14th, 1877, till the Treaty of Berlin on July 18th, 1878, and it is true that early in Febru-

16

ary of the latter year the rumour of the entry of the Russians into Constantinople was circulated in London; but that will never excuse the authorities for sending out such youngsters to the Cape to oppose the bravest savages in the world, or for expecting the poor boys to be good at bush-fighting, a game that requires seasoned soldiers who will work when not under the eye of an officer, and whose reliance is on their own coolness and skill. It is well to mention these things; it is ill to condemn any one unheard, because of panics to which the most experienced troops are as liable as the rawest.

Colonel Evelyn Wood and Major Redvers Buller joined the ship at Plymouth as special service officers. The staff thus numbered six, including the general; a modest following it will be allowed, considering the numbers that have been authorised for preceding and subsequent expeditions; but I was the only one of us who had not been on the warpath before; the rest were veterans. The War Office had provided us with numerous blue-books, we had Silver's *Guide* to tell us about the country, and a precis from the Intelligence Department on the manners and customs of the Kafirs; everyone owned a copy of *The Soldier's Pocket-Book*, most had Galton's *Art of Travel*, and there were Kafir grammars and dictionaries on board.

There was a judge also among the passengers, the Cape Attorney-General, a member of the Legislative Assembly, and some men from Port Elizabeth who could talk Kafir; so, our guides to knowledge were many. Triple expansion engines had not then been invented, and instead of sixteen days we were twenty-five on the voyage; but you cannot get much into your head in that time. We had not Theal's excellent *Compendium of South African History and Geography* then, and getting up history from blue-books is a very slow process. We learned what we could of the history, the language, and the manners of the country we were bound for, but I am afraid it was not very much, except that the war had been caused by a fight between Galekas and Fingoes at a marriage feast.

General Thesiger was going out to relieve Sir Arthur Cunynghame, who had been recalled at the instigation of the Colonial Office, Mr. Molteno, the Cape Premier, and Mr. John Merriman, the Minister of Public Works, having refused to allow the general commanding Her Majesty's troops to command the colonial forces in the war. The Colonial Office had given ear to certain colonists at home and abroad who considered Sir Arthur's protest as mere obstruction, and hence the change of generals. Could there be a more ridiculous proposition than to have two commanders operating each at his own will against the enemy? Dual command, dual commissariat, two parties bidding for supplies in the same market! The governor, Sir Bartle Frere, cut the knot before we landed by dissolving the Ministry; but let us hear what the two factions in Parliament thought of the matter.

After the dissolution of the Ministry the new Premier, Mr. Sprigg, speaking at King William's Town, said that the late ministers, Messrs. Molteno and Merriman, while acknowledging the governor to be the Commander-in-Chief of Her Majesty's troops in the colony, contended that His Excellency did not hold the same position with reference to the colonial forces; they maintained, in fact, that they alone were entitled to direct and control the colonial forces, quite apart from the governor.

The general commanding and the governor were therefore kept in ignorance of proposed movements; and consequently, there was no possibility of joint action, each branch of the military forces in the country working in ignorance of the others. For fear Mr. Sprigg's account of the crisis should be denied by the other party, we quote Mr. Merriman's resolution in the House of Assembly in the following June. The Speaker having called attention to the fact that Mr. Merriman's resolution was unconstitutional as containing a direct censure on the Governor for dismissing the late Ministry, the following clause was substituted by Mr. Merriman:

"That the assumption of the command of colonial forces by Sir Arthur Cunynghame in January last, contrary to the advice of the Ministers, was not justified or advisable under existing circumstances."

It will thus be seen that governors and generals have no easy time of it in our "self-governing" colonies, where the ministers have the ear of the Colonial Office; the only wonder is that governors can be found to accept the situation, and that imperial troops are sent there at all.

Ours was a busy voyage, and we had hardly time to look at Madeira, Teneriffe, Gomera, or Cape Verde. The *American* was a slow old boat, with a poop on her which made her much by the stern; but she was comfortable, though crowded. A voyage or so after she fractured her main-shaft and sunk off Ushant, but all her passengers were saved; so much for trying to drive a boat up hill. The captain was a very cautious navigator, and there was a yarn about him on board which if not true is at least amusing. The ship was going up channel one night when the Channel fleet with its many lights appeared on the port bow.

"Hard-a-port," said the skipper; "we must be running into Brighton, but I never knew they had so many chemist shops there."

Young officers will have their jokes about their skippers, so one need not take all such yarns as even verging on the truth. At any rate he was a very good fellow, and told us a lot of things about the Cape and the East Coast.

We reached Cape Town on the 25th, and there we first heard the history of this little war so far as conflicting interests would allow, and it may be well to give a short summary of what had occurred since the marriage-feast of the Fingo.

Sir Bartle Frere, being luckily on the frontier six hundred miles from Cape Town, sent a message to Kreli, chief of the Galekas, to keep quiet, as any disturbance would be punished. Kreli replied that he could not restrain his young men, upon which the governor gave orders for the Frontier Mounted Police to assemble as rapidly as possible under Commandant Griffith on the borders of and between Fingoland and Galekaland. On September 27th the Galekas attacked the Fingoes and one hundred and twenty Police, but were routed and pursued.

On the September 30th Commandant Griffith with a force of two hundred Europeans and two thousand Fingoes was attacked by several thousand Galekas; the enemy was in the end defeated, but it became evident that the revolt was spreading. Sir Arthur Cunynghame had been in the Transvaal, but in October he came to King William's Town, took command of the imperial forces, and gave orders to the *Burgher* forces, now being called out, which were not obeyed.

The Gaikas, settled in British Kaffraria, soon joined the outbreak under their chief Sandilli, and the Tslambies under Mackinnon and Dhimba, also located in British Kaffraria, were not slow to follow; so that by December, 1877, there were three tribes in revolt, but all the fighting up to that time had been in independent Kaffraria, the boundary of British Kaffraria being the River Kei. Commandant Griffith, with Police, Volunteers, and Fingoes, swept Galekaland with several columns, and by the middle of November had driven the insurgents over the River Bashee into Pondoland, where it was not thought politic to pursue them.

The imperial troops during this first Galekaland campaign, as it was called, consisting of the 1st Batt. 24th and part of the 88th Foot, garrisoned posts within the colony and kept open the line of communication with King William's Town. Commandant Griffith was rewarded with the Order of St. Michael and St. George, and some said

THE SOUTH AFRICAN WAR OF 1877-8.

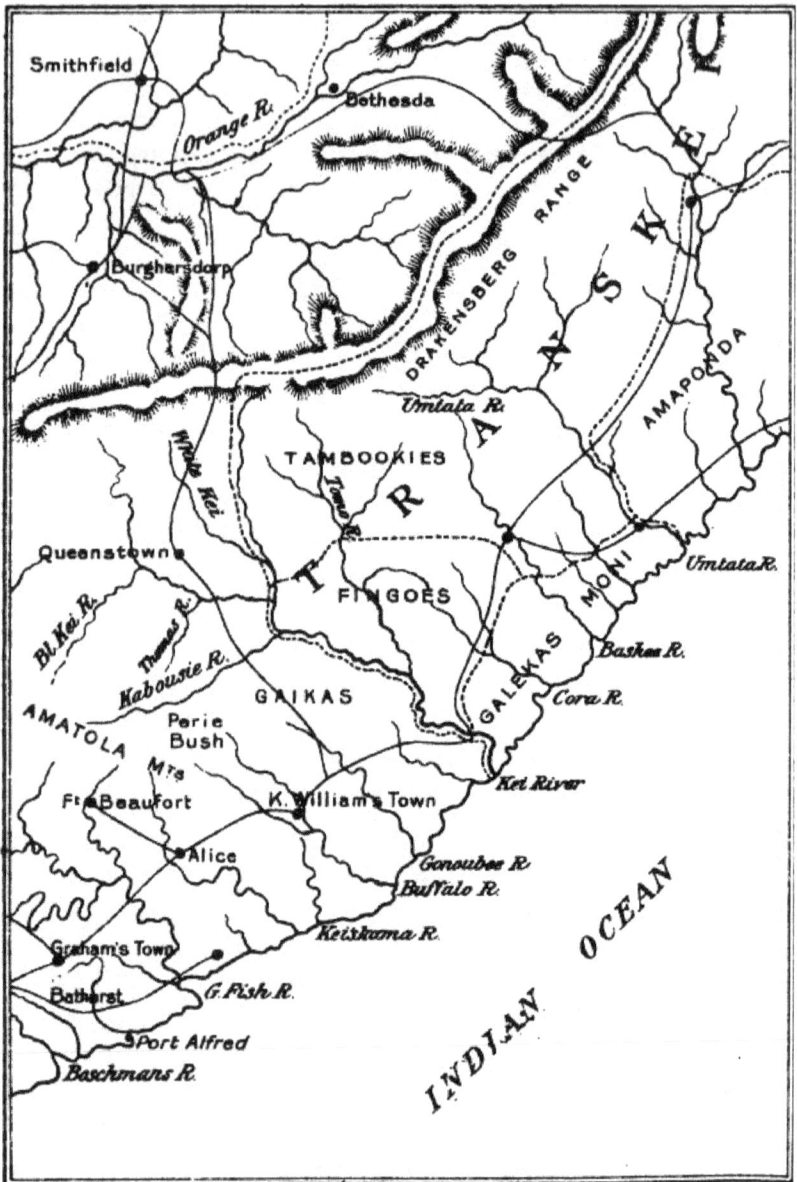

Smithfield

Bethesda

Orange R.

DRAKENSBERG RANGE

Burghersdorp

Umtata R.

TAMBOOKIES

White Kei

Tao R.

T R A N S K E I

AMAPONDA

Queenstown

FINGOES

Umtata R.

Bl. Kei R.

Thomas R.

Kabousie R.

GAIKAS

MONI

Bashee R.

GALEKAS

Cora R.

AMATOLA

Perie
Bush

Mts

Ft. Beaufort

Alice

K. William's Town

Kei River

Gonoubee R.

Buffalo R.

Graham's Town

Keiskama R.

Bathurst

G. Fish R.

Port Alfred

Boschmans R.

INDIAN OCEAN

"Campaigning in S. Africa"

Scale of English Miles

0   10   20   30   40   50   60   70   80   90   100

the war was over. It had in fact not really begun.

The mine was thoroughly sprung on the last day of 1877, when a special magistrate, his brother, and a field-cornet (corresponding with the American sheriff) who had gone to a Kafir *kraal* within the colony to inquire after some stolen cattle which had been tracked there, were murdered by the Kafirs; and at the same time some of Sandilli's Gaikas crossed the River Kei into Fingoland, killed many natives and one European, set fire to twenty villages, and carried off more cattle. A post-escort had been attacked and some men of the 88th killed the day before. Then the war-cry went throughout the land: the settlers gathered into the nearest town or *laager*; the *burghers* looked to their horses and arms, and banded together under trusted leaders; and stores of provisions and ammunition were collected.

There is nothing more piteous to see than the result of a Kafir outbreak. Farms in that country are large, say from one thousand to four thousand acres: they are occupied by pioneer farmers, discharged soldiers of the old German Legion, and other military settlers, who with their families live far apart; and it is only by their known good marksmanship, and the respect inspired by a white face, that they hold their own among hundreds of black men. When a man has laboured on his farm for the greater part of his life, when he sees his homestead burned and all his cattle swept off, when he has barely been able to save the lives of his wife and his children, it is small wonder, when he and his comrades go on the war-path in revenge, that he should be a greedy fighter and avow his determination once and for all to make an end of it.

The Kafir gives no quarter; why should he? The ways of the soldiers may be noble; but when the work is done, they go home and leave him surrounded by the old dangers and the certainty of another outbreak in time. He has heard of, if he does not personally remember, the ill-results of the government agreements formerly. Whenever a beaten chief sent to say, "I desire that blood shall cease to flow," the reply was, "There is no more war between the English and the Amaxosa"; and the savage settled down unmolested to bide his time, as in 1851 and 1857.

To take but one instance of what a Kafir war means to the settler, here are the experiences of a well-known man who lived in the East London district within the colony. On January 4th, 1878, a large body of Kafirs swept his farm completely; they burned his houses and out-buildings, and carried off twelve thousand sheep with many cattle and

THE CAFFRE WAR—A FINGO SENTINEL

horses. From affluence he was reduced in an hour to destitution. He had grown grey with long toil, and was too old to begin life afresh. Does even the Aborigines Protection Society wonder that this man should have occupied a conspicuous place at the front during the war, and would they be surprised to hear that the motto of such men was, *Slay and spare not?*

In the new year fights came fast and furious. Sir Arthur Cunynghame had moved to Ibeka in the Transkei, and had assembled a force in four columns to sweep Galekaland, the regular troops being the 1st Batt. 24th, who had been quartered at King William's Town, and part of the 88th with blue-jackets and marines from the *Active*, the flagship on the Cape station; there were also police, volunteers, and Fingoes. The line of communication with King William's Town, by way of Butterworth, Kei Drift, Komgha, and Draiibosch, was kept open by posts of the 88th, while to overawe the Gaikas and keep them from their old battleground among the Amatola Mountains, posts were established in a north-west direction from King William's down to Cathcart.

There were skirmishes every day, and important fights at Draiibosch (where Major Hans Garrett Moore of the 88th won his Victoria Cross), at Quintana Mountain, at the Chichaba Valley, at the Kabousie River and other places on both sides of the Kei; and about the end of January the Tambookies, under Gongabele, threw in their lot with the rebels, which resulted in more fighting near Queenstown and in the valley of the Thomas River.

While Galekaland was being swept for the second time, the rebels were collecting in two main bodies in the Chichaba and the Kabousie bush in the valley of the Kei. When the Chichaba had been harried, the force there moved up the Kei valley to join that in the Kabousie, from whence the enemy was believed to be moving higher up to the Thomas River. It looked as if they were making for their old fastnesses in the Amatola Mountains, and Commandant Griffith collected all the colonial forces that he could muster to prevent it.

It was a feather in the cap of the Intelligence Department to have published, in its precis on the eastern frontier, the following note of warning, derived from the report of an officer of the 32nd Light Infantry, a regiment which had only just been sent home after a sojourn of three years at the Cape.

It is very probable that in the event of a Kafir outbreak the Gaikas would attempt to seize their old strongholds, the Amatola

THE CAFFRE WAR—A GALEKA CHIEFTAIN

Mountains and the Waterkloof, proceeding by way of the Kabousie, as they could push through under cover of bush nearly
all the way.

Precautions, it will be seen, were accordingly taken; nevertheless,
the Gaika Kafirs actually carried out the movement later, taking advantage of a gap left in the line from King William's Town to Cathcart
by a force of colonial troops losing their direction during an attack on
the Thomas River bush.

Such then was the news that greeted us on our arrival. Briefly
it amounted to this: that Galekaland had been twice cleared; that
Kreli was in hiding either in Galeka or Pondoland; that Sandilli was
somewhere near the Thomas River; that Tini Macomo, who had also
revolted, was in the Waterkloof; but that little further resistance was
expected, and that the crisis was supposed to be passed. We heard also
that Messrs. Molteno and Merriman had been ordering about the
colonial forces at their own sweet wills; that the Ministry had been
dismissed; and that now Commandant-General Griffith commanded
the colonial forces under the orders of the Lieutenant-General commanding Her Majesty's troops.

The imperial forces had been strengthened. In the middle of February, the 90th Light Infantry from England had relieved the detachments of the 88th, who had returned to garrison Cape Town, except
their mounted infantry which remained at the front. The 90th had
been sent to Fort Beaufort to operate against Tini Macomo in the
Waterkloof. The colonial forces were decreasing, six months being the
time for which volunteers and *burghers* had engaged; such as remained
were being instructed to take orders from the lieutenant-general, but
isolated cases still existed where local forces preferred to look after
their own districts.

A characteristic story is told by one commanding officer of Volunteers who was ordered by a member of the Legislative Council to
guard a threatened farm where his wife and her native servants per-
sisted in remaining. He went, off-saddled in the yard, and was asked in
to dinner with the officers. "Oh, we always live like the men, and we
have our rations," was his answer.

"But dinner is ready for all of you," said the hostess; so, in they all
went. After the meal a charge of two shillings was handed to each officer; whereupon the officer commanding asked, as paymaster, for a
general receipt for all. That evening a document, *To eight dinners, sixteen*

shillings, received same time. Emma ——, was forwarded to the governor with the comment, "Dear Sir Bartle, I send you this to show how ——'s wife treats her defenders."

With all our new information we left Cape Town on February 28th, stopped at Mossel Bay and Algoa Bay, and arrived off East London on March 4th. Now at this port the current, running south-west down the coast, keeps a ship broadside on to the rollers. With a south-easter every ship puts to sea, and with a steady breeze from that direction you seem as if you would roll your yards under. Luckily for us the sea was moderate.

The general, Crealock, and Gosset landed in the port life-boat; they were nearly upset at the bar, where the rollers follow each other in such quick succession that hard pulling and very good steering are required. The lifeboat's crew are highly paid, are white men of the worst class, are generally drunk, and their language even when sober has been described as a marvel of profanity. They pay little attention to the coxswain, and when on this occasion I from the ship saw the boat with my chief for a moment broadside on to the bar, I own to feeling a most uncomfortable sensation.

I had to follow in a surf-boat with the baggage. A surf-boat there is a lighter of eighty tons, decked, with one centre hatchway; the cargo or passengers are below, and battened down in even moderate weather. When loaded it is towed by a small steam-tug to a buoy; this with its attached rope is hauled up and at the end is found a coir hawser, one end of which is anchored inside the bar and the other end out at sea. The hawser is passed over sheaves in two posts on deck and kept down by iron pins, then the crew—natives as naked as they were born with one white fellow in command—begin to walk the hawser aft, and you are on your way to the bar.

We got through well enough; we bumped on the bar, and the next roller shot us over into smooth water, a little wet but no harm done. A few days after, in landing some of the 24th, the hawser broke and a boat containing the band got broadside on and was turned over the bar into the haven, the mouth of the Buffalo River.

I found on landing that the others had gone on by special train to King William's Town; so, with a fatigue-party from Fort Glamorgan I got the baggage landed, carted it over the Buffalo by the ferry-boat from East London to Panmure, put it into a railway-truck for the seven o'clock train next morning, and then looked about for a lodging. I found a certain Phoenix Hotel, got myself some dinner, and then sat down to smoke on a bench outside, placing my hat beside me. In half a minute it was gone. "*Ach, de* boys jumps *de* hat!" exclaimed the German proprietor when I complained; and then I learned all about the South African verb *to jump*, which signifies to take on loan, only to return if discovered. You may jump anything in Kaffraria, a horse, a pipe, a hat, a gun, and if you return it when caught you are all right. In other countries you are called a thief if afflicted with this playful habit.

My friends were very glad to see me arrive with the luggage and servants, for the place was full of what our soldiers call Brass Hats (*i.e.* staff-officers), and our party up to this had been in their travelling-suits. Sir Bartle Frere with his staff and several members of the Ministry, and Sir Arthur Cunynghame with his staff were at King William's Town; so, we heard all the news, and sorry enough we were to be told that everything was over, and that we should probably be back in Cape Town in a month or so.

It is always awkward when a general is sent out to relieve another whose period of employment is not yet expired. We all thought that Sir Arthur Cunynghame had been badly treated by the Colonial Office, and we did our best to avoid giving any offence to him or the officers of his staff. I had known his military secretary, Colonel Forestier Walker, in Mauritius; his two *aides-de-camp*, Captain Grenfell of the 60th Rifles and Lieutenant Coghill of the 24th, were such excellent fellows that it was easy not to give offence. I only trust we all succeeded in our easy task. Sir Bartle Frere I met for the first time at dinner that night.

He had a wonderfully quiet, deliberate manner of speaking, never hesitating and never at a loss for the right word, giving you the idea that whatever might be the subject of conversation he knew much more about it than any of his audience. He impressed us all as a most cool-headed diplomatist, and we recognised that he was one who was doing his best for the good of the State, and one who had the will, the determination, and the power to carry out any policy that he thought would be for the best. To us he seemed a model proconsul.

Our first business was to buy horses; I secured three animals of a kind for £25 apiece, and the others were also soon suited with riding and packhorses. We had brought with us pack-saddles of Otago pattern, but these are too large and heavy for the Cape horses, at least for the stamp of horse you can obtain there on an emergency like this. The small light pattern with leather bags, used by the officers of the Frontier Mounted Police is the thing for South Africa; the other is more fit for a seventeen-hands mule. None of our head-stalls would fit, being all too long in the cheek; and all the girths wanted a reef in them.

We secured seven *Hottentot* grooms from a corps of volunteers named Pulleine's Rangers which had been raised by Lieutenant-Colonel Pulleine of the 24th; they were *quadroons* or *octoroons*, rejoicing in such names as De Munk, Hendriks, Chun, Caesar, Frank, etc. These worthies received from the Colonial Government half-a-crown a day and their rations, which was galling to the British soldier, and especially to our soldier-servants, who had to put up with the shilling a day of the Home Government. The men we brought from home, though all bearing good-conduct badges, were with two exceptions of little use. Within six weeks mine had gone to swell the ranks of the 24th, and from that regiment I got in his place a young Welshman named Noot, as good a soldier as I ever want to see.

As for the enemy, we were told that the Galekas had been driven over the Umtata River into Pondoland; that Colonel Glyn with the 1st Batt. 24th, Mounted Police, Volunteers, and Fingoes was patrolling Galekaland; that the Gaikas, Tslambies, and Tambookies were surrounded by Commandant-General Griffith with police, *burghers*, volunteers, and Fingoes in the Thomas River bush and must shortly surrender; that the 90th had gone to Fort Beaufort and suppressed Tini Macomo in the Waterkloof district; finally, that the 2nd Batt. 24th was expected to be at King William's Town from England within the week.

★★★★★★★★★★★★

Let us now see what sort of people these Kafirs were, with whom we were still hoping to measure our strength, once if no more. Each tribe has its own great chief whose person is inviolable, and to whom the offer of any indignity ensures the gravest consequences. The people are the property of their chiefs, so for an offence against any of them a man by rights pays the chief a fine; but he may escape to another chief and will be protected by him. Fines and death are the only penalties. Each chief is assisted by councillors, to whose advice he is compelled to listen. A Kafir may have as many wives as he can afford to buy and keep. In the case of chiefs, the highest wife in rank (a neighbouring chief's daughter, for instance), is termed the Great Wife, and her eldest son is the heir.

Other two of the wives are named, with the consent of the councillors, the Wife of the Right Hand and the Wife of the Left Hand. Their sons may be, and generally are, older than the heir, so the tribe often splits into three clans; if the sons manage to get along without

28

fighting, the Great Wife's son is recognised at the chief's death as the paramount chief; but the others pay him no tribute, and usually settle down at some distance, so that the number of petty chiefs and small clans is great. However, for a war against the *Umhlungu*, or white man, they combine under noted fighting chiefs of the tribe.

The Kafir is a splendid man physically, but weak in the arms, for he only attends to the cattle and milks the cows, while the women do such field-work as is necessary. The men's dress in hot weather is nothing at all; in cool weather skins or blankets are wrapped round them; the chiefs wear an ivory band round the arm above the left elbow. Married women wear a skin kilt always; unmarried girls are content with a string and a bunch of beads; all wear necklaces and bangles. Their huts are like beehives; there is a very small opening, no chimney, and a fireplace in the middle of the floor; a collection of huts is called a *kraal*. This description refers only to the tribal Kafirs; those living in towns or in service are forced to dress; mission Kafirs have doors and windows to their circular huts. Tribal Kafirs may not enter a town till they have got a blanket to cover their nakedness.

The wealth of the Kafirs consists in cattle. The men and boys alone tend and herd them, and milk the cows; a woman may not enter the cattle-enclosure. The milk is put in skins, soured, and drunk almost in lumps. Mealies and Kafir corn are their cereals, and from the latter they make Kafir beer, which is drunk grains and all. The cattle are taught to follow a whistle, and the control the men have over their herds is extraordinary.

The boys are circumcised when about fifteen years old, and then rank as men. But after that they must be daubed all over with white clay and live apart for a month or so, when they are brought before the old men to be lectured, after which they are allowed a period of freedom from any control whatever; and as licentiousness is no disgrace to either sex, the immorality after these annual ceremonies is appalling.

The weapons of the Kafir are one short broad-bladed stabbing-*assegai*, half-a-dozen long, tapering, throwing-*assegais*, a *knobkerrie*, or club, and now generally a gun; perhaps an old Tower musket dated 1835, a trade "gas-pipe" gun, or sometimes an Austrian rifle with two triggers. Out of these they fire iron pot-legs, slugs, stones, or any heavy thing that will go down; and the musical notes of the various missiles in a Kafir fight is a thing to hear.

When the Kafir goes on the warpath he stains his body and his blanket with red clay and grease; he is then *Isahombe*, a red Kafir, and

A Kafir warrior

an awkward brute to meet in the bush. The women follow as beasts of burden with cooking-pots, mealies, and babies; and the boys drive and herd the cattle for their fathers, leaving them free to fight unencumbered.

The throwing-*assegai* of the Kafir will wound seriously at forty yards; the *coup de grace* is given with the stabbing-*assegai* in the abdomen so that the corpse shall not swell, it being their belief that if a body swells the hand of the slayer will suffer also. With the exception of certain educated Kafirs, mostly sons of chiefs who can afford to buy rifles, there are very few good shots among them. If they see you from the bush against the sky-line, and have time to take a steady aim at a few yards' distance, you will probably suffer, so the plan is always if possible, to attack them up hill; but as a rule, a Kafir with his *assegai* and *knobkerrie* is more to be dreaded in the bush than the one with a gun.

The fellow has a hide like a rhinoceros; the wait-a-bit thorn, that tears pieces out of your clothes, merely makes a white scratch on his bronze or reddened skin. His movements are therefore unheard; you may be surrounded by a crowd of Kafirs in the bush, and unless you have come across their *spoor* you may be quite ignorant of their proximity till, with a rush, a red form with a quivering-*assegai* appears within a few yards of you. Then your coolness and your firearm, Snider-carbine, or Winchester-repeater for choice, decides if you are to be ripped open or not.

It is difficult for white men with their clothes, their great helmets, and their boots, to move through the bush at any pace; and so, a glade, or at least a bush path, is sure to be chosen if it leads in the proper direction. Your enemy knows this well enough, and will line the path in wait for you. When he shows himself there is only one thing for you to do, to go straight at him into the bush with a cheer. You are then both in semi-obscurity and on more even terms, and he is almost sure to run; at any rate if he does not on account of numbers, you can see him to shoot at, and are not firing wildly into darkness. White troops moving in the bush should always have friendly natives as scouts to precede and flank the column. A broken twig, a blade of grass turned over, or a stone that has been moved, is as good as a signpost to them; whereas your men take months to learn such woodcraft, and would blunder on at first into the most open ambuscade.

If in the bush with a small party, and you think you are followed along the path, imitate the buffalo. Move into the bush at the side, go back parallel with the path for forty yards or so, and then lie down in line quietly with rifles at the ready. Your foe will come along after your spoor; he will see no break in the trail, and will make to pass you. When abreast of you your time has come to fire. He will not come at you if he does not know your strength: a few rifles make a great noise in the bush; and moreover, you are not playing fair, you have learned his own game, and he does not like it. This stratagem is to "forelay," not to "waylay" as we should call it in England.

Again, if riding in the open and you see a suspicious red object, for the red Kafir is exactly the colour of the red earth, ride on to within range, halt, and, keeping your eye upon it, take careful aim with a carbine or rifle. You need not fire; that would indicate your whereabouts to more prowlers. If it is a Kafir, it will run away or at least move to get cover; if not, it is a rock or ant-heap, and you can lower your firearm and continue at your leisure.

The white helmet and accoutrements of the regulars show at great distances even in the bush. They should be coloured with coffee or boiled mimosa-bark, and when wanted for parade again can be pipe-clayed up as neat as ever. Smooth brown leather does not do for regular soldiers. A touch of grease brings out black spots which can only be removed by careful treatment with oxalic acid and recoloured with saffron; hardly a process for the field.

A general's scabbard is the best mark for an individual in a sunny climate, and the *aides-de-camp* are never at a loss to find him if he is moving about on a fine day; it is six-sided, and the two outer flat faces reflect the sun's rays like a heliograph. Rifle-barrels, buckles, and other scabbards are rounded or bevelled, and reflect little spots of light; but the general's scabbard looks like a planet among stars.

Finally, never be induced to try and capture a few head of cattle grazing in a glade. It is the commonest Kafir trick to set such a trap. Colonial troopers are mad after looting cattle for the sake of the prize-money; and many have had to pay the penalty for going after a few beasts by finding the surrounding bush swarming with Kafirs. Beat the bush around such a place by all means; you are certain of a find, and can make your arrangements accordingly.

CHAPTER 3

We Take the Field

A few days after our arrival at King William's Town, Sir Arthur Cunynghame left for England, taking Lieutenant Coghill with him as *aide-de-camp*. Sir Bartle Frere also left for Cape Town, taking Colonel Walker. Sir Arthur's military secretary, on his own staff in the same position. Captain Grenfell was made Deputy-Assistant-Adjutant-General, for Colonel Bellairs, the Deputy-Adjutant-General, had been working throughout with a single assistant. Everyone was glad that such a man was to be retained at the front.

We had heard very little news from the front since our arrival. Griffith was hemming in Sandilli, and it was daily expected that the news of his capture would be reported. On March 9th the *Himalaya* arrived with the 2nd Batt. 24th. which was at once moved up to King William's Town; not before they were wanted, for on that very day Sandilli showed that he was not yet finished with.

On the 8th Commandant-General Griffith had attacked the rebels in the Thomas River bush; to increase the force for the operation he had taken all available men from the line of posts from Cathcart to Stutterheim, which line stopped the way between the Thomas River bush and the Perie bush on part of the Amatola Range, the scene of the operations in the wars of 1835 and 1851. Griffith reported no resistance, and that he had captured twelve hundred head of cattle; but a portion of his force had taken the wrong road, leaving a gap in the circle surrounding the Kafirs.

Sandilli at once took advantage of this, and on the morning of the 9th, the thirty men left to guard Stutterheim were astonished to see large bodies of Kafirs, within a few miles of the town, making for the Perie bush. The Kafirs luckily did not attack the town, but contented themselves with burning outlying farms and killing their German occupants in passing. Mr. Fleischer, the magistrate, at once rode out with his small garrison to attack, but could do no good; and after they had passed, he rode on to Grey town to telegraph Sandilli's escape to the general at King William's Town.

The news came in at midnight, and immediately all the mounted volunteers that could be assembled, about one hundred and twenty in all, were sent off to Stutterheim, some thirty-five miles away, under Captain Gardner of the Albany Volunteers. Captain Cosset was sent with them as staff-officer, to report and advise, not to take command; for however well colonial commandants and volunteers may fight, they never will report their proceedings or their whereabouts, and it was necessary now, for a very large surrounding chain had to be drawn, that headquarters should be in touch with each force. The same night reinforcements were sent off to Kabousie, Fort Merriman, and Keiskamahoek, and a large force to Isidengi on the top of the Buffalo Range.

Steps were also taken to form a cordon of posts round the Buffalo Mountains, a circumference of about sixty miles, to hem the rebels in there and prevent their further inroad into the colony; for the loyalty of other tribes, further west, was rather doubtful. That night and the following days were busy ones. It required some days to get the troops into position, and much work by the commissariat to distribute supplies to posts at such distances from King William's Town; for the motto of South Africa should be *Wait for the waggon*, the ox's pace being about two miles an hour. From the top of the Buffalo Mountains the country to King William's Town is all plainly visible, and trains of waggons approaching the Perie bush had therefore to be escorted for fear of the enemy appropriating the stores and oxen.

The noted Perie bush extends for twenty miles all along the south-eastern slopes of the Buffalo Mountains, these mountains being connected with the Amatolas, which lie to the north-west, by the Kabousie neck. Only two roads cross it from south to north, those from King William's Town to Stutterheim on the east and to Keiskamahoek on the west, and they are seventeen miles apart. The range from north to south is about eight miles wide, broken up in the most extraordinary manner into hills and valleys, *kraantzes* and *kloofs*, table-land and precipices, pasture and bush.

****

It may be well here to give the explanation of some of the South African terms and phrases. A *kraantz* is a bare rocky slope, so steep

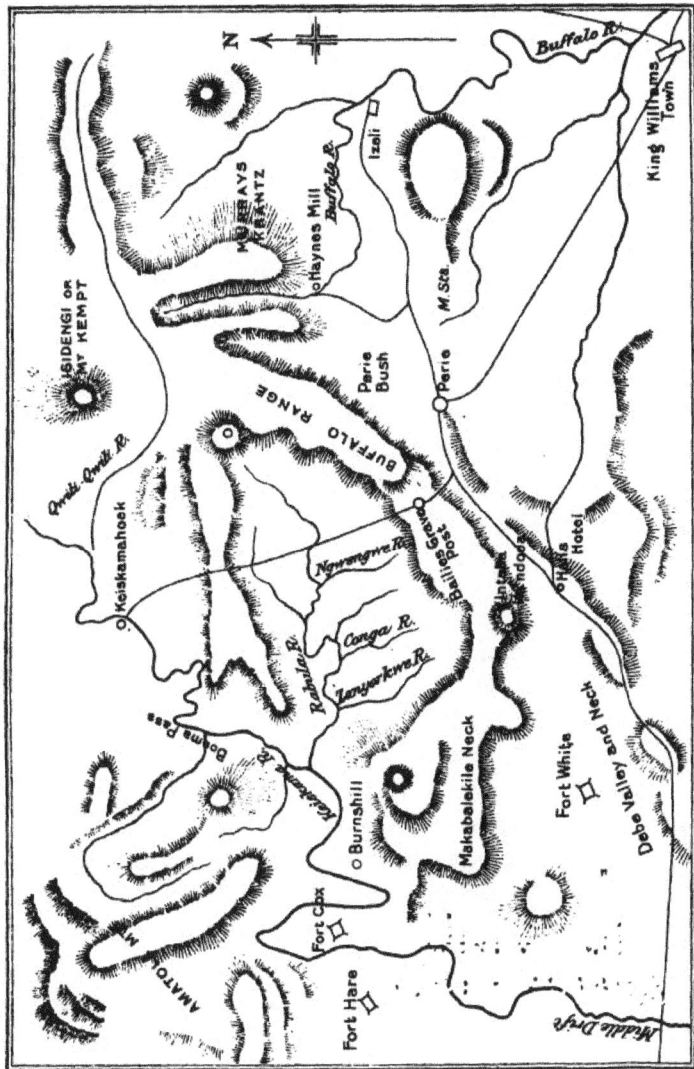

ROUGH SKETCH OF GEN. THE HON. F. A. THESIGER'S OPERATIONS,
In the Buffalo Mountains and around Intaba Kaindoda 1878.

Scale about 5 miles to 1 inch

A.J.R. Cashlewood, Printers Blackheath.

'Campaigning in S. Africa.'

Buffalo R.

King Williams Town

Izali

M. Sta.

Perie

MURRAY'S KRANTZ

Haynes Mill

Buffalo R.

ISIDENGI OR FORT KEMPT

Perie Bush

BUFFALO RANGE

Ponti-Ponti R.

Keiskamahoek

Ngwangwe R.

Grays Hotel

Kabula R.

Ball's Post

Conga R.

Lanyarkwe R.

Bolbs Pass

Keiskama R.

Makabaleikile Neck

Burnshill

Fort White

Debe Valley and Neck

AMATOLA M

Fort Cox

Fort Hare

Middle Drift

N

that trees can seldom grow upon it, the rocks which have fallen from above forming caves and passages at its base. A *kloof* is literally a chasm, what would be called a *cañon* in the Western States of America. There is generally a stream at the bottom, but often not if the sides are bare of bush. A *poort* (Dutch for gate) is the lower end of a *kloof*. The Bush is the primeval forest. Enormous trees overhead keep off the sunshine, while dense undergrowth with multitudes of creepers, or monkey-ropes, and wait-a-bit thorns make movement difficult and limit the view to a few yards.

As nearly all the transport at the Cape is by ox-waggon, and the beasts must graze to live, public halting-places are reserved throughout the country, where you may *outspan*, and they are marked on the maps with the noun of that ilk. The converse of this verb is to *inspan*, or, as we should say, to harness. When on horseback to *off-saddle* and to *saddle-up* are the words used. No one trots at the Cape; a walk or a canter are the only paces, or if you can secure a good *trippler* (a horse that can trot with his fore legs while he canters with his hind) you will be easiest and most in the fashion. In riding' any distance you walk your horses for half a mile or so and then canter.

At the end of an hour, if you are near water, you off-saddle, and knee-halter your horses by tying their head-stalls down to within eighteen inches of one knee by their *riems* (headropes of raw hide). You strip off the saddles at once, to the dismay of new arrivals from home, and turn your horses loose to feed. They will first roll in the dustiest place they can find, then drink, and afterwards feed off the *veldt* (grass). In half an hour you saddle-up and ride for two hours, then off-saddle for one hour, and so on for the rest of the day. By this means a horse is never more than two hours without food, and will cover many miles a day.

Of course, the *veldt* is not green like English grass, being more or less burned up by the sun to the condition of hay; but the principle is to let your horse eat and drink as often and as much as he likes; at night give him oat-hay (oat-straw cut green with the oats left in it) and mealies (maize), or at a pinch Kafir corn (millet) chopped up and bruised, and he will do double the work of an English horse without losing condition. To *ring* horses is to tie their heads together at night by their *riems*, so that they may stand in a circle with their heels outwards.

To *trek* is to march with a column of transport. A transport-rider is the owner of the hired waggons, and he employs a *voorlooper* and a driver for each waggon. Every mounted man has saddle-bags which will hold food and a change of linen, and these are strapped to D's on each side of the seat of the saddle. Cruppers are generally used, the Cape horses being low in the withers; they are never shod behind and often not in front, for the roads, except in the towns, are the bare ground, and unshod they can get over smooth rocks better. A rasp occasionally is all that is required.

Every *kitchen* (or tame) Kafir is a *boy*; and a *hunter*, as in the Old Testament, is not a horse but a sportsman. A store or shop is a *winkel* and a grog-shop is a canteen. A *laager* is a fort, or a convoy of waggons drawn up in a defensive form. A *commando* is a levy of *burghers* under the command of a field-cornet. To *spoor* is to track; a *drift* is a ford, and a *donga* is a dry watercourse with steep sides, corresponding to an Indian *nullah*.

The colonial does not fall in for parade or fatigue duties; he *rolls up*. He prefers to do his work on horseback, and when he fires, he calls it *letting rip*. Finally, *footsack* is equivalent to *be off!* The term is usually applied to a prowling dog or pilfering Kafir; and it is said that an author who had lived a few days up country, wrote on his return home:

In the Cape every dog is called *Footsack*, and runs away when you call him.

British Kaffraria revels in strange names for localities. Murderer's Kop, Bailie's Grave, Deadman's Drift, and the like show what hard times the early settlers had, and are as good a history of the country as are Gibbet Lane and Hangman's Clump in the neighbourhood of Bagshot Heath.

★★★★★★★★★★★★

From the 9th till the 14th of March all our time was taken up in forwarding troops and supplies to the posts surrounding the Buffalo Mountains: these posts were Keiskamahoek, Fort Merriman, and Stutterheim on the north; Perie mission station and Izeli on the south; Frankfort on the east, and Bailie's Grave Post on the west. As the periphery was some sixty miles, and the nearest post was ten miles from King William's Town, the delay was unavoidable. On the 14th the general made a reconnaissance of the south side of the rebel's fastnesses from Izeli to Perie mission station.

On the 15th he inspected the line on the west to Keiskamahoek, and on the 16th the east side, Frankfort and Peelton, coming back to King William's Town for office-work each night. Riding over a hundred miles in three days of hot weather, reconnoitring, inspecting, and giving orders all the time, and finding office-work to settle at night on one's return, is no joke after a month on board ship.

On the 16th, before starting for the day's work, I accompanied Commandant Frank Streatfeild, who had marched a native levy of Fingoes up from the Chichaba Valley, some way out of the town to put him on his way for Keiskamahoek, where he was proceeding in hot haste to join a force under Commandant Lonsdale, late of the 74th, who had just raised another corps of Fingoes. Both of these corps were to be placed under Colonel Evelyn Wood's command. He had some of his own regiment, the 90th Light Infantry, with him, they having been sent back from Fort Beaufort, as the rebels in the Waterkloof under Tini Macomo had been dispersed and those parts only wanted patrolling and watching.

Streatfeild's head-man at once became the mouthpiece of the levy. "*Baas*, is that the *inkos inkuhi* (great chief)?" "No, *Inyati* (buffalo), he is *induna wangasenkosini* (a captain of the great chief's)." "Oh, may we sing our *igwatyu* (warsong) to him?" "*Hai, amadoda, tutu!* (no, boys, keep silence)." They were quiet for a bit, and then came the request that they might take off their boots and carry them; this was granted, and tying them together by the laces they slung them over their guns.

In five minutes, there was another request; might they take off their trousers now that they were beyond the town? This also was granted, and their nether garments being tied round their waists and the legs knotted in front, they went on at twice the pace in perfect content-ment. Streatfeild knew how to manage savages, and his men would have gone anywhere and done anything for him.

On March 17th the Headquarter Staff left King William's Town to form a camp at the Perie mission station. Here the worthy missionary informed us that all his converts were loyal, but we soon found that they were in communication with the rebels in the bush. Now, as our forces were few in number, and as it would have been suicidal to let the wily Kafir hear where the sentries were to be posted, as he must have done at every relief in the ordinary methods of our service, the general issued the following order, to inspire the young soldiers with confidence and to guard against their being cut off on outpost duty in the bush or in bivouac:

> The men to be told off into permanent groups of fours, either according to the regulation mode of sizing, or by selection; or,

as is considered to be the preferable mode, by the men choosing their own comrades irrespective of sizing. Companies when working in extended order, or in attack formation, to preserve the groups of fours.

This system need not interfere in any way with the instructions laid down in the drill-book. On outpost duty the group of fours will take the place of the double sentry, thereby saving two men per sentry, one man remaining on the lookout (stationary), while the other three lie close down behind him. The groups of fours must have a leader who will regulate the relief of sentries and take general direction on all occasions.

He also pointed out that outpost sentries must trust to their eyes by day and their ears by night, and that if the sentries patrol, they cannot use their senses properly. Visiting patrols of course were employed, but were told to be quiet over their work and to arrange a secret sign with the sentry groups.

The plan worked very well: you cannot keep touch in the bush, but four men together were found to be more confident, and not easily cut off; while on outpost duty the plan was liked by the soldiers, who were quite happy and alert in their little bivouacs of four.

Our official instructions for outpost duty were then almost word for word those authorised for the Peninsular War. They may be very excellent against civilised troops, but ridiculous against the savage, who can wriggle like a snake almost noiselessly through the grass, and whose delight is to display a stained *assegai* to his own dusky maiden, to show that he has washed his spear in some poor sentry's blood. The Kafirs' ways are like those of the Red Indians; you must employ loyal natives, or mend your own ways entirely to be even with them.

The following is the disposition of the force previous to the concentric attack on the Perie bush:

NORTH SIDE.—(1) *Keiskamahoek*, Colonel Evelyn Wood, V.C.

90th Light Infantry	65	
Mounted Volunteers	210	
Fingoes	125	
		400 men.

(2) *Fort Merriman*, Commandant Frost, with Major Redvers Buller as adviser.

Mounted Volunteers	488	
Fingoes	200	
		688 ,,

39

(3) *Isidengi*, (on the top of the Buffalo Range, to which post the Stutterheim Force had been moved). Commandant Scherm-brucker, with Captain Gosset, A.D.C., as adviser.

Mounted Volunteers	269
Fingoes	400
	669 ,,

SOUTH.—(4) *Perie Mission Station.* Colonel Law, R.A.

2nd batt. 24th.	290
Mounted Volunteers	46
Fingoes	300
Two 7-pounder guns	
	636 ,,

[At this post there were also some sailors with tubes and 24-pounder rockets].

EAST.—(5) *Gwengwe Post* (on the east of the Buffalo Range to which the troops from Izeli and Frankfort had been moved). Lieut.-Colonel Degacher.

2nd batt. 24th	200
Some Natives	
Two 7-pounder guns	
	210 ,,

WEST.—(6) *Bailie's Grave Post.* Commandant Brabant.

Mounted Volunteers	162
Fingoes	125
	287 ,,
Total	2890

There were thus, it will be seen, less than three thousand men to search more than one hundred square miles of very difficult ground.

In getting into position the troops had several brushes with the Kafirs. Patrols had kept up connection between the posts, and those from Isidengi fell across Matanzima, Sandilli's son, who, with a body of men and large droves of cattle, was on his way to join his father. Fifty Kafirs were killed and part of the drove taken.

Though the surrounding force was small, it does not do to let the Kafir rest, and the order was accordingly given from the camp at Perie mission station to attack next day, March 18th, at daybreak. The plan was as follows. Colonel Wood was at first to direct the attack, and, when his force from Keiskamahoek came abreast of Brabant's and Frost's on the plateau, they were to join on his right and left respectively, and sweep the plateaux and *kloofs* eastward, driving the Kafirs into the great *kloof* known as the Buffalo Poort. When this had been done, it was intended to let Colonel Law's force at Perie mission station join the right of Brabant's line, and the whole of the four detachments, wheeling slightly to the left, were to drive the great Buffalo Poort in a north-east direction, the outlets on the north and east being guarded by Schermbrucker and Degacher.

To make sure that his orders were understood, the general left his camp at four a.m. and rode to Bailie's Grave Post. He reached it before daybreak, saw Brabant, and then returned to camp, reaching it at ten a.m. All that day we waited anxiously at Perie mission station, hearing firing to the west, which, however, did not seem to advance. A few Kafirs appeared in sight on *kraantzes*, and a rocket or seven-pounder double shell were sent at them to keep them moving; but not a sign of our forces appeared. In the afternoon the general rode to Hayne's mill at the bottom of the Buffalo Poort, and then on to Izeli, but not a movement was to be seen nor any sounds to be heard; so, we returned to Perie mission station, reaching our camp at six in the evening.

I forget how the truth reached us; I think it came that evening by an officer who rode out from King William's Town, to tell us that one of Brabant's lot had galloped into the place saying the attack had been repulsed, and that we were all in full retreat.

It turned out that the spirit of cattle-lifting, the curse of South Africa, was responsible for the failure of the scheme. Brabant, with his Volunteers and Fingoes, finding there was cattle in front, would not wait for Wood to come up in line, but went on at once, the temptation being too strong for undisciplined men. They fell into the ambuscade, and were so roughly handled that they ran away.

Some reformed behind Colonel Wood's force, but others went on the fifteen miles to King William's Town, and bred the panic that I have narrated. Frost, finding an action in progress on the plateau below him, tried to send help, but his men were stopped by a *kloof*; he then joined Colonel Wood, but could not do so till half-past three in the afternoon on account of the ground, when it was decided that it was too late to organise a second attack.

It appeared now from the reports of spies that the rebels in the bush, about two thousand in number, were in three divisions. Matanzima, Sandilli's son, had their right wing; Sandilli and Gongabele, chief of the Tambookies, were with the centre; and Edmund, Sandilli's eldest son, had the left wing, the latter had been brought up as a Christian. He had been a magistrate's clerk at Middle Drift, and had worn a frock coat and tall hat on occasions; but such is the force of Kafir custom that he changed his clothes for a blanket, daubed his body red, and took to the bush to join his father. When asked afterwards why he had done this, he could only answer, "My chief called, and I had to obey." There is an instance of self-abnegation; for he had never been circumcised, and his tribe would never have recognised him as paramount chief.

About this time Commandant-General Griffith joined General Thesiger from Thomas River, the levies he had commanded having been detailed to the various posts round the Perie bush. He was a great accession to our party, knowing the language, the people, and the country so thoroughly; he had been many years at border work, and there was not a trick of the Kafirs that he was not acquainted with. In a day we were all the best of friends, and my Chief afterwards at Cape Town owned how much he had owed to Griffith's local knowledge. He told us, among other things, that the Kafirs had lost their former daring, and that our camps would not be molested at night. This turned out to be correct; the only times our sentries were alarmed were when parties crept out of the bush at night to rob the surrounding mealie-fields or cattle *kraals*.

I often wondered at the enemy's lack of enterprise; had he come from his central position on one of our posts in strength, we should have had enough to do to hold our own. Sometimes it seemed as if the Kafir thought the whole thing a joke, for when we shelled the bush, the women would all troop out to us, sit down behind the guns, and watch the effect, sometimes even applauding a good shot. When it was over, they would try to return; but this was not allowed, as they were really the intelligence, commissariat, and transport departments of the rebels.

It was decided to send them down to King William's Town and East London, and thence by steamer to Cape Town, where some of them were taken into service till the war should be over. This greatly damped the rebel's energy, and also saved many a woman's life; for many would have died of starvation in the bush, a sort of wet season prevailing, and they could not light a fire except at night, since the smoke attracted the attention of our gunners. The Fingoes wanted to take them as wives, saying that the Gaikas would rob them of theirs if they got a chance.

The women regarded the idea very stoically, perhaps having changed hands before; but they were sent away under a white guard and, I believe, made themselves happy enough at Cape Town.

While on this subject, I must say a word in praise of our enemy, and tell a story related by some friends who had been in the Galekaland fight. One day in a skirmish there, a young Kafir, whose arm-ring showed him to be a chief, was shot, and his men began to retreat, except one tall grey-headed old fellow, who threw all his *assegais*, then his *knobkerrie*, and finally heaved stones and dirt at the white men. Their officer ordered them not to shoot him, and an interpreter told him that if he would surrender, he would not be hurt. His reply was worthy of any race:

"This morning I left the great place with my young chief; you have killed him. I, a councillor, cannot return to his father without him; I will follow him"; and he continued advancing and throwing, till some man, who got a crack on the head, put up his rifle and shot him. This, and the episode of Edmund Sandilli, show that, though their ways may be barbarous and though they never give quarter, they have a certain feudal system and sense of honour attaching to it that would put a civilised Socialist, or even a Radical, to shame.

On March 19th, Brabant, Wood, and Frost, who had now combined, advanced and drove the Kafirs from the plateau into the Buffalo Poort; but the general, on account of the difficulty of communication, had no notion of what they were doing until he heard the firing above Perie mission station. We had left camp before six o'clock that morning, leaving the guns and an escort there, for Haynes's saw-mill which is on the Buffalo at the open end of the Buffalo Poort, and Mr. Haynes had promised to have one hundred and fifty Fingoes under a head-man ready to work the lower part of the bush.

These Fingoes did not seem to like the job; they did not assemble till noon, and then the head-man was absent. Haynes proposed to guard his mill himself, and sent his son, aged about sixteen, as leader. The general asked me if I would take them, and sent ten men of the 90th under an officer to give the Fingoes courage. We started for the bush, and when young Haynes had shown me the road into the *kloof*, I sent him back, after he had picked out a man for me as interpreter.

I took the bearings of the *kraantz* we were to make for, and then we extended and entered the bush. For all I knew everything was going well, till after about a mile we emerged on a clearing which had been planted with mealies, and there I found only about forty Fingoes with me, the rest having made a strategic movement to the rear thus early. I assembled the remnant and asked what their comrades were about. They had every sort of excuse under the sun: "This was a most unlucky day for a fight, the moon was so-and-so"; "If the Inkos' would only let them wait for their head-man, they would charge like wounded bush-bucks"; "They would rather wait for him even till to-morrow, and they would be ready when the sun was only as high as half my hand,"—and so on, and so on.

On bidding them advance all together, one pointed his gun at me; I had to take it away, and rub his nose with the muzzle of my revolver. It was clear to me that semi-civilisation at the sawmills had taken all the stiffness out of their constitutions. But loth to give up thus early, I took two men of the 90th with me in front, told the Fingoes to follow in a lump, and the remaining eight soldiers to drive them on from behind. The interpreter then became very entertaining. First, he discovered the spoor of some cattle, and said we ought to return as there must be red Kafirs about, as if he did not know we were after them; then followed other excuses, and finally he said that a red Kafir had just passed and bent the grass down.

I was just taking a look at my compass, when bang went a gun waking up the echoes of the forest, and the whole lot of Fingoes turned and went down the path as if the Evil One was after them. I could not tell at first if it was a Kafir who had fired, or if one of the Fingoes had let his gun off by accident; but we could see nothing under the bush, and as all seemed quiet, it was evident that the Fingoes had been themselves the cause of the stampede. There was now nothing to be done but to get out of the bush as quietly and quickly as possible, which we accomplished without accident, after a lot of useless exertion, and without rendering any help to those on the plateau. So much for the Fingo!

We afterwards heard that on this day Wood, Brabant, and Frost had cleared the plateau, with the loss of one colonial officer, Captain Bradshaw, and two Fingoes killed, and a few Fingoes wounded, and had occupied the ground gained; Frost's force bivouacking there for the night, while Wood's and Brabant's returned to their original positions a mile off. Captain Bradshaw was killed by Dukwana, one of Sandilli's best shots, who before the war had been elder of the Emgwali mission station; and the worthy missionary, when his convert disappeared, could only suggest that he had gone to convert the rebels.

On the 20th the general moved headquarters from Perie mission station, going by Haynes's mill, Izeli, the Gwengwe Valley, and Sugar-bush Flats, to Isidengi, calling on the way at Colonel Degacher's camp for a mounted escort. At the Sugarbush Flats the signs of recent fighting began to be seen; swollen corpses of Matanzima's following were lying all about; and one especially ghastly sight, the body of a warrior who had fallen back with his arms extended right on to a bush, and who looked as if he had been crucified. Dead rebels were never buried during the war, unless near enough to a camp to be unpleasant; the ground was so rocky that it took hours to dig a grave, and while you were about it the chances were that some live Kafirs would be stalking you.

The columns under Wood, Brabant, and Frost had now exhausted their three days' supply, and, it being impossible from the state of the ground for waggons to reach them, they had to return to revictual. While such transport as they had, took the track down to Bailie's Grave Post, Wood, with the greater part of the men, drew the bush on the south side of the plateau, having got information that the Kafirs were breaking back westwards and crossing the open at Bailie's Grave Post towards the Intaba Ka'ndoda Mountain, otherwise called Tslambies Kop.

On the 21st, therefore, he sent Brabant's force down into the bush above Perie mission station with orders to beat westward: Frost was to hold the edge of the plateau facing south; while Wood's force was nearer the road between King William's Town and Keiskamahoek. Two officers of the Diamond Field Horse, Captains Ward and Donovan of Brabant's force, were killed this day by Kafirs concealed behind rocks, and some of their men were wounded.

General Thesiger left Isidengi Camp on the 21st, and getting news of this retreat for provisions, was obliged to postpone the general attack. He therefore moved over Mount Kempt to Bailie's Grave Post, reaching it at ten in the evening, where he could confer with Colonel Wood. He had been trying to get the Volunteers, who had engaged to serve for six months, to extend their service, but very few could be induced to do so. They would probably enrol themselves again, but six months was enough at a time; for the present they were off home to see their friends and spend their pay.

Having now got a good notion of the difficulties of the country and the smallness of the force that would remain to search it, there was nothing to be done but to raise fresh levies of Volunteers, to get a thousand Fingoes from Fingoland, and while watching and harrying the Kafirs as much as possible, defer any combined movement until the reinforcements arrived.

That night we all slept in camp with Streatfeild and his Fingoes. I am afraid the younger members of our party did not turn in till long after midnight. We had plenty to talk about with that best of good fellows, and when you have been in the saddle for sixteen hours at a stretch, a little joviality after dinner, when it is cool, does you no great harm. However, six o'clock, the hour to saddle up, came all too soon next morning, and we were off to King William's Town, to confer with Sir Bartle Frere and the Colonial Secretary, and to raise fresh levies of Afrikander Volunteers and of Fingoes, if His Excellency should approve.

Headquarters remained in King William's Town till the 26th of March. The raising of the new levies was approved, and the colonial authorities agreed to the proposition that all the mealie-fields near the bush, whence the Kafirs got their supplies, should be destroyed. In the meantime, Colonel Wood was making a practicable' road from Bailie's Grave Post on to the plateau, while Schermbrucker and Degacher were widening the tracks from Izeli past Isidengi to Mount Kempt. By the 27th the conferences were over and the office-work done, and much to our delight, we were again on the road to Isidengi, Commandant-General Griffith accompanying headquarters.

By the same date Colonel Wood and Brabant had revictualled and returned to the plateau, bringing tents with them this time; it was determined therefore to harry the enemy, though deferring the general attack till the arrival of the Transkei Fingoes. The Kafirs had returned on to the lowest part of the plateau from the Buffalo Poort, but in reduced numbers as we judged from the smoke of their fires. Two seven-pounders had been got up to Mount Kempt, with which we attempted to shell them from their position; but though we sunk the trails in the ground, the distance was too great.

Colonel Wood therefore moved down and drove them off, while Allan Maclean's Fingoes, a new levy, worked up the Buffalo Poort from Haynes's mill, and emerged on the plateau, having missed the enemy in that enormous tract of forest. Though our shells could not reach them, we could hear their war-cry shouted from time to time, so clear was the atmosphere and so great our height above them.

For some days more a desultory warfare was continued. Wood's force cleared the lower plateau, thereby confining the enemy to the Buffalo Poort, and portions of the bush were beaten each day; but we could not discover Sandilli's hiding-place, only killing a few Kafirs and finding groups of starving women and children. During this time Captain Gosset and myself were engaged in cutting a road through a *kloof* to join Mount Kempt with the plateau below, and in trying to survey the chain of mountains; for the small-scale maps had been evidently filled in from imagination, while those on the large scale contented themselves with leaving the Buffalo Mountains to be represented by blank spaces.

In the latter work I must confess that we were not successful. Theodolites and plane-tables were impossible when nearly everything had to be done from the back of a horse, with a couple of orderlies keeping a sharp look-out while we observed and recorded; but the road did well enough, giving easy access to Wood's camp, so our six days' work was not quite in vain.

At last, on April 3rd, the thousand Transkei Fingoes arrived, under their magistrate Mr. Ayliff, and the grand attack was arranged for the 5th. The plan was for the white troops to hold the plateaux while the combined Fingoes were to beat the bush from Mount Kempt to Haynes's mill; the signal for the drive to commence was to be three shots from the seven-pounders at Mount Kempt. Captain Gosset and myself got leave to join Commandant Streatfeild for the day's bush-driving, and as it was to begin as soon as it was light enough to see, we joined his bivouac overnight. There was a grievous smell there, and next day a dead woman was found close at hand.

On the 5th at daybreak the guns were fired, and packing up our blankets and coats we prepared for the fray. Streatfeild had to wait to let Lonsdale's men get level with him, so we had time for a light breakfast, and to watch the Transkei Fingoes on our left perform their war-dance. Directly they were formed up, they fired off their guns into the air and began dancing like maniacs.

"What is all this row for?" asked Streatfeild of Ayliff. "You will spoil the beat."

"Oh, they always do that to tell the enemy they are coming, and as a hint for them to get out of the way. I can never stop them," said Ayliff, who was one of the finest, handsomest, and pluckiest of the magistrates in those parts, and who was mad at the behaviour of the people he governed and now commanded.

However, we started at last, about six o'clock, our Fingoes numbering about eighteen hundred in all; and from almost the beginning our white comrades lining the plateaux above must have thought we were engaged in a terrific battle, Every bush-buck or blue-buck that was viewed got a tremendous volley, the men firing right or left or back, whichever way the beasts went, regardless of wounding or killing their comrades or officers; yet they carefully avoided the bases of the *kraantzes*, the very places where the enemy might be expected to hide. They were so untrustworthy that I was not surprised to see the white officers of each corps invariably keeping together. Four white men with carbines can make a good defence; a company of Fingoes with one officer would probably run if attacked, and leave their white leader to his fate.

During that day we passed through the wildest forest scenery. Enormous yellow-wood trees, some of them as much as twenty feet in girth, kept the sun off, while our way lay over enormous rocks at one moment, through dense bush at another, interspersed with glades full of gorgeous butterflies; pebbly streams in one place, deep bogs in others, and then a *kraantz*, only to be surmounted with the aid of monkey-ropes, would temporarily bar our way, while a perpetual *feu-de-joie* kept us always on the alert. But the longest day has an end, and after eleven hours hard labour we emerged at Haynes's Mill, having nominally marched eight miles. Many of the men had joints of bucks; not a man of the Transkei force had a single round of ammunition left, and as a thousand men started with sixty rounds each, this day's work meant the expenditure of over sixty thousand rounds; while the Kafirs killed, some ten in number, were decrepit old men, too rheumatic to escape the stabbing-*assegai*.

During the 5th the general and his reduced staff had moved from Isidengi to Haynes's Mill, expecting that, as the Kafirs were driven into this southern corner, the final resistance would be somewhere near that point. When at length we emerged from the *poort*, and reported the rebel loss at ten all told, he was much astonished, thinking from the tremendous noise that had been going on all day that we had at last found our enemy in force. "What on earth have you been shooting at?" he asked. We could only point at the numerous joints of bush-buck, and report that the Transkei Fingoes were useless.

It now became evident that the bulk of the Kafirs had got away westward, or we should at least have got some cattle during our day's work; and this was borne out on the evening of the 5th by a report from Captain Warren, R. E., commanding the Diamond Field Horse at Debe Nek, that he had had an engagement with Kafirs of Jali's, Kama's, and Seyolo's tribes, who had left their homes on the north of the Keiskama River, between Fort Wiltshire and the sea, to join the other rebels in the Intaba Ka'ndoda bush. Of these Seyolo, who had been well known in the war of 1851, was named the Lion on account of his courage, and was undoubtedly still the bravest of our foes. Kama was a Christian and an ordained minister: he did not turn out with his men, but took no steps to stop their going on the warpath; while, curiously enough, Siwani, a very near relation of Seyolo's, not only refused to turn out but actually came over to our side, bringing a levy of Gaikas with him.

On hearing of this fresh outbreak and the concentration of the Kafirs around the Intaba Ka'ndoda, the general that night gave orders for all available forces to march against Seyolo next day. Streatfeild's and Lonsdale's Fingoes were sent up a path over Perie mission station to rejoin Colonel Wood on the plateau—a pleasant night's climb after their day's work: the Transkei Fingoes were ordered to march at one in the morning for Bailie's Grave Post; a company of the 24th and two guns under Colonel Law, R.A., were ordered to move on to the same place at daybreak; and a message was sent by the returning Fingoes to Colonel Wood, to assemble all the men he could and move down from the heights and by the valley of the Rabula to the neighbourhood of Burnshill to stop the rebels from getting to the Amatola Mountains.

The general and staff left Haynes's mill early on April 6th for Bailie's Grave Post, where three companies of the 24th, two seven-pounders, and one thousand Transkei Fingoes were now assembled. The force was then moved westward, and got into position at noon; the bush on the southern slope was shelled and cleared by the Fingoes without any difficulty; the guns and the infantry were then moved on to the eastern *kraantz* of the Zanyorkwe Valley, which runs north and south from the Rabula Valley to Intaba Ka'ndoda. Our allies, under Wood's command, were to beat towards us; but they had such a long march that they could not get into their places till four in the afternoon.

Seeing that cattle were grazing at the head of the Zanyorkwe Valley, and knowing that Kafirs must be thereabouts, the general lined the edge of the plateau with the companies of the 24th, and sent the Fingoes to beat the wooded slopes below. As luck would have it, they came right on Seyolo's following; he, behaving like a hero again, took charge of the Kafir rear-guard and twice repulsed the Fingo rush, while the bulk of the rebels scaled the opposite slope on to a plateau, where they were received by volleys from the 24th on our side of the valley, and dispersed into a further stretch of bush. Our Fingoes suffered severely when they were driven back into the open glade by Seyolo, Captain Webster and three men being killed and thirty wounded, nearly all severely. From above we could see and hear everything; but as friends and foes were mingled, we could not help with musketry. Commandant-General Griffith, who was with us, translated the sounds to us.

One sight was terrible, as we could do nothing in aid. A wounded Fingo lay on the ground, and an arm-ringed Kafir approached him. "Mercy, mercy, oh my chief, and I will tell you all about it!" was the despairing cry. "*Inja* (dog)!" said the Kafir, and ripped him right open with his stabbing-*assegai*, the curious shout that the Kafir gives when administering the death-blow and the dying yell of his victim rising together to the heights in fearful unison.

Colonel Wood's force had now arrived on the opposite plateau and prevented the Kafirs escaping there; but it took so much persuasion to induce our Fingoes to enter the bush again that darkness put an end to the contest.

When our wounded were brought up to the plateau there were some curious scenes. The only doctor with us was a man who had formerly been a chemist's assistant at Grahamstown. This disciple of Æsculapius was discovered with half his hand inside a Fingo who had been wounded by some ragged shot in the abdomen, and who was taking his awful punishment without a single groan. He was stopped, of course, for there was not the slightest doubt that the wound was mortal, and it was no use giving intense pain by roughly searching for the missile. "Oh, I know these n———s well: he will most likely pull round," said the fellow, who seemed quite grieved when his experiments were stopped.

The wounded man was given Liebig and water by some of our fellows, bandaged up, and told to keep quite quiet and to eat nothing. But in the night, he actually crawled half a mile away to his comrades' camp, gorged a lot of tinned meat, and did not die for two days; so, the Grahamstowm man knew something about them and their cast-iron interiors. Poor Webster's body was carried up on an extemporised litter after dark; it was evident that he had been shot with a Snider rifle, for there was but a very small blue hole in the centre of his forehead, while the whole of the back of his head had been blown completely away.

When the Enfield rifle was first made, the bullet had a solid, oval-shaped head, and a boxwood plug expanded the cup at the base under the pressure of the powder on discharge, so as to take the grooving.

Later on, a second piece of boxwood was let in at the apex of the bullet, so as to keep the weight as near as possible round the circumference, to sustain the rotation longer. Later still, to reduce the cost, a baked clay plug was substituted for the wooden plug at the base; and the plug in front discontinued, its place being left hollow in casting with a small lead lip round it, this being spun over the hollow by machinery; so that the point looks solid, but is really hollow, as can be seen by cutting off the point.

These bullets are as bad as explosive ones. On impact with a soft body, they open out, and the wound on exit is frightful. The bullets of the solid, hardened Martini and Magazine rifles go in and out so cleanly that they must touch a bone or a vital organ to disable; but few can stand up on the touch of the soft lead expanding missile, and for bush-fighting against savages I think the Snider will remain the favourite arm. We do not want to blow our enemy to pieces; but when that enemy is a savage, we do want to stop his rush and keep his stabbing-weapon at a distance.

If at this time the force had been strong enough the rebellion could have been suppressed in a few weeks; but the six months' Volunteers, some of whom had been induced to extend their service for a fortnight, were leaving in large batches, the Transkei Fingoes were so useless and insubordinate that they had to be disarmed and sent home to be disbanded, and there were only sufficient men remaining to hold the various posts round the mountains. The Kafirs therefore got breathing-time, and were joined by various waverers who thought they must have got the best of it in their war with the white man. The order was accordingly given for Lonsdale's and Streatfeild's Fingoes to receive ten days' leave; they came originally from Keiskamahoek, and were disbanded there temporarily, being told to guard their own homes and mealie-fields.

The forces of Commandants Frost and Schermbrucker were sent to look after the rebels in the Thomas River bush. Colonel Palmer of the 90th was ordered to send all the men of his regiment to join Colonel Wood, and, as Tini Macomo had left the Waterkloof, to patrol it with volunteers and *burghers* only. It was not considered advisable to reduce the forces in the Transkei, for Kreli was still somewhere thereabouts in hiding. Kreli, by the way, was never caught, but Tini Macomo was captured in May.

CHAPTER 4

An Old Ironside

On April 8th the general and staff returned to King William's Town to superintend the raising of new levies. There we stayed till the 14th, during which time the troops from the various posts around the Perie bush were employed cutting roads through it. Levies were being raised of volunteers, *burghers*, and Fingoes by Commandant von Linsingen (field-cornet of the East London district), Captain Sampson of Grahamstown, Captain Vintcent of Berlin, Captain Ronald Maclean of Von Linsingen's district, Captain Comley of Somerset district, and others; while Lonsdale's and Streatfeild's Fingoes were repairing damages and commencing to reassemble, for their *commandants* were popular, and the men did not seem to care much for leave, preferring the plenteous food of the imperial commissariat; these latter therefore were soon again at Colonel Wood's disposal.

On the 15th, pending the assembly of the forces, the general left King William's Town for a tour westward to Fort Beaufort, inspecting the south side of the Intaba Ka'ndoda Mountain *en route*; he wanted to see how things were going in the Waterkloof, and to prevent the Kafirs getting back to one of their strongest retreats in the old war of 1851. On the evening of the same day, we reached Debe Nek, where Captain Warren, R.E., and the Diamond Field Horse were stationed, patrolling the south side of the bush.

After dinner heavy firing was heard to the westward, and a vedette galloped in with the report that the Kafirs had made a raid at sunset on some Fingo *kraals* and were driving the captured cattle northward to the bush.

Part of the force was sent after them, but the herd was safe in the bush before they could be intercepted; and our men returned in the dark discomfited, with the loss of two horses shot by a parting volley. The Kafirs had fired all the Fingo huts as they retreated, carrying firebrands in their hands, and ought to have presented a good mark

FORT BEAUFORT

to our men; but though many killed rebels were reported, none could be found next day.

Early on the 16th the general with a small escort visited the burned villages. It soon became certain that the Christian Gaikas of the Reverend William Shaw Kama were implicated in the raid, so we went on to that reverend Kafir's farm with our witnesses, placed posts round his village, and ordered him to assemble all his men with any arms they possessed.

Of course, he protested that all remaining with him were loyal, and that such Christian people had no arms; but *assegais* were seen in the huts, and our Fingo witnesses identified men who had assisted at the cattle-lifting the night before.

Some of his flock were accordingly arrested before his very eyes, and all his people's huts searched for arms, when of course guns, as well as *assegais*, were found in the thatch. It was a wet day, and we were all well soaked by nightfall.

On April 17th we left Debe Nek for Middledrift to meet Colonel Wood. It was there decided to push on to Alice, and, leaving our tents behind and sending the kits on by mule-waggon, we reached that place at six in the evening. Two companies of the 90th were encamped here; there was an excellent hotel, and the village was the prettiest we had seen since landing. Close to Alice is the Lovedale mission station, the best of its kind in South Africa. They do not imagine there, as most missionaries seem to believe, that the singing of hymns translated into the Kafir tongue will turn a wild man into an angel.

The Kafir is fond of singing; he usually has a splendid voice, and when chanting loudly and rolling his eyes, he looks so intensely devout that ordinary missionaries think that he is regenerate. Mr. Theal of Lovedale goes on a different system. He catches the Kafirs young, teaches them to read, write, and sew, turns them into the workshop, shows them how to make chairs and tables, then into the garden to irrigate, sow, and reap; later on, he lets them help to print the local paper in their own dialect, or work the telegraph, the wire of which runs through the establishment; all the while the Christian belief being gradually laid before them.

The Kafir sees of course the utility of the things he makes and does, and naturally argues that, as the white man knows so much that is beneficial, doubtless what he says about religion must also be beneficial; in fact, he gets to believe in the missionary first, and then in the religion that he practises. How hard a task even such a man as this

54

has in overcoming tribal influence was shown afterwards. Sometime later, all our efforts to catch the rebels *en masse* proving ineffectual, and our messages going by wire through this station, suspicion fell upon the native clerks. False information was accordingly telegraphed purposely to Colonel Wood; and the Kafirs were found in the very place where the message had said that the troops were not to be employed.

On April 18th we left Alice for Fort Beaufort, which place previous to 1835 had been, with Grahamstown, the headquarters of the Eastern Frontier Force, the dividing line up to that year having been the Kat River to its junction with the Great Fish River, and thence along the latter to the sea; but after the war of 1835 the country, as far as the Kei River, had been proclaimed a British Province, and as such had been divided into the districts of Victoria East, Peddie, King William's Town, and East London.

We were surprised at the English appearance of Fort Beaufort. It has two or three churches, a park, a fort, several hotels, and the streets were planted with trees. The hotel was good enough, but monstrously dear, the landlord evidently going on the principle that he did not see a general every day. We were more fortunate, however, than the governor, who had been charged £50 when he went through the place a short while before.

It was now decided that operations should be resumed on April 30th, and the general, on his return to King William's Town, was busily engaged in arranging for the concentration of our motley forces. He made a further visit to the southern posts on the 25th, to Hall's Hotel, Green River, Debe Nek, and Fort White; but he gave out generally that he would attack the Perie bush on the 30th, for he had ascertained without doubt that nearly all the rebels were massed in the Zanyorkwe Valley and the Intaba Ka'ndoda bush, and he intended to surprise them there.

The new dispositions were as follows:

It was now my turn to go as *amanuensis* to a colonial *commandant*; so, when, on April 29th, the staff rode out to Bailie's Grave Post, I

EAST......*Bailie's Grave Post*, Lieut.-Colonel Degacher,
2nd batt. 24th.
Royal Artillery (Major Harness), four
7-pounders.................................... 60
2nd batt. 24th (Major Black), four
companies............................... 320
——
380 men.

WEST.....*Burnshill*, Colonel Wood, V.C., C.B., 90th.

Royal Artillery (Captain Smith), two 7-pounders	36
90th (Major Cherry), five companies	540
Diamond Field Horse (Captain Warren, R.E.)	118
Streatfeild's Fingoes	500
Lonsdale's „	500
	—— 1694 „

NORTH...*Rabula Valley*, Major Buller, C.B., 60th Rifles.

24th, one company	75
Frontier Light Horse	80
Somerset Volunteer Horse (Captain Comley)	175
Alan Maclean's Fingoes	600
	—— 930 „

SOUTH....*Debe Nek*, Commandant Von Linsingen.

Buffalo Volunteer Horse	105
Grahamstown „ „	76
Humansdorp „ „	60
Vintcent's „ „	40
Panmure „ „	39
Ronald Maclean's Fingoes	500
Siwani's Kafirs	300
	—— 1120 „

Total 4124 men.

left them *en route*, and with my *Hottentot* boy and a packhorse joined Von Linsingen at Debe Nek. After five minutes' talk, we were like old friends.

"Well, my boy," he began, "I know why the general sends his staff-officers away to colonial *commandants*. He wants his orders obeyed, and no cattle-lifting! Do you know Chobham? Yes? Well, I was Brigade-Major of the German Legion there in 1853, so you see I know the regulations. But I am glad you have come; it will remind me of old times, and you shall tell me what you think of my plan for tomorrow. I see you have brought a carbine; that's right, I always work the bush on foot with my men. I know most of them would rather be riding, so one has to set an example, though I am getting an old man now to clamber about on foot.

"You know the general has told me to leave Sampson's Graham-stown men in the open to keep Seyolo and his lot from escaping to their locations; there will be a few details left to look after the horses and the camp, that will leave me about two hundred *burghers*, mostly Germans. Siwani has sent me three hundred Gaikas, and there are five hundred of Ronald Maclean's Fingoes.

"Siwani was loyal in the old war, and he has sent a half-caste rela-tion of his own, one Jem, to help Captain Clarke lead the men, but one must make quite sure of them; so, tomorrow I shall post Siwani's men in the middle of the front line, put two hundred and fifty Fingoes on their right and the same number on their left, and the two hundred Germans dismounted in their rear as second line; and I shall tell the Germans, who are all rare good shots, to watch Siwani's, and if they turn against us, to shoot them down to a man.

"If there is only some blood-letting between Siwani's and Seyolo's Kafirs, it will make the 'loyal' Gaikas stick to us for ever, for being of the same extraction, there will then be a sort of blood-feud between them; besides, some of Siwani's own men have joined Seyolo."

Of course, I approved of the arrangement. Then said the grim old warrior: "We will have supper and then I shall read prayers, at which you will be welcome. I always have prayers at night in the field, and it is curious how glad the roughest are to attend. After that we will have a tot of rum and turn in, for we must be off at four o'clock in the morning."

He was pleased to see an addition of one to his congregation after supper; and by eight o'clock the old Ironside and I were trying to drown each other's snores.

The next morning the guard woke us all too soon; but after a mug of coffee and a biscuit, we stripped to leggings, breeches, shirt, and cap, telling our boys to keep our pack-horses with food, coats, and blankets near Sampson's patrols, and be ready to join us wherever we might bivouac. Then with carbines and bandoliers of cartridges, we paraded the motley forces as well as it could be done in the dark, and stepped out in our two very irregular lines at four a.m. It was a good two miles to the scene of action, through grassy, broken ground, and we were wet to the knees in five minutes from the heavy dew.

However, we reached the bush before it was thoroughly light and lay down to get the men more or less aligned; then, with the centre directed straight at Intaba Ka'ndoda Peak, we went ahead as quietly as might be and watched Siwani's men keenly.

We soon struck the track that had been made on the night of the 15th, when the Kafirs had looted the Fingo cattle; and a fine track it was, just as if an avalanche had started half-way down the mountain and flattened everything but the big trees. The hill rose twelve hundred feet above the plain, and the bush was so dense that a bill-hook would have been our best friend. I don't know what hour it was, but I should think from the sun about eight o'clock, when our centre was stopped by a regular wall of rock some two hundred feet high, while the right and left reported they were on ridges on its flanks.

It was evident this pulpit-shaped rock was not to be scaled from the south; but while we were looking for a road, Siwani's Kafirs discovered some of Seyolo's scouts in among the rocks at its base, and with yells of delight killed seven, whose names they seemed to know. Von Linsingen's joy was unbounded; he told Captain Clarke and Jem he would reward the men with his own hand, and report to the general how well the officers had behaved; and then he said very quietly to me:

"Now Siwani's men are my children; they cannot live with Seyolo's anymore. You may let the general know their loyalty is assured, and, as you see, they can fight. I think you will say I am a good recruiter."

It was then decided to let the Fingo right wing go round to the east side of the peak, while the centre and left moved to the west side, so as to feel the forces on the right and left before moving down into the Zanyorkwe Valley; when very heavy firing of musketry, and then of artillery, on our left front told us that Colonel Wood was busily engaged. Our centre and left then executed the plainest and best of manoeuvres; they marched straight for the sound of the firing.

What a race it was! Into holes, out again, hands and faces bleeding from thorns, knees punctured, and shirt-sleeves in ribands, till after about an hour of it our left came out on the open plateau west of the Zanyorkwe Valley, and our centre force hit off the bush covering the valley's western slope. Finding that Colonel Wood had extricated his column from the bush and had assembled it on this west plateau, we waited to let our Fingoes on the right complete their movement round the Intaba Ka'ndoda Peak and again get touch of us. We were too late to intercept any of the Kafirs that had opposed Wood, but our left came out near the path up the Makabalikele Ridge, where he had been engaged, and during our halt we went to see the ground.

The path was wide enough for guns, and the order of march had been one company of the 90th leading, then two seven-pounder guns followed by another company, and then the rest of the force. The flank had been protected by men of a *Hottentot* levy, moving thirty paces within the bush parallel to the column; but these fellows had either been outstripped by the column moving in the open path, or, thinking discretion the better part of valour, had laid down. Whichever happened, the Kafirs managed to form in the bush parallel to the path and close to it; and when Captain Stevens's leading company arrived abreast of them, it was greeted with a volley which wounded its captain dangerously, and killed and wounded some men.

Lieutenant Saltmarshe took command and was immediately afterwards killed; and so, daring did the Kafirs now become, that some came out in advance on the open path and fired into the head of the column. The company however forced its way through on to the open ground, which gave room for the two guns of the Royal Artillery to gallop out, and unlimbering within thirty yards of the bush, they fired case into it parallel with the path, and cleared out the ambushed Kafirs. I don't know how the defaulting *Hottentots* could have liked this; they were probably too far off to be hurt and lying very low. This short skirmish cost the 90th an officer and four non-commissioned officers and men killed, and an officer and three men wounded.

When Von Linsingen's men had got in line again, we worked the west side of the Zanyorkwe Valley northward, killing a rebel here and there until we met Lonsdale's and Streatfeild's Fingoes at the mouth of the Tutu Kloof, where we wheeled threequarters-left-about and, when they had joined our right, advanced up that valley. Major Buller crossed the valley from the east side, now well cleared by Alan Maclean's Fingoes, to the west with a company of the 24th and the Frontier Light Horse which had now joined us, placing the soldiers to line the top while the Fingoes and Colonials beat the bush below. When it was getting dusk Von Linsingen's force joined Colonel Wood on the plateau, and afterwards returned by the Makabalikele Nek, reaching camp between seven and eight at night.

In this very broken country, it was impossible to know what everyone had done, the forces on the plateaux being alone able to flag-signal across the Zanyorkwe Valley to each other; so that night we only knew that we had accounted for some twenty-five rebels, and that the 90th had lost both officers and men; but it was afterwards ascertained that about one hundred and thirty Kafirs had been killed, and that our loss was twenty-two natives killed and wounded in addition to the loss in the 90th. In a despatch home on this day's operations, the

The 24th in Zululand

general reported how necessary it was to employ signallers in South African warfare.

Now about three p.m. on this day we had passed a message back to the boys with our pack-horses to return to camp and await us there. On reaching Debe Nek, my boy and a pack-horse were missing; the other fellows explained that he chose to consider head-quarters his camp, and had somehow made his way there from Sampson's patrol, so I found myself without a coat, outer garments, or blankets. Von Linsingen lent me a pea-jacket to sleep in, and wanted me to take one of his blankets; but thinking that, after dinner and a pipe, I should be all right, I just lay down on the ground in the tent as I was, and to this day have not ceased to regret it; for with the morning came a chill, two days after tobacco was distasteful, and in two months' time I was insensible with typhoid fever.

On this day a curious case of suicide occurred. An infantry sergeant, one of the company lining the edge of the Tutu Kloof, had been quite rationally directing the men near him to aim at Kafirs who were breaking out of the bush; suddenly he exclaimed to a man near him, "Goodbye, Jack," and placing his rifle to his own head, blew out his brains. He was buried with difficulty there and then in a shallow grave, for the ground was very rocky; but in the night the Kafirs dug him up, took away his boots, and left him in a sitting position, where we found him next day and had again to bury him.

That night we had nothing to do except guard our camp, but Lonsdale's and Streatfeild's Fingoes were posted so as to prevent the scattered Kafirs breaking back into the Perie bush. A party of Kafirs stumbled right on to Lonsdale's men, who bolted in a panic, firing like maniacs and leaving their commander alone in the camp; the Kafirs, equally frightened, also bolted, dropping blankets, guns, and *assegais* all over the place. Plucky enough by daylight, neither set of natives was ever of any use at night.

I now rejoined headquarters, glad enough to get back to my clothes and blankets, but the mischief was already done. It was known that Seyolo, two of Sandilli's sons, and great numbers of their followers had been in the bush before the 30th; but we had not come across them during the two days despite a rigorous search. The parties which had been known to have escaped at night did not account for one tenth of their force; so, it was decided to continue the search, and while the general and staff rode around the cordon of posts on May 2nd, Von Linsingen's men and Colonel Degacher's companies were sent down

61

to beat the valley. On our return pretty late, a report reached us that a cave had been discovered in the valley, where some chiefs and a large following were supposed to be hiding.

It appeared that the place had been several times passed during the day, but the Kafirs keeping quiet had not been discovered. As our men, however, were being withdrawn at dusk, one of Siwani's loyal Kafirs had passed close to it, and, being recognised as a renegade Gaika, had been shot dead by Seyolo's men, who could not resist the temptation. It was too dark to attack them, so Von Linsingen posted his men for the night in a semi-circle round the place, which was backed by a steep *kraantz*, and lit fires. He talked to the Kafirs, found that Seyolo was actually there, and endeavoured to induce him to surrender, but without avail.

The next morning, we were up early, to visit the cave before returning to King William's Town. We rode to the edge of the valley, and then, leaving our horses, clambered down through the bush. An approach had been made at day-break, and another of Von Linsingen's men shot; so, he had bid them get such breakfast as they had before going on. We could not stay to see the affair out, but rejoining the chief rode by Perie and Haynes' Mill to the town; for there was now no doubt that most of the Kafirs had escaped and were reassembling in the Buffalo Range, and new dispositions were necessary for a further attack on this bush. A message came in later that the cave had been taken and twenty-one Kafirs killed, with a loss on our side of four; that the chiefs had escaped during the night by a winding path up the *kraantz*; and that only one man of note, an old councillor who had fallen while climbing, had been captured.

To keep the intended attack on the Perie bush secret, the general remained at King William's Town till the 8th of May and then rode out very early to Haynes' Mill. The plan of attack this day was as follows:

(1) Colonel Wood, with 751 Europeans, 760 natives, and two seven-pounder guns, was to move from near Keiskamahoek to the Gozo Heights. This was the new name given to the plateau on the Buffalo Mountains east of Bailie's Grave Post. The Kafirs call the Perie bush the Forest of Hoho, after a former *Hottentot* chieftainess who led her race in their last battle against the Kafirs; and the pronunciation had been corrupted by ourselves.

(2) Colonel Degacher, with 775 Europeans and 550 natives, from

Haynes' mill to the plateau west of the Buffalo Poort.

(3) Commandant Von Linsingen, with 184 Europeans and 800 natives from near Perie Mission Station to the same plateau, keeping to the left of Degacher's Force.

(4) Major Buller, with 293 Europeans and 500 natives, from Mount Kempt by a bush path cut in April to the same plateau.

(5) Commandant Schermbrucker, with 285 Europeans, from Isidengi to Mount Kempt, and then to follow Major Buller.

(6) Captain Surplice, with 80 men of the 24th and 200 of Haynes' Fingoes, was to be conducted by Haynes himself to beneath the western *kraantz* of the Buffalo Poort, to forelay the path that the Kafirs, when driven from the plateau, would take.

At daybreak on the 8th the forces moved off; all went well, and they reached their assigned positions, except Captain Surplice's detachment which had Haynes of the mill as its guide. As this man Haynes knew every inch of this bush, having cut timber in it for years, he had been chosen for guide, notwithstanding that he had shirked a job some little while previously. He had been shown the exact spot for the ambush on the day before by Major Buller; yet he misled the company and rendered the whole plan abortive. He was a bit of a braggart, too, which makes me relate this little accident of his.

The other parties got into position and drove the Kafirs off the plateau; but they escaped through the gap, their retreat being covered by a few determined men. In searching the ground below, near which Surplice's party was supposed to be in ambush, Major Buller's force was surprised by the Kafir rear-guard and suffered severely. Captain McNaughten and three men being killed, and Captain Whalley and five men wounded. During the sharp fighting that ensued Major Buller earned the highest praise, the general's despatch stated:—

He set an example of intrepidity and calm courage to his men under very trying circumstances, and although the operations of this day were not attended with all the success I expected, he did his best by personal example to secure it.

His force at length turned the Kafir's position, drove them out and killed fifteen of them.

Colonel Wood was now instructed to build a fort on the Gozo Heights for a garrison of two companies and two guns, to command the Perie bush plateaux; and another fort was constructed on a plateau east of Intaba Ka'ndoda for one company and two guns to command the Zanyorkwe Valley. The Kafirs were thus kept from coming into the open: the various colonial and Fingo levies divided between the two positions worked the bush daily; and Schermbrucker at Stutterheim looked after the Thomas River district.

The end was now near at hand. Sandilli, constantly sending in with offers of peace but refusing to surrender himself, was killed by a stray shot at Isidengi; Dukwana, the Christian and Elder, the best shot they had, fell with his chief; Seyolo was killed by Von Linsingen's men in the Fish River bush; Tini Macomo was captured near his old haunts in the Waterkloof; and the only men of note remaining in arms at the end of May were Umhala, Dhimba, Edmund Sandilli, and Matanzima. Gongabele, chief of the Tambookies, and some of his lesser chiefs had surrendered to the magistrate in Anta's country north of the Thomas River in April, and were now safe in gaol at Queenstown.

With the deaths of Sandilli and Seyolo, the paramount and the fighting chiefs, the rebellion collapsed. The people of King William's Town would not own it, for they were growing rich by the war; but the general decided that the finishing touches were more properly work for Police and Irregulars, and gave instructions accordingly. For the time, however, he kept troops at Keiskamahoek, Bailie's Grave Post, Perie mission station, and Izeli, the two former points separating the Pirie and Intaba Ka'ndoda forests, and the two latter keeping watch between King William's Town and the Buffalo Mountains, with an eye on the Christian Kafirs; for, regardless of the Reverend Mr. Ross's protests, his men were on several occasions convicted of assisting the rebels.

The general now determined to visit Galekaland and the Gaika Location, for though Ngubo, Kreli's witchdoctor, had been surrendered by Umquiliso the Pondo, with whom he had sought asylum, the chief was at large and might cause trouble there. Leaving British Kaffraria therefore in Colonel Wood's charge, he set out on May 23rd for a tour in the Transkei where Colonel Glyn commanded.

It was on this tour that we met with that institution of savage South Africa, the *bongo*. Every chief of note has one; a man of loud voice and great powers of oratory who goes before the savage, singing praises of his beauty and his valour. Veldtman, a Fingo leader who had behaved very well in the first Galekaland campaign, had been rewarded by some wags with the present of a bright plum-coloured suit of corduroy, garnished with gold lace off a tunic, and an old gold-laced staff-cap. Carried away by this, he had stuck a feather or two about him in addition, and set up his best shouter as *bongo*; and one day, when we were on the road, he came thus to meet us and pay his respects to the general.

His *bongo* came along, a mile ahead, shouting like an Egyptian cavass, "Clear the way for the great man," regardless of the fact that the road was nowhere but, as an American would say, "where you darn please to go." This was too much for our native guide, who began to shout in his turn that there was a bigger personage about; and the two orators nearly came to blows. Before the crisis, however, Veldtman cantered up, with his big toes only in the stirrups, and made obeisance; but on many occasions, *bongos* have met and had a round or two with their clubs before their lords could arrive and discuss the question of precedence.

After perambulating Galekaland, the general went into Fingoland, where our Transkei levies had been raised. We stayed the first night at Ncamakwe with Mr. Ayliff, who made us most comfortable, and showed us what the land could produce when irrigated. He had diverted a little stream through his garden, and there was not a vegetable you could name that was not easily grown; the fruit, especially the passion-fruit, was splendid; only a little energy is required to make those parts where water is available a very paradise in appearance.

While on this subject it is impossible not to comment on the different ways of Dutch, English, Germans, and Kafirs at the Cape. The Dutchman, or Boer, recognises South Africa as his home; he is said to be lazy and behind the times, but he only wants to live and let live, not to make money as fast as he can and then pack up for home. He has his flocks and herds; he plants enough corn and grows enough tobacco for his own needs; he irrigates enough land to make a garden of fruit trees and vegetables for himself, but none to spare; with his skins and his wool he can buy the coffee, the sugar, and the *schiedam* necessary. He diverts streams into his few villages and plants trees for shade; what does he want more?

The Englishman, on the other hand, is hoping every day to be off home again. He is after diamonds or gold, or else he is a trader. He may buy a farm, if he thinks he can sell it at a bargain tomorrow: if he is an old settler who has had a free grant, he wisely sticks to it; but if he can't get it free, he leaves the land severely alone and tries, shop-keeping. His villages and towns are uncared for: there is no water in the gutters; dust, corrugated iron, and stones reign supreme; trees are few and far between, and everything is hideous.

The German is a trader, if a Jew; but on the eastern border he is a soldier-settler of the old German Legion or descended from one. He is the only market-gardener there. His wife works as hard as he. They keep cows and goats; they grow vegetables, and but for them half the population of King William's Town would suffer from scurvy; to that town they come in on their bullock-carts with garden-produce, butter, and a little milk. As settlers they are worth more than half a dozen of any other white men; for they are the most law-abiding people, though if called out by the field-cornet for service they soon show that they have lost none of their military instincts.

The Kafir is a lazy fellow, and the Fingo is only one shade better. Flocks and herds, as I have said, are their wealth; and their soured milk, with the little maize and millet they grow, keep them in food and drink. Though the demand for milk is great in the towns they have none to spare; the Germans cannot supply enough, and condensed milk from Switzerland is imported in thousands of tins to this purely pastoral country. During 1878 a great demand arose in our camps for milk. Markets were established in them and the safety of the purveyors guaranteed; but the natives were too idle to milk their cows, and were detected, when the bidding for the real article grew high, in selling Liebfraumilch which did not come from the Rhenish vineyards. There was of course an immense rise in the Swiss condensed milk trade as soon as this story got abroad.

All the time we had been employed in Kaffraria the rest of South Africa had been very much disturbed. The Pondos had been threatening; the Basutos had been stealing; the natives of Griqualand west and Bechuanaland, west of the Transvaal, had broken out into rebellion; the Zulus, east of the Transvaal and north of Natal, had been very impertinent; Sekukuni, in the north of the Transvaal, had broken out; and finally, the Boers of the Transvaal were, like the Irish, agitating for a Repeal of the Union. The general therefore decided to go down to Cape Town with his military secretary to confer with Sir Bartle Frere, and then to return up the coast to Natal.

Gosset and I were to remain to pack up the Headquarter Staff kit and get it, with the horses and servants, to Natal; while Colonel Wood was to march a column composed of the 90th Light Infantry, Harness's battery of the Royal Artillery, and Buller's Frontier Light Horse, right through Independent Kaffraria to Kokstad, and thence over the Umzimkulu River into Natal, to overawe the mixed tribes on the east coast between the two colonies, and if necessary give a lesson to Umquikela the Rondo, who was always fighting with his loyal nephew Umquiliso, and had now threatened to fight Her Majesty also.

But now the excitement was over I collapsed, as completely as the rebellion. The very afternoon my chief left, on June 24th, I went to lie down for a while, and recollect little more till the end of July; but I find I smoked my first pipe on August 2nd, exactly three months after the previous attempt on May 2nd.

While I was ill Edmund Sandilli and Matanzima were captured, Umhala and Dhimba surrendered, and the farms were again occupied throughout Kaffraria. Wood's column had got close to Natal. An amnesty was proclaimed on July 1st with a free pardon to rebels who surrendered at once. The trials of the captured chiefs took place early in the same month. The general left Cape Town for Natal on August 1st, and Gosset left to join him on the 14th.

I got out on crutches on September 1st, and a Medical Board at once ordered me to England. They kindly informed me that pyaemia had supervened on enteric fever, that I had at one time reduced the government's store of quinine by sixty grains a day, and that I had better walk softly for some time to come. Indeed, I felt like doing that and no more. The worst part of this vile disease is that it goes either to the lungs or the bones always; and it gave me a turn of both pneumonia and periostitis.

I took my passage in the *German* of the Union Line, commanded by Captain Coxwell, one of the best of his kind. Like a fool I refused to be hoisted up in the basket, with the result that, between the surfboat and the rolling ship, I managed to splinter the bone of my shin, for I was too weak to climb up the side quickly. This gave me food for reflection, and I was glad enough to sit quiet and look at nothing while we were loading up from the 18th to the 22nd, on which day we sailed. The captain was kindness itself; he recommended all the fresh air possible, and rigged up a little tent on the quarterdeck as a lounge. There were very few passengers on board, and it was difficult to make up a rubber of whist; but Coxwell at last persuaded a most extraordinary individual, who had rushed on board the last moment at Cape Town in a tall hat and frock coat, and with only one portmanteau, to join us.

The stranger demurred on the ground that he objected to gambling, and besides was in bitter grief on account of his mother, who was sick unto death, and whom he hardly expected to find alive on his return; but on our promising to play for penny points, he was induced to take a hand. He was a curious fellow; between paroxysms of woe he would tell stories of all sorts of countries and people; he knew the Transvaal and Natal, had been in the Free State and at the Diamond Fields, and used to toss about a big yellow uncut diamond of about twenty carats, explaining that its value was much lowered by a flaw, and that he had sent home many worth more.

His anxiety for his sick mother increased as we neared Madeira; and on arrival there he jumped into the first boat, went ashore, and told us on returning that he had telegraphed home and found a message awaiting him, saying his parent was worse, but happily not yet gone. When four days after we fell in with a fishing boat near the Lizard, he asked to be put on board, as his mother was in Cornwall; it was done; away he went, tall hat and all, and that is the last I saw of him. Shortly after landing at Southampton I met Coxwell in London.

"You remember," he said, "the fellow with the big diamond who would only play for penny points? Well, the next ship put on all speed, got to Madeira five days after us, and cabled on to arrest him; but he has got away. He has robbed a bank at Cape Town of £6,000, and is wanted at other places. That's the sort of man who calls whist gambling."

A Medical Board gave me four months' leave: a leading London surgeon told me time only was required to complete my cure; and following his advice I lived quietly, amusing myself by working out culminations of stars suitable for observation for position in 30° south latitude and 32° east longitude during all the months of 1879. Zululand was quite unknown except to a few officials and traders of Natal, and if I could ever get there, this would save much calculation when map-making in rough times.

On my arrival in Cape Town, I had heard that I had got promotion to captain in the ordinary course, on July 4th after thirteen and a half years' service; and therefore, expected that, if any rewards were given for the Kafir War, I might fall in for a brevet. However this was not to be, for the *Gazette* of November 28th promoted or decorated every staff-officer but myself. I went to see the Military Secretary on December 3rd to ask if there was any chance for me, and was told that I had so recently attained the rank of captain that a brevet was out of the question. Sir Alfred Horsford was such a charming man that one could take no from him in better part than yes from many; so away

THE DIAMOND FIELDS HORSE AT CROW'S FARM

I went, determined to go to Natal as soon as fate would allow and have a try again; but I could not help contrasting my case with that of an *aide-de-camp* of the Ashantee War, who, after his first campaign and with only ten years' service, was given his captaincy and brevet-majority in the same *Gazette*.

CHAPTER 5

The Zulu Army

During the latter part of 1878, the general commanding the forces in South Africa had not been idle. He, with the commodore, had visited St. John's River in Pondoland on its annexation, and left a garrison there to support a newly appointed Resident. He and his Staff had worked out a volume of Regulations for Field Forces in South Africa, had compiled an account of the Zulu Army, and a pamphlet of hints on dealing with natives for the use of commandants of Natal Native Levies (popularly called *Bellairs Treatment of Natives*). He had drawn to Natal and the Transvaal all the troops that could be spared from the Cape Colony, leaving only the 88th to garrison British Kaffraria and to send a detachment to Mauritius

The South African Republic, commonly called the Transvaal, had been annexed by us in April 1877, at the request of certain of its inhabitants who were townsmen, and against the will of certain others who were farmers. The annexation was inevitable; for Sekukuni, who was of Basuto descent though a vassal of the Zulu King, had in 1876 routed the Boers when they attacked his stronghold in a quarrel over what was known as the Disputed Territory on the left bank of the Blood River; the Boer force had dispersed, and the country was hopelessly disorganised and bankrupt, the treasury being found to contain the princely sum of twelve shillings and sixpence.

While the Boers held the Transvaal and the English held Natal, the Zulus had been friendly with us. The king had sought our advice against the aggressions of the Dutch farmers, and by our good offices he had been persuaded to restrain his young warriors from washing their spears in the blood of these white landgrabbers. To do ourselves justice, we had not attempted to take land from the Zulus: the Tugela and Buffalo Rivers had been our boundaries since the proclamation

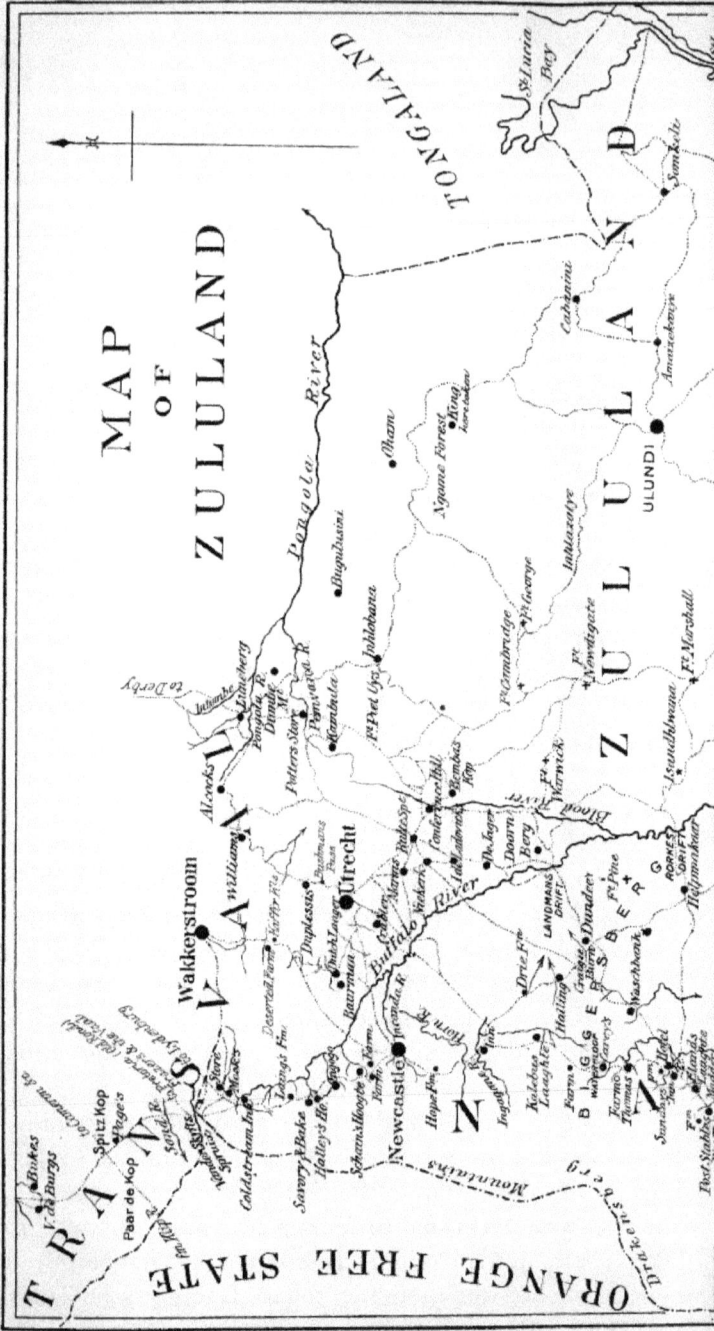

MAP
OF
ZULULAND

INDIAN OCEAN

BASUTOLAND

Scale 25 Miles to 1 Inch
5 0 10 20 30 40 50 Miles

S.& B. Stat. Lim.sch Printers Edinburgh

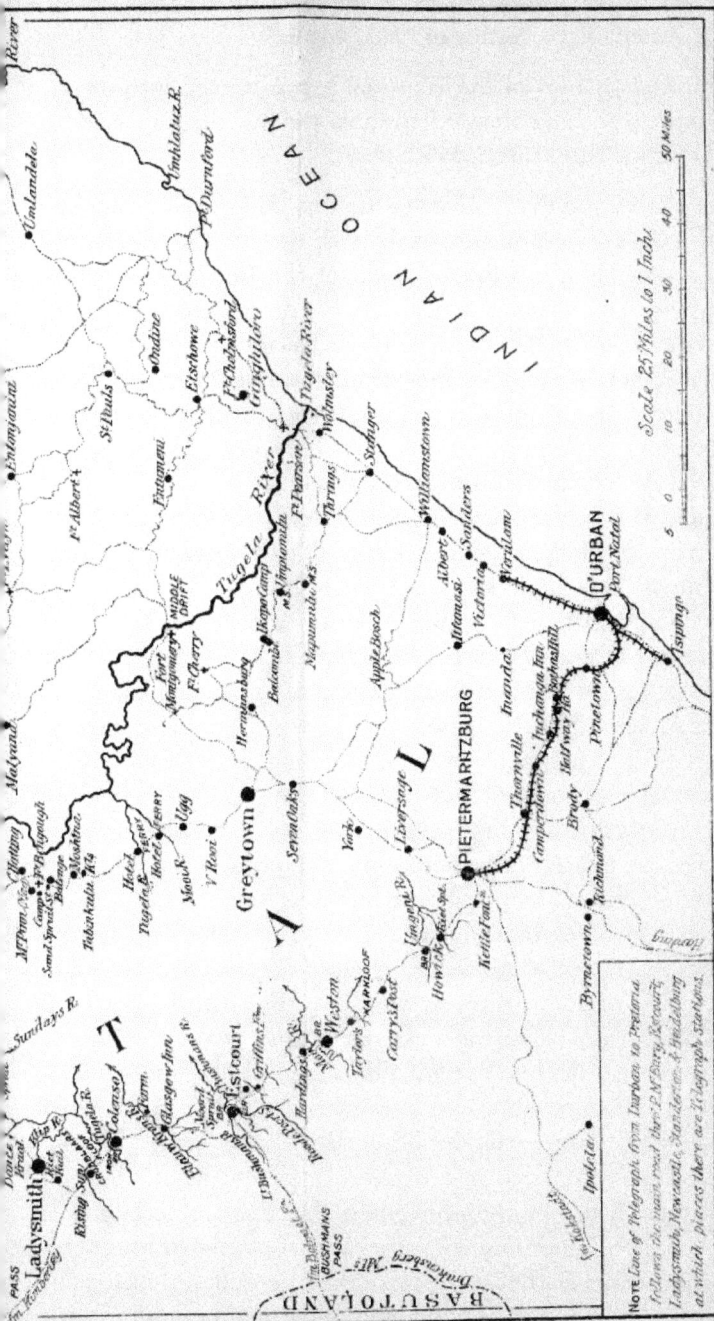

NOTE Line of Telegraph from Durban to Pretoria
follows the main road the 'P.M.Burg Network,
Ladysmith, Newcastle, Standerton & Heidelberg
at which places there are telegraph stations.

D'URBAN
Port Natal

PIETERMARITZBURG

GREYTOWN

Ladysmith

River

Tugela River

Umhlatuzi R.

Durnford

Gingindhlovu

Fort Pearson

Tugela River

Wolmsley

Stanger

Williamstown

Verulam

Isipingo

Pinetown

Botha's Hill

Inchanga Inn

Inanda

Thornville

Camperdown

Brody

Hellway Inn

Richmond

Byrnetown

Ixopo

Kokstad

Victoria

Albert

Ntomasi

Saunders

York

Umgeni R.

Liversage

Howick

Nottingham Rd.

Kettle Fontein

Carys Post

Weston

Harrisons

Taylor's

Nappwood

Griffin's Kr.

Estcourt

Mooi R.

Glasgow Inn

Colenso

Frere

Chieveley

Ennersdale

Elandslaagte

Waschbank

Sunday's R.

Dundee

Glencoe

Helpmekaar

Nqutu

Isandula

Rorke's Drift

Middle Drift

Fort Montgomery

Fort Cherry

Kranskop

Greytown

Seven Oaks

Nqumene M.S.

Apple Bosch

Nagpumube

Balcomb

Fort Albert

Patgmeni

St Pauls

Eshowe

Elsfontein

Ondine

Endingyanizi

Umlandela

Nchanga

Tugela R.

Moschtrok

Helpmekaar

Tuboskata M.S.

Mount Prospect

Sand Spruit M.S.

Balsorge

Rising Sun

Platrand

Driefontein

Bushman's River

Bushman's Pass

Drakensberg Mts.

Pt. Albert

Melmoth

T

A

L

of 1845; and for over thirty years we had been at peace with the nation on the left banks of those rivers. It had been otherwise with the Boers. The Lieutenant-Governor of Natal wrote:

> Bit by bit, the farmers of the Transvaal had advanced into the Zulu country, pushing forward towards the sea till they had almost hemmed the Zulus into a corner.

After the annexation the relations of the Zulu King and of Sekukuni his vassal were at first not unfriendly with us as the new rulers of the Transvaal; but being no longer afraid of the Boers, these chiefs were not now so anxious to conciliate us. There was now no excuse for a large standing army, but it could not be disbanded without being first conquered, all the traditions and organisation of the nation being bound up therein; and as the younger men, hot-headed and impetuous, were burning for a fight with anyone so as to be allowed by the king to marry, the situation was naturally a delicate one.

The Zulus, or more properly Amazulu, were a comparatively insignificant tribe until their famous Chief Chaka (properly spelled Tyaka) organised them about the year 1820. (Chaka means *bastard*, but since the accession of that king such a person is called *umlandhwane* in Zulu.) He was rather a bloodthirsty person, but had great military talents, and was eighth in direct descent from the Chief Zulu, whence the name of Amazulu for the nation. He formed all the able-bodied men of the tribe into regiments by ages, gave them regimental (*Inkosi*) and company chiefs (*Induna*), and localised them in military *kraals* about the country, forming new regiments every three or four years from the boys, and linking these with some old corps of married men to inspire them with military traditions and lore.

Each man had a cowhide shield, half a dozen throwing-*assegais*, one stabbing-*assegai* and a *knobkerrie*, or club. The married men had head-rings, made of *acacia*-gum, worked into their matted hair and blacked and polished with burnt sticks, and carried white shields; the boys (bachelors) had no head-rings, and carried black, tan, or particoloured shields. Regiments could only marry with the king's consent, and this was seldom given until the particular regiment had distinguished itself.

Each regiment had a distinguishing dress: thus the *Umlambongwenya* (Alligator River) regiment might wear a band of otter skin round the forehead, a blue-crane feather in centre of the forehead, and earflaps of green monkey-skin; while the young boys of the regiment, afterwards attached to the same *Kraal-Umxapu* (the Sprinklers), might be given a band of leopard-skin round the forehead, plumes of black and white ostrich-feathers on the head, a bunch of split Kafir finch-feathers at the back, ear-flaps of green monkey-skin, and bunches of white cows' tails hanging from the neck over the chest and back, and so on.

The *Indunas* wore a short kilt of civet and green monkey-skin reaching half way from the waist to the knee; a more magnificent kilt would mark an *Inkosi*; and the king (*bayete*) alone would wear a leopard-skin robe and carry one immense spear only. The Zulus are not circumcised, and are therefore a distinct race from the Amaxosa Kafirs.

In one of the earliest of Chaka's fights, one of his *impis* (regiments) ran away and attributed their defeat to the fact that they had thrown all their *assegais* and had no more to hurl. The king was equal to the occasion; he took away all the throwing-*assegais* from his army, leaving every man his stabbing-*assegai* alone; and he gave notice that every man who returned without his *assegai* should be killed, and every man who returned without having washed his in the blood of an enemy should be punished. This, of course, meant close quarters and *l'arme blanche* with a vengeance; and as usual the side in which every man meant business succeeded, till the Zulu *impis* became invincible.

Natal at that time was densely peopled; the various native tribes are said to have been "numerous as the blades of grass spreading over the hills and filling the valleys"; but Chaka crossed the Tugela and "ate up" those people, so that in 1824, when the first English settlers arrived, the land was practically depopulated. Chaka who had been friendly to the settlers, was succeeded by Dingaan about 1828, who was succeeded by Panda in 1840: it was in the latter's reign that Natal was ceded to us; and Cetewayo succeeded Panda in 1872.

They all maintained the same military organisation; and it says much for this warlike race that never since the cession, and but once before, had they attacked the English; and this was only in return for an attempted invasion of Zululand made by some of the settlers in 1837.

Cetewayo, alive to the fact that white men were generally successful on account of their firearms, did all he could to get guns for his warriors. The trade was prohibited by the people of Natal and the Transvaal; but when diamonds were found in Griqualand West in 1867, a very large population of all nations soon assembled there, native labour became necessary, and Cetewayo saw what he thought was his chance. He gave his men by turns leave to work at the mines, on condition that each brought back a gun.

Cetewayo *c* 1875

The cunning traders soon discovered that they could sell an old musket worth nothing for thirty shillings, and they drove a roaring trade, for the native labourers' wages were high. The Transvaal Boers protested, and stopped all armed men when they could; but with the Bechuana tribes on the west hostile to them and Sekukuni, a vassal of Cetewayo, in the centre, it was easier to run arms across the country than might be supposed; and after the annexation of the Transvaal in 1877 the trade went on more openly.

The Portuguese at Delagoa Bay were also not averse to coining money out of old smooth-bores, so that by 1878 there were few Zulus who did not possess a gun of some sort. In that year the Zulu Army, composed as it was of the entire nation capable of bearing arms, was by the best authorities estimated at over forty thousand men formed in fourteen corps of most irregular numbers: the Udukuza corps, for instance, formed of one of Chaka's regiments and one of Panda's, was in all only five hundred men; while four of Panda's regiments (including the *Tulwana*, or Royal Regiment) of four thousand men, and the Nkobamakosi of six thousand, made up the Undi corps to about ten thousand men. This corps was organised by Cetewayo and garrisoned Ulundi and its neighbourhood. Cetewayo, then aged forty-five, belonged to the Tulwana regiment commanded by Umavumengwana.

Now a gun is an excellent thing when you have been taught how to use it, and have the right ammunition, and of course a rifle is better for fighting on account of its longer range; but if you fire nails, stones, slugs, and potlegs out of your gun you will not do much harm to the enemy; and if you have no notion of the theory of motion of projectiles, or sufficient rule of thumb from constant practice, you will not hit your mark with a rifle.

This was the weak point of the Zulu Army in 1879. Finding ammunition scarce, they used any missile they could get; when they captured some breechloading-ammunition they broke it up to load their smooth-bore guns; when they used a rifle with its proper ammunition, and found that by elevating the backsight and aiming over it they got greater range, they thought that raising the flap gave the gun greater power to kill, and so they always used it and generally shot over your head.

Using a gun meant stopping to fire; it broke the successful rush, and if the Zulus had had no firearms in 1879, but had stood by their old tactics of closing at once and stabbing, it would have gone worse with us in that year than it did.

Now, as has been said, when we annexed the Transvaal, we inherited also the quarrel between the Zulus and the Boers over the disputed territory.

This quarrel had arisen as follows:—in 1861 two of Panda's sons had left Zululand for the Transvaal in fear of their brother Cetewayo, then practically regent for their father Panda; and, on condition that the fugitives were surrendered, Cetewayo is said to have promised the Boers a slice of Zululand on the left bank of the Blood River. In 1864, when a Border Commission of Boers began to mark out the new boundary, Panda denied ever having alienated the land.

The quarrel dragged on till the annexation, when (in February, 1878,) we proposed, and Cetewayo agreed, that the matter should be settled by arbitration; but a decision was not given until the following November.

In that same month and year Sekukuni was ordered by Cetewayo to send an *impi* to make a raid on a native chief in the Transvaal, named Pokwana, who was friendly to the English. The British Commissioner for the district remonstrated, but all the answer he got was that the white men must leave, as the chief was ready for war.

The only imperial troops in the Transvaal were three companies of the 1st Batt. 13th at Pretoria, and they could not be spared from the capital, as a portion of the Dutch population were openly agitating against the annexation. At the request of the Administrator of the Transvaal, three more companies of the 13th and three companies of the 90th were sent from Natal; but though volunteers were raised and native contingents enrolled, Sekukuni still remained in open revolt.

In August, accordingly, the 80th Regiment was sent up from Natal, and all the troops in the territory put under the command of Colonel Rowlands, V.C., who was soon reinforced by the Frontier Light Horse, our old friends of Kaffraria, under Lieutenant-Colonel Buller, but they were only about two hundred strong.

It had been intended to attack Sekukuni, but the exceptional dryness of the season prevented the advance being successful, and the troops were withdrawn to the borders of Zululand and to certain towns in the Transvaal.

This encouraged Cetewayo in his contumacy: in April he had warned all the missionaries to leave Zululand; in July an *impi* had crossed the Buffalo into Natal, had carried back and killed two native women who had sought British protection; in September a government surveyor was captured on the Natal side of the Tugela, and kept prisoner for a time; the settlers in the Luneburg district of the Transvaal had been ordered to leave their farms by a Zulu chief, who said that the king wanted the land. Everything pointed to war.

At this time the 1st Batt. 13th and the 80th were in garrison in the Transvaal; three companies of the 90th were at Utrecht, just outside the disputed territory; and three companies of the 2nd Batt. 3rd Buffs and the 2nd Batt. 24th in Natal. While the column under Colonel Wood, V.C., which had marched overland from King William's Town, composed of the remainder of the 90th, the mounted infantry of the 24th, and N Batt. 5th brig. Royal Artillery, was at Kokstad on the borders of Pondoland, where it had been halted to frighten Umquikela, the 11th Batt. 7th brig. Royal Artillery being at Pietermaritzburg. A large force truly to guard two hundred miles of a hostile frontier, to overawe the coloured population of Natal, three hundred thousand leavened by only twenty thousand white settlers, the Pondos, two hundred thousand in number, and last, but not least, the disaffected Boers of the Transvaal.

The general naturally asked for more troops from home, and particularly for a regiment of cavalry; in answer he received the 2nd Batt. 4th and the 99th Regiments, the second and fifth companies of Royal Engineers, and some special service officers. He concentrated the Buffs, bringing three of its companies from Mauritius; the 2nd Batt. 24th was brought to Natal, leaving one company only to guard the fort at the mouth of the St. John's River in Pondoland; British Kaffraria was held by the 88th which also garrisoned Mauritius, and Cape Town was guarded only by volunteers. In November the flagship *Active* landed a Naval Brigade of one hundred and seventy sailors and marines, with two twelve-pounder guns, a Gatling, and two rocket-tubes. They were sent to the Lower Tugela Drift.

Sir Bartle Frere, the High Commissioner, gave his award on the disputed territory in November. It was certainly favourable to the Zulus, giving them for their boundary the left bank of the Blood River from its junction with the Buffalo River to its source, and thence direct to a round hill between the two sources of the Pongolo River. The boundary marked off by the Boers in 1864 was considerably within this line, so Cetewayo could have had nothing in that respect to complain of; but it was resolved that certain demands should be made at the time of explaining the award, "as the aggressive bearing of the Zulus, and the known power of their army, had produced a condition of affairs which their European neighbours found to be intolerable."

In justice to Sir Bartle Frere, I must say that I do not believe there was a white man in South Africa who was not thoroughly in accord with this opinion.

The demands were: (1) That the sons of the chief who had violated Natal territory should be surrendered for trial, and a fine of five hundred head of cattle paid for the outrage; (2) That a fine of one hundred head of cattle should be paid for the outrage on the surveyor; (3) That Umbelini, who had with his men made a raid into the Luneberg district, should be surrendered; (4) That the Zulu Army should be disbanded; (5) That all Zulus should be free to marry; (6) That the administration should be reformed; (7) That a British Resident should be received; (8) That the missionaries should be allowed to return; (9) That all cases against white men should be heard in the presence of the Resident.

On the 11th of December Cetewayo's deputies were told of the award, and of the demands as an ultimatum; a reply was to be sent by December 31st, and the persons and fines demanded to be given up on January 10th, 1879. They were satisfied with the award, but pretty plainly said that the king was unlikely to comply with the demands, least of all with Nos. 4, 5, and 6. Two Zulus afterwards described the question thus:

> The Zulus, all of them, do not wish to fight. As to the marriage-law, when all Zululand was assembled a while ago, the king not being present, the Indunas spoke to them words which they understood to be from the Governor of Natal, proposing that they should all be allowed to marry, and the *Indunas* approved and said this should be agreed to. But the king said: 'Is there any people without an army, and what army is allowed to marry. Is the English Army allowed to marry?' Thereupon there was disagreement on that point. They would like well enough to be allowed to marry, but are quite content to remain as the king wishes. He says that they are boys.

In case of war the first thing was to secure Natal and the Transvaal from invasion. The frontier between Natal and Zululand is broken, mountainous, and covered with forest for a length of about one hundred miles; a Zulu force could easily assemble unseen for a rush across on Durban or Pietermaritzburg; the obvious plan therefore was to attract the enemy away from Natal by at once assuming the offensive. The Transvaal border was open country; notice of a forward movement in that direction would be at once reported, and the enemy could be opposed with greater effect.

The local Natal Forces were eighty Mounted Police and three hundred Mounted Volunteers. All natives in the various locations in Natal are liable to service; seven battalions of a thousand men each were accordingly organised, but as the natives are akin to the Zulus their loyalty was at first doubtful, and only ten per cent, were given firearms, while each battalion had nearly a hundred white men as officers and under-officers.

The organisation of our forces was in five bodies, as follows:

(1) *Right Column at Lower Tugela Drift.* Colonel Pearson, 3rd Buffs.
   Royal Artillery, two 7-pounders.
   Royal Engineers, No. 5 company.
   2nd batt. 3rd Buffs.
   99th Foot, six companies.
   Naval Brigade, two 12-pounders, Gatling, and rockets.
   Mounted Infantry, one squadron.
   Native Infantry, two battalions.
   Native Pioneers, one company......... 4,750 officers and men.

(2) *Centre Column at Rorke's Drift.* Colonel Glyn, C.B., 24th Foot.
   Royal Artillery, N–5, six 7-pounders.
   Royal Engineers, No. 2 company.
   1st and 2nd batt. 24th Foot.
   Mounted Infantry, one squadron.
   Natal Mounted Police.
   Natal Mounted Volunteers.
   Native Infantry, two battalions.
   Native Pioneers, one company 4,709   ,,   ,,

(3) *Left Column at Utrecht, Transvaal.* Colonel Wood, V.C., C.B., 90th Light Infantry.
   Royal Artillery, 11–7, six 7-pounders.
   1st batt. 13th Light Infantry.
   90th Light Infantry.
   Colonel Buller's Frontier Light Horse.
   Swazies, one battalion 2,278   ,,   ,,

Two bodies were organised for the protection at first of Natal and the Transvaal ; one under Colonel Durnford, R.E., at Middledrift, the other under Colonel Rowlands, V.C. at Luneburg. After the advance into Zululand they were to act as ordered.

81

(1) Colonel Durnford's Force at Middledrift.
     Mule rocket-battery.
     Mounted Natives, one corps.
     Native Infantry, three battalions.
     Native Pioneers, one·company...... 3,871   ,,   ,,
(2) Colonel Rowland's Force at Luneburg.
     One Krupp and two 6-pounders.
     8oth Foot.
     Transvaal Mounted Volunteers.
     Native Contingent..................... 1,565   ,,   ,,

Total of all arms.........17,173   ,,   ,,

The 2nd batt. 4th Foot was on the march to join the centre column near Rorke's Drift.

Headquarters were to accompany the centre column. The three columns had an average of about fifteen hundred British infantry in each, but there was not a single British cavalry-trooper in the whole of South Africa, and as we had lived at peace with the Zulus for over thirty years, the mounted contingents in the right and centre columns at least had little knowledge of what to observe and how to report it.

My prologue takes us to the end of 1878. At that time hardly a soul at home seemed to know, or care, that some five thousand Englishmen stood face to face with forty thousand trained warriors of the most fighting race of South Africa, or of the restlessness and hatred to the white men existing among the other tribes in that country. I heard from my friends in Natal from time to time; but as the ultimatum of December 11th was only given a month to run, I knew no more than the rest of us as to its terms or their effect till on the morning of February 11th, 1879, all England was shocked by the news of the destruction of the camp at Isandhlwana on January 22nd.

Early on that morning my man (Private Noot of the 2nd Batt. 24th) rushed into my room with *The Times.* "Oh, sir, the regiment has been cut up by the Zulus, and Mr. Pope (who commanded Noot's company) and a lot of the officers killed. Read this—do you think they will let us go out?—Don't let them send me to the depot."

The man was mad with rage. I read the account, ordered breakfast to be got ready at once, that I might be in Pall Mall as soon as possible. "We will see if we can't go out together," I added; and at this the good fellow began to look less mournful.

The Horse Guards were willing, provided that the Medical Board would pass me sound; and on the same conditions the War Office promised me a passage for myself and servant by the first ship. There was a tremendous bustle in Pall Mall, for it had been already decided to despatch to Natal two regiments of cavalry, four batteries of artillery, six infantry battalions, with other details, including four generals and staff, making a total of ten thousand men all told. And yet three months before the Secretary of State for War had refused General Thesiger's request for a single regiment of cavalry—a rude awakening for those wiseacres at home who are so prone to confute the opinions of men on the spot!

The Medical Board passed me. On the 15th came my orders to sail in the *Manora* of the British India line, and on the 22nd we were off—a motley company, soldiers, sailors, and civilians, with all sorts and conditions of stores, but principally ammunition.

On March 17th we were at Simonstown, and there we heard the news in detail. Cetewayo not having complied with the High Commissioner's demands by the 11th of January, the three columns had accordingly advanced into Zululand. Their progress had been slow, as there were no roads for waggons, and the weather had been very wet. Each column had been opposed, the first at Inyezane, the second at Sirayo's Kraal, and the third near the Zungi Range.

On January 22nd, as we already knew, the camp of the second column had been destroyed at Isandhlwana. The first column had therefore been halted at Echowe, and was now besieged there; what was left of the second being at Rorke's Drift and Helpmakaar, and the third (Colonel Wood's) having retired to Kambula. The general, we were told, was starting for the relief of Echowe in a day or two, and I might possibly be in time to join him. The great difficulty was want of transport, for all with the second column had been lost, and there was such a panic now that transport-riders would not engage to let their waggons and teams of oxen.

Everyone had a different tale to tell of the disaster of January 22nd, but all agreed that our soldiers had fought gallantly, and accounts were rife of heroic actions from the "last man" at Isandhlwana to the heroes of Rorke's Drift. All English-speaking people know the story of the latter; that of the former, full of pathos as gathered later by Mr. Osborn our resident, needs a place here.

He struggled on and on, retreating higher up the hill till he reached a small cave, or recess in the rocks, into which he crept, and with his gun kept off the enemy. The ground in front of this little cave falls steeply down, and the Zulus, taking advantage of the stones and rocks scattered about, endeavoured two or three times to approach and shoot him. The soldier, however, was very cool and wary, and invariably shot every Zulu as he appeared. He did not blaze away hurriedly, but loaded quietly, took deliberate aim, and killed a man with every shot, till at last, the Zulus being now very tired, a number of men, good shots, were brought up with guns, who fired simultaneously at the unfortunate man and killed him. This lasted far into the afternoon, and the shadows were long on the hills before this man, who was the last to die, met his fate.

Before leaving the subject of Isandhlwana, which has been talked and written about much more by those who knew nothing about it than by those who were in the country, I would say a few words and ask a few questions. Is there a single English officer who, being given eight hundred white men armed with breechloading-rifles and any amount of ammunition, with a place to put his back against would not willingly face any number of natives unskilled with firearms? If there is, we have lost our ancient renown; but it is not so; the need was skilful handling and obedience to orders. The orders were in writing to the effect that the vedettes were to be kept far advanced, but the line of infantry outposts drawn in closer; and that if attacked the commander was to act on the defensive.

Now there is a valley six miles north-east of Isandhlwana hill, and there a Zulu Army lay on the night of the 21st of January. Thirteen thousand strong it had marched from Ulundi on the 17th and had reached the Isipezi hill, twelve miles east of Isandhlwana, on the 20th. Our vedettes in both these directions were three miles from our camp, and on the 20th and 21st patrols had been sent in both directions beyond the vedette-line. On the early morning of the 22nd the general with four guns, six companies of the 2nd Batt. 24th, the Mounted Infantry, and the Native Pioneers, moved off to reinforce the volunteers, police, and Native Contingent on the Ndhlazgazi hill, south of Isipezi.

He left in camp thirty Mounted Infantry, eighty Mounted Volunteers and Police, two guns with seventy men of the Royal Artillery, six companies of the 24th (five of the 1st and one of the 2nd Batt.), four companies of the Native Contingent, and a detachment of Native Pioneers; and he gave orders for a force of five troops of Mounted Basutos, the rocket-battery, and two companies of the Native Contingent of Colonel Durnford's force (which had moved from Middledrift to Rorke's Drift on the advance of the columns into Zululand), to move to Isandhlwana, where it arrived at ten a.m., making the total in camp eight hundred white men and nine hundred natives. Lieutenant-Colonel Pulleine of the 1st Batt. 24th was to command till Lieutenant-Colonel Durnford, R.E., arrived.

There has been printed an official account of that day, from which I shall quote only that the Zulus, advancing with two out-flanking columns, or "horns," and a "chest," as is their method, overwhelmed the force left to defend Isandhlwana camp by two p.m.; that at nine a.m. our vedettes to the north-east, three miles from ours and three from the enemy's camp, had withdrawn; that at one time the left company of our infantry was a mile away from the camp, that at another the right company was three quarters of a mile away in the other direction; that when the attack developed about one p.m. we were extended over three thousand yards, and at this time the mounted men with the commander were holding a position two thousand yards from Isandhlwana hill.

Was this, I ask, carrying out orders? Will anybody, I also ask, believe that a good cavalry regiment—say the 19th Hussars, as one then at home and available—would have withdrawn an important vedette, or would not have discovered an enemy, thirteen thousand strong, which had been within twelve miles of us for two days, and the last bivouac of which was only three miles from our own vedettes?

I want to reopen no wounds, to revive no quarrels; but I want to be just to the living at the same time respecting the dead, and to say that it was the case of General Wyndham at Cawnpore over again. The party, left behind to guard, went out to fight on its own account. Fifty-two officers, eight hundred and six white men, and four hundred and seventy-one natives fell, rallying into compact bodies till, their ammunition being expended, they were overpowered and died where they stood. They fell like heroes; that is their absolution. Those who were in Zululand unanimously absolved the Commander of the Forces; but a scape-goat had to be found for the popular indignation, and to aim high will always pass for independence. The opinion of one who was with the column, written shortly after, may be worth quoting:

> The whole business rests in this; had the force been kept together in a good position they could not have been cut to pieces as long as their ammunition lasted; they could have done

ZULU WARRIORS

as was done at Rorke's Drift. They sent their mounted men to fight, instead of keeping them to break the enemy's advance. A head was wanted; they lost their lives through overconfidence and pluck. It was when trying to get back to a good position that the Zulus closed on them, and their formation once broken they were at the mercy of an enemy vastly superior in numbers.

I suppose it is unreasonable to expect that all our hereditary and elected legislators should confine themselves to subjects within their own knowledge. In both houses men, who knew nothing of what they were talking about, were not loth to air their theories in bitter words; I have quoted here the theory of one who was on the spot, who was not bitter, and knew thoroughly what he was talking about.

★★★★★★★★★★★★

The Naval Squadron at the Cape had been unexpectedly reinforced by the frigate *Shah*. Captain Bradshaw, who commanded her, was returning home from the South American station, but having called at St. Helena had obtained news of the disaster from a passing steamer. He, on his own responsibility, and after an interview with the governor, picked up a company of the 88th and a battery of the Royal Artillery, and carried them off to Natal; a very timely reinforcement, in fact the first to arrive.

Five days later, on March 11th, the *Tamar* came in with the 57th from Ceylon, all old soldiers, a battalion to be proud of; the *Pretoria* had passed with the 91st, the *Dublin Castle* with six companies of the 3rd Batt. 60th Rifles, and the detachment of the 88th in Kaffraria had already marched for Natal. It looked as though the relieving column for Echowe would be off before I could reach it.

The *Manora* lost no time in coaling or on the way, and on the 21st we dropped anchor off Durban. There I found my old friend Gosset at the general's office up to his eyes in work and furious at the bad luck which had given him a fall a short time before, dislocated his elbow, and so confined him to the desk. We went off forthwith to the remount depot, where we found only a fine collection of cripples, for good nags were at a premium. I picked out what seemed the only decent pair—Pampas and Poll Evil I christened them from their respective diseases—and with a veterinary surgeon set to work to lance the gums of the former and to anoint the head of the latter with paraffin, gave them both double rations, fitted the saddlery, and at last made them look quite presentable.

That night after dinner Gosset told me of the unfortunate affair at the Intombe River, where a convoy of waggons, guarded by two officers and one hundred and six men of the 80th, had been surprised by the Zulus on the morning of March 12th, and the officer commanding and sixty men killed. In short, to put matters in scientific military language, the Zulus, acting on interior lines, had in succession struck at every column, showing that they were no mean strategists.

I found that a post-cart with letters and despatches was to leave Saccharine on the 24th for the Lower Tugela; so, I sent my man Noot off next morning (the 23rd) with the two horses to ride and lead alternately by Verulam and Stanger to Fort Pearson. On the 24th I left Durban by rail at nine a.m., found the post-cart waiting at Saccharine at eleven, and after three changes of horses reached Fort Pearson at midnight, passing, as I had anticipated, my man and the two sorry beasts on the road.

The outposts were soon satisfied, and I was glad to hear that there was no order for a general advance on the day we were just commencing. Headquarters was pointed out to me, and making up to the only tent in which a light was burning, to my delight I found it occupied by my old friend and school-fellow Hart, who made me welcome to supper and a bed, and gave me all the news of the camp. Want of transport had been the great difficulty, as we had heard at Durban and matters were not being mended by the rains. Our available strength was as follows:

Naval Brigade (from *Shah*, *Tenedos*, and *Boadicea*), two Gatlings, two 9-pounders, four 24-pounder rocket-tubes.

57th Foot.

3rd Batt. 60th Rifles, six companies.

91st Foot.

99th Foot, five companies.

Mounted Infantry and Volunteers under Barrow.

Native Infantry, two battalions.

The force was formed in two brigades under Lieutenant-Colonel Law, R.A., and Lieutenant-Colonel Pemberton, 3rd Batt. 60th Rifles. One hundred and twenty-five carts and waggons were ready with provisions; and it was hoped that the river would allow us to cross in time for a start by the 29th. Captain Ernest Buller of the Rifle Brigade had taken my place on the staff, and Milne of the *Active*, flag-lieutenant on the Station, had been appointed naval *aide-de-camp* to the general for the campaign. My friend Hart was Colonel Law's Brigade-Major, and Buller was filling the same position with Colonel Pemberton's Brigade. Commodore Richards had come up with the Naval Brigade; and Major Barrow, my old friend of the 19th Hussars, commanded the divisional troops of one hundred and fifty mounted Europeans, one hundred and thirty mounted natives, and one hundred and fifty native foot-scouts.

The whole force consisted of three thousand three hundred and ninety white men, and two thousand two hundred and eighty natives. No tents were to be taken. We should be opposed to a certainty, and except for the big convoy of waggons, there was little doubt of the result; but the country was so heavy and the rivers so swollen that it was hard to move the waggons at all, and there was always the danger of their straggling in the bushy part of the route, for now that the Zulus had plenty of ammunition and a good stock of Martini-Henry rifles they thought themselves sure of their prey; in the language of the camp, "*they had got their tails up.*"

CHAPTER 6

The Advance into Zululand

From March 25th to the 29th we were hard at work all day and half the night ferrying the force over the Tugela by the pont. The Naval Brigade worked the machine and were quite in their element.

It would take only one waggon and its team at a time, so that more than a hundred trips over and back were required for the transport alone; and as the river when high is about half a mile wide, it will be understood that the Blue-Jackets had no light task. A fort, called Tenedos, had been constructed on the Zulu side, while Fort Pearson, one hundred and eighty feet above the water, covered the ferry on our side. By the night of the 28th the whole force was across, and bivouacked on the left bank in a terrific storm of rain, which put out all the fires and turned the ground into a swamp.

On Saturday, March 29th, the leading brigade advanced at daybreak, hoping to reach the Inyoni River only nine miles off. Reach it we did, for the oxen were fresh, but the tail of the column had only got half-way by noon, and that night the waggon-drivers, who had had no practice in *laagering*, got so out of hand that the *laager* was made anyhow, and would only hold one third of our oxen. So much for our first trek and our first *laager*.

******

When I returned from Natal in 1879, a friend asked me to give him some notes on *laagers* for use in a text-book on field-fortification which he had been commissioned to draw up. I did so, but as towards the end of 1880 his book had not yet appeared, and as affairs between ourselves and the Boers of the Transvaal were very much strained, I got his leave to send a copy of my notes to the secretary of the Royal United Service Institution. They were accepted for the journal and published in vol. xxiv.,

The Naval Brigade in the Zulu War

p. 806, just in time, as it happened, for the Boers revolted in December, and those who wanted to know what a *laager* meant, and how it was to be made, were not without the information.

★★★★★★

The next morning was so wet and foggy that the oxen could not be turned out to graze till five o'clock, and no start was possible before eight. However, in spite of one shocking bad drift, over which only one waggon could be got at a time, we were all *laagered* and entrenched on the Amatikulu River by half-past five that afternoon. This was better than the previous day's work: we had done seven miles in seven hours, and the *laager* this time was large enough and fairly well made; but the performance was not good enough for the critical eye of John Dunn.

John Dunn was the son of a Scotchman who had settled at Port Elizabeth in Cape Colony. Being of an adventurous frame of mind he had come to Natal about 1850, had been made interpreter to the Governor of Durban, and somehow got mixed up in the Zulu civil war of 1856, when Cetewayo defeated his brother, Umbulazi, on the Tugela. Though Dunn had been on that occasion with the losing side, he seems later on to have become most friendly with Cetewayo, and with his brother, Dabulamanzi, whom he taught to ride and shoot with a rifle.

The king gave him land near the Lower Tugela and wives, and he was now a chief over a tribe. He had warned Cetewayo against fighting us; but when at the beginning of 1879 he saw war was imminent, he went over with his tribe into Natal and remained neutral. The general had asked him to come with us to Echowe as guide, for he knew every path and every bit of bush on the way. He would not promise, but when we had started, he set off after us, and of course all the fighting men of his tribe followed their chief. We welcomed them warmly, gave each a red handkerchief for his head, and employed them as scouts.

John Dunn was a handsome powerful man of about forty years of age, a perfect rider and rifle-shot, rode an excellent *jagd paard* (shooting-horse) on all occasions, had the best of saddlery, breeches, boots, and other clothes (which he always got from England, though he had never been there), and but for his large wideawake hat and tanned face might have been taken for an English country gentleman. Familiarity with the Zulus had not bred contempt in him. Almost the first thing he said to me on the 29th, when a bad *drift* had temporarily lengthened our column, was, "We shall have to do better than this if we are

92

JOHN DUNN

to beat Cetewayo's *impi*."

On the 30th, when Zulu scouts were observed on our left flank, he was much relieved to find that practice had got our heterogeneous set of conductors and foreloopers into some sort of order, able at least to understand and to obey. With waggons and teams each of forty yards in length one mistake may upset the whole column; for each vehicle takes such an enormous space to turn in that unless a *laager*-master is regularly told off, and given an assistant to catch each conductor as he comes up, a block is almost a certainty.

That night it rained in torrents again, and there lay the Amatikulu right in front of us. Anywhere except in South Africa, if you were told that a river was "down" you would understand that it was lower; but in Natal or Zululand the term means exactly the reverse, and that the water is "down from the mountains." The Amatikulu was down with a vengeance; it was forty yards wide and four feet deep; in that depth an ox has no power, and the current was running like a mill-stream. Every single waggon would have to be double-spanned (thirty-six oxen instead of eighteen), and it was clear that the passage alone would be as much as we could do that day.

The chief therefore decided that our next camp should be only a mile and a half on, where the river, reaching a sharp bend just above the drift, runs nearly north and south, so that the left flank of the column would be partially protected by it after crossing. Barrow's mounted men and Dunn's scouts began the passage; then followed the first brigade, and then the convoy of waggons and carts. The brigade took two hours to cross, the waggons six, losing an ox or two, but on the whole making the passage in fine style. The second brigade brought up the rear, wading up to their arm-pits, rifles and pouches on their heads. The whole column was in camp before five, after nearly eleven hours' hard work, everybody as wet as a sponge.

The enemy's scouts on our left were more numerous this day, and the *laager* at night, though better, was not perfect. It was decided, therefore, after due consultation, that for the future the *laager* should be an exact square of one hundred and thirty yards (thirty waggons and carts to a side), and that the shelter-trench should be fifteen yards in front of the sides. This would hold about two thousand men in close order two deep; and as we had just over three thousand all told, this arrangement gave us one thousand for outposts, reserve, mounted men, and casualties. I was told off for *laager*-master next day, and John Dunn promised to show me a good camping-ground.

Next day accordingly, April 1st, Dunn and I, with my four mounted orderlies, cantered on ahead of the column to an open space near Ginghilovo Kraal, five miles from our late camp and one mile short of the Inyezane River; it was only slightly commanded on the south side, with regular glacis-like slopes on the three others. I at once placed my four mounted points: the column soon appeared; and the *laager* was finished and the shelter-trench marked out in no time. The distances worked out beautifully; we had guns, rockets, or gatlings, at the angles of the trench; an opening in the middle of each face to let the horses and cattle in and out, with four waggons ready to run in and close it at any moment. The men then went to their dinners before digging the trench.

Barrow's scouts (who had done beautiful work this day) had reported that there were small but organised bodies behind the Umisi Hill to the west of us, and Dunn had an idea that there would be some to our left front up the valley of the Inyezane; so, when the *laager* was finished, he asked me to come out with him and reconnoitre. I got leave, was told to take care of myself, and off we rode. Now the man came out:

I am sure that is not all mist; there is smoke with it; I want to keep along the stream, cross it at a place I know, leaving you with the horses, and see what is over the rise on the other side. Now you know we are in for a dangerous job, and as I have never been out with English officers before, I should like to be certain, before I start across, that our ideas are the same. In Africa a white man must stand by a fellow while there is life in him; if his friend is dead, then he may save himself. Do you agree?

I managed to satisfy my companion on this score, and then we took to the soft low ground near the bush and rode on in file silently, for Zulus have eyes like vultures and ears like watchdog's.

The rain began to fall again in perfect torrents, which was all the better for us, as any scouts about would be likely to crawl back to their fires. After a couple of miles Dunn turned off into the bush, pushed through it to the Inyezane, and stopped to listen. Not a sound was to be heard but the patter of the raindrops and the roar of the river. Beckoning me up to hold his horse, he stripped, tied his clothes up in a bundle which he gave to me, took his rifle, swung himself into the torrent and, holding on to the branches of a tree that had fallen across it, landed on the other bank and disappeared. The good old horses

INSIDE A LAAGER AT GINGHILOVO

stood like lambs; but a Kafir crane found me out on his peregrinations in search of a dinner, and made off with rather more noise than I thought necessary.

It was rather uncomfortable work as the dusk began to fall, and I was not sorry to see my naked friend wriggling down through the grass on the farther bank. I don't know how he managed to get back, for the river had risen ten feet in the hour, and the trunk of the tree was submerged; but he swung himself across somehow, landing blue with cold. We were soon on the march again, he drying his rifle and changing the cartridge as we made our way through the bush, and as soon as we reached the open, away we went at a gallop for the *laager*.

As we rode, he told me that he had seen an *impi* and a lot of bivouac-fires, that he had been nearly discovered by one of their scouts who, when the clattering crane rose, had advanced to within a few yards of where he lay, that he had been obliged to lie low till the fellow was satisfied and went back, and that he wanted a gallop now to warm himself.

When we reached the *laager* the trench was completed but full of water in places, and the state of the ground inside it defies description. When five thousand human beings, two thousand oxen, and three hundred horses have been churning up five acres of very sodden ground for two or three hours, it makes a compost neither pretty to look at, easy to move about in, nor nice to smell. There were unpleasant reptiles about also, for two puff-adders had just been killed close to our waggon. Dunn's report, combined with Barrow's, told us pretty well what we might expect on the morrow.

As it was clear that the ground would not permit the waggons to be moved for at least a day, it was decided that the oxen should be kept at home next morning, and that our two native battalions should be sent out to attack the enemy at daybreak, with orders to fall back behind the *laager* when the Zulus were well stirred up, so that the latter might come on at our shelter-trench, manned, as it would be, two deep, shoulder to shoulder, by British soldiers and sailors.

The morning of April 2nd broke over Ginghilovo *laager* in quite a cheery way; it was not raining, and a white mist presaged a hot day. The Zulus did not need much stirring up, for at six a.m., just as our natives were being let out to do it, the outposts began to fire and fall back. Soon the mist cleared a bit, and we could see black bodies of men across the Inyezane River and on the top of the Umisi Hill, opposite our front and left faces. "Stand to your arms—saddle up—

no independent firing—volleys by companies when they are within three hundred yards," were almost the only orders. From a waggon I could see the Zulus advancing in the usual formation— two encircling "horns" and a "chest," with the "chest" hanging back at first.

We were in luck: there could be no doubt about the day now; but what had induced them to leave us alone on the march and attack us now, when we had all our oxen safe inside and all our fighting men ready outside, passed my comprehension. I suppose they had watched us, seen that the oxen were let out to graze before the march, expected we should do it today, and laid their plans accordingly; for, if the oxen are captured, the column is ruined; that must always be your weak point when fighting with an enemy who has no transport but women and boys, who in fact always fights *en l'air*.

Not a shot was fired except by the outposts as they hurried back; but when our front was clear the petty officer in charge of the Gatling gun at the left-front angle implored Ernest Buller to let him have one turn at a body of Zulus that had formed in full view half a mile away. "Beg your pardon, sir," he said, "last night I stepped the distance to that bush where those blacks are, and it's just eight hundred yards. This 'no firing' seems like throwing a chance away. I've got her laid true for them; may I just give her half a turn of the handle?"

The chief, who was close by, did not object to the range being tested, providing he stopped at once. A final sight, and, I am sure, quite two turns of the handle was the response, and there was a clear lane cut right through the body of men. The effect of the fire of a machine-gun is awful if it is served by a cool hand; the gun has no nerves, and, provided the man is steady and the cartridges do not jamb, nothing can live in front of it. The captain of this gun was a veteran, and afterwards during the fight his exhortations to his crew would have made, when carefully expurgated, an admirable essay on behaviour under fire.

The first attack came from the north on the front face of the square, and the extreme left horn swinging round attacked part of our right face a moment later. The other horn from the Umisi Hill was a little behind in attacking the left and rear faces of our trench; but the attack was fairly simultaneous, and the shouts of the Zulus could be heard even amid the roar of the volleys.

It was hot work on our right front angle. Some rocket-tubes were there, and from our saddles we could see the Zulus' behaviour in the long grass. Rockets look awful instruments of destruction; but they do none at all except when used to frighten horses or to set tents on fire. The Zulus evidently thought them living devils, for I saw many men fire at them as they passed over their heads. As one went skimming just above the grass, and the Zulus in that direction fell back a bit from its flaming tail, the general told Barrow to take out the Mounted Infantry on the right face and keep them on the run.

But the Zulus, quickly recovering from their panic, and showing no fear of the horsemen, and the attack, which had come on our left and rear, extending round to our right face, the chief, fearing Barrow might be cut off, ordered me out to recall him. It was done only just in time, for we had to fight our way back. One fellow missed me at close quarters, and paid the penalty by a revolver bullet in his forehead, but another shot straighter; the bullet entered poor old Lampas just below the seat of the saddle; he carried me over the trench and then succumbed, sending me headlong into the miry mess. Barrow and two of his men were wounded; three horses were killed and three wounded.

It is a curious sensation when a horse going at a gallop under you gets a mortal wound. He falters in front, picks himself up and drops behind, gets his hind-legs under him once more, makes one supreme effort, and then turns a complete somersault; it is much the same sensation as trying to sit the mechanical horse when bucking, an exhibition that I had visited in London in my youth. My poor brute lay still but alive; so, I gave him his quietus, cleared him of saddle and bridle, and saw under the saddle on the opposite side to the wound a lump like a warble; one touch of a knife and the bullet dropped out, a very badly cast spherical thing, half hollow, with the waste lead still left on it.

With my load I staggered through the mud, round the *laager* to the left face where my man and other horse were. Noot was sitting on the top of the waggon alongside John Dunn, loading for him and beaming with joy. "Here's about the first man killed on our side," he said as he got down. "It's our *forelooper*; he went and lay under the waggon in a fright; I told him to come out as it was all luck, and that minute a bullet hit him in the head. And there's the first drunk man," he added, pointing to one of the Native Contingent who lay under a commissariat-waggon breathing stertorously. A Martini bullet had pierced a cask of rum, and the nose of a native had detected the well-loved smell even amidst the "villainous saltpetre"; he had caught the stream in his mouth and was, when discovered, quite insensible.

"I tell you that gentleman is a fine shot," my man went on; "he never misses them; he has his own and my rifle; he shoots, I load"

"Well, get on with the other horse, and clear as much of the filth off the saddle as you can," I said, and mounted up alongside Dunn.

"I've picked out an *induna* or two," was his only remark, as I took Noot's place as loader. The Zulus were now on their stomachs in the long grass, rising to their knees to fire. The men in the trenches could not see them, and had ceased firing, kneeling at the ready in case of a rush; but up above we had a clear view and could fire over the soldiers, and many a Zulu fell to Dunn's rifle that day.

When Poll Evil was saddled, I went out to look for the general. The 57th were hotly engaged now, their volleys ringing out as clear as if they were at Aldershot. If every regiment had possessed such seasoned men as those, we could have walked to Echowe and back without having to burrow into the ground like ant-bears. The Native Contingent were squatting on their hams between the waggons and the trenches; some of them, I am afraid, occasionally getting rather roughly handled by their officers. They had been ordered to keep their muzzles pointing to the sky and not to fire at any price, their white officers being in front of and facing them; but they are an excitable race, and gun after gun was let off in the air, sometimes at no very great elevation. Then came bad words and hard boots; cracks on the head are no good; you might as well hit a cocoa-nut.

I found the general, reported myself as dirty but not hurt, and that Barrow's men were all back. Crealock was the only one of the staff hit, luckily not severely. As they were mounted and outside the waggon-square during the whole engagement, it is a miracle that they escaped so well. Just as I reached them at the front face, Lieutenant-Colonel Northey, of the Rifles, was hit in the shoulder by a Martini bullet. I thought it was slight, for he told the next senior and walked away to the ambulance-waggons; but though the bullet was extracted, the shock was too much, and four days later he was dead.

An hour and a half of this work had pretty nearly convinced our foes that there was no chance for them this day. They were now evidently wavering; so, the general sent Barrow at them again, and ordered the Native Contingent out to pursue. The Zulus gave the mounted men a few shots and then turned and fled; the Native Contingent followed, and the foe that threw away his arms when overtaken by the horses found short shrift at the hands of our allies. It is a very common trick with savages to feint a retreat, and then turn on you in the disorder of the pursuit. The strictest orders had accordingly been given that neither soldiers nor sailors were to leave the trenches.

The commodore had been impressing on his Blue-Jackets the awful things he should be obliged to do to them if one of them moved; but this was too much for him. "Come along!" he said to his flag-lieutenant, and away they went hacking and slashing on foot, while the tars, who obeyed orders and never stirred, yelled with delight. "Go it, admiral!" they would shout. "Now you've got 'em! Look out, sir, there's one to the right in the grass!" till everyone was roaring with laughter. Sailors are the best of comrades in rough times; nothing puts them out; I suppose because the ship is their home, and a run on shore is always and in any circumstances a holiday to them.

There was one warrior who would not fly, but set his back to a thorn bush and defied his foes. "Leave him to me," said a sergeant of the Greys who was instructor in the Mounted Infantry. A ring was formed and at it they went, sword mounted against *assegai* and shield dismounted. The soldier was the more skilful, but the Zulu was in better condition. Cutting was tried at first, but it was turned by the shield invariably; at last, a point went through shield and man, and the hero found the death he courted.

The loss on our side was returned at nine men killed, six officers and forty-six men wounded, twelve horses and thirty-four oxen killed or wounded; and from five to six rounds a man had been expended. The Zulus were calculated to have lost about twelve hundred killed. Upwards of four hundred guns and rifles were picked up, some of them Martinis with the stamp of the 24th regiment on them; and in the dead Zulus' pouches and bags was found stationery captured at Isandhlwana, which they had been using as wadding for their smooth-bores, ration-returns, letters, English newspapers, and all sorts of odds and ends.

From off one Zulu an English officer's sword was taken and brought to the chief. Crealock's clerk, who had been an assistant in the orderly-room of the battalion annihilated at Isandhlwana, at once recognised it as having belonged to Lieutenant Porteous of the 24th; it was accordingly preserved and sent to his friends. The total number of Zulus engaged was ascertained to have been about ten thousand. Somapo was in command, with Dabulamanzi, Cetewayo's brother, next under him.

The garrison from Echowe now flashed us their congratulations, to which the chief replied, and we all felt very pleased with ourselves.

This was my first experience of these savages, and I was certainly astonished at their pluck. Before an *impi* marches to battle, every warrior is given an emetic and then some witchdoctor's stuff. This would not raise the courage of a white man, who prefers to fight on a good breakfast; but it seemed to act well with them; there could be no question of their pluck, and they were as active as cats.

After the fight we let out the oxen and set to work to reduce the *laager* to one hundred yards square, leaving out the carts that were to accompany us onward the next day. The trenches had to be levelled first, then the oxen inspanned, and the left and rear faces of the waggons moved in thirty yards. While we were all hard at work the most appalling yells were suddenly heard, and thinking the foe might be mustering for a fresh attack, every one stood to their arms, not without an anxious thought for the grazing oxen.

It turned out, however, that one of our native battalions had come across a crowd of wounded Zulus in a patch of bush, and with the chivalry peculiar to the nature of the semicivilised, were killing them in cold blood and celebrating the heroic deed by a war-song. Employing natives was a horrible necessity in Zululand; their behaviour at a crisis was contemptible; at other times they were filthy and cruel, and their white officers could not be everywhere to guard against it.

Next morning the chief started at eight a.m. with the 57th, the 60th Rifles, the 91st, part of the Naval Brigade, the Mounted Infantry, Dunn's scouts, and fifty-eight carts, to march the fifteen miles to Echowe; leaving two companies of the Buffs, five of the 99th, part of the Naval Brigade, and two battalions of the Native Contingent, besides details, to defend Ginghilovo *laager*.

Four miles from Echowe Colonel Pearson came out with part of his force to give us a helping hand in case there was any fighting; but as our scouts could find no enemy, the general told him to send the troops back. The staff stayed with us, showed us a short cut, and gave us a concise history of the seventy days. I think the universal cry was want of tobacco, tea-leaves and coffee-grounds being carefully preserved, dried, and smoked; otherwise, they were not in actual want, but coast-fever and typhoid had claimed many victims, while rough fare, watchfulness, and anxiety had set their mark on all.

We reached Echowe at half-past seven, but the rear of the column was not in till midnight. To add to the fame of the British Army and navy not one man fell out that day, though they had been sixteen hours on their legs, and, according to my pocket-aneroid, had climbed fourteen hundred feet in the fifteen miles. This sounds perhaps no very hard day's work to those who climb in the cool air of Europe; but in a semi-tropical climate the fatigue of getting a convoy over it must be felt to be believed. None of the regiments had their bands on this expedition; but the 91st had their pipers, who played their best as they marched past Fort Echowe to their bivouac amidst thundering cheers from both relieved and relievers.

Fort Echowe was to be evacuated on the 5th, for it was evident that a better route to Ulundi could be found nearer the coast, by way of St. Paul's, than by keeping to the track through Echowe. That morning we inspected the fort. It was an irregular hexagon of weak trace but strong profile, and if all its ditches had been flanked could have defied the whole Zulu Army. They had been too wise to run their heads against it, even as it was; and there is no doubt that its continued occupation had so impressed them that it prevented them from invading Natal.

From some spies it was discovered that after the fight at Ginghilovo, Dabulamanzi had returned to his *kraal* at Esulwini, which was only about six miles north of Echowe. The general determined to show the king's brother that he too had a long arm to strike with; so, about eleven that morning all the mounted men were sent oft at a gallop to try and surprise him, the staff going with them to see the fun, Dunn, of course, as it was supposed, making one of the party. But as I was on the point of starting, I came across Dunn sitting on the ground in the middle of an *umkumbi* (circle) of his men.

Apologising for the interruption, I told him that the general had just started. "He did not ask me and my men to come," was the answer, and it was evident that the chief and his men were highly indignant. I told him that a notice had been sent round the camp, and that orders had been given to show it to him; that he knew of it was obvious, from the fact of his being offended.

"Of course, the general wants you to come with him," I said. "I'll gallop on and get the invitation from him direct if you won't believe me." He relented, was on his horse (with his "after-rider" close behind him) in a moment, and away we went while the men stood up, raised their right hands to the sky, groaned *Inkos*, and raced after us. It is necessary to be most particular in your behaviour to a Zulu chief; and Dunn, while amongst his men, could not afford to waive any portion of his dignity. He had by this time, moreover, assimilated many of his people's habits and modes of feeling; and I fancy they would all have thought it more correct if the general had sat upon his hams every morning with an *umkumbi* of all the heads of departments round him, hearing their reports, and deciding on the day's operations.

We soon overtook the staff; a few words put all to rights, and then it was a race to the Entumeni Mountain and Esulwini.

There is a high *kraantz* at the back of Esulwini Kraal from which the Zulus must have kept a pretty good look-out, for when we reached the place, fat Dabulamanzi was on the top out of danger, though there were some men still climbing who shouted their war-cry in defiance at us. We killed two loiterers, took one prisoner, and set fire to the huts. There must have been many loaded guns left in them, for the explosions became so frequent that we all moved some distance off, and were standing in a group when, noticing that Martini bullets were dropping around us with great regularity, we became aware that the fellows on the *kraantz* twelve hundred yards off were making some uncommonly good practice at us.

They were just on the skyline; Milne had a naval telescope and Dunn the best of eyes; he plainly recognised Dabulamanzi, and then commenced a duel with Martinis. Dunn shot better than his former pupils: with the glass we could see them duck as the shots reached them; but as there was nothing to be gained by this sport, we destroyed the mealie-fields and made our way back to Echowe.

Pearson had marched on the 4th with his garrison four miles towards the Inyezane and *laagered*. On the 5th we followed him, reached his camp at eight, and halted till ten to let his rear proceed. But the road was worse than ever, and at last the general told him to take command of his old column and move it by its original route straight to Fort Pearson, while the relief column struck off to the left and made a road for itself towards Ginghilovo *laager*.

This was a most trying day from the heat, the long grass, and scarcity of water. The men, too, now that the excitement was over, were falling out every moment. There was no shamming: they did their best; but as one old soldier said to me, "Now those chaps are relieved you seem to begin to feel yourself, and I'm just as if I had no heart left at all and no legs." It was plain that we could not reach the *laager* by night-fall, so Crealock and Dunn went ahead and chose a place near the Inyezane for a camp. The column was all in by half-past six, when we entrenched in a rectangle and lay down for the night.

The entrenchment was guarded by pickets from each regiment three or four hundred yards in advance of it, and Dunn's scouts were sent to occupy some mealie-fields just beyond them. We had kept the tents lent us by Pearson, and after getting our dinner, Dunn and I turned in to one of them, and using our saddles as pillows were soon asleep. Early the next morning some outlying man fired a shot by accident, when the scouts and one of the pickets began to fall back, the latter soon making "a strategic movement to the rear" at full speed, leaving its officers standing alone. The men in the trench opposite them fixed their bayonets and, unable to distinguish friends from foes in the dark, met them with the point, the result being that five soldiers were wounded, and of Dunn's men two killed and eight wounded.

At the sound of the shot we were up; at the sound of the rush, we were outside the tent and on our way to the trench. It was heartrending to hear the wild appeals of those outside to those within to keep cool. The poor scouts were the worst off, their only distinguishing mark from the enemy being the red cloth round their heads. They had been drilled by Dunn to answer "Friend"; the best they could manage was "blend," and shrieks of "Fiend" were heard above all the din, yet they were stabbed unmercifully. Dunn was mad. "They are killing my people! Are the men fools? Can't they hear them calling out? Oh, my children!" he cried as he ran towards the trench; and then the soldiers recovered their wits, and we did what we could for the wretched victims of funk.

No one can account for the madness which seizes upon bodies of men at times. It is no use saying' it is only young soldiers that are thus affected; old ones may be less liable, but they are not impervious to it. One has only to read Froissart's account of the siege of Tournay in 1340, where one night:

Four thousand Flemings, lying in their tents asleep, suddenly felt such a fear in their hearts that they rose, beat down their tents and fled, not abiding for one another, without keeping of any right way.

Or to read Napier's account of the panic that seized the Light Division one night in a cork wood during the Peninsular War; or, if those be considered too ancient examples, Sir William Russell's account of the last bivouac at Old Fort in the first year of the Crimean War, where:

The picquets fell back tumultuously at the sight of a few Cossacks, and later on fell back firing and wounding each other when there were no Cossacks at all.

105

The history of war is full of such examples; and, as he is the best general who makes fewest mistakes, so we may call that the best army which has the fewest panics.

Before we marched, we could see Echowe in flames, so there had been no long delay in avenging Dabulamanzi's burned *kraal*. We reached Ginghilovo *laager* at half-past eleven; but the air and water were so contaminated by the still unburied bodies of men and horses, that the general moved a mile and a half further on, and gave Colonel Pemberton, who was to be left in command here, orders to move his *laager* to new ground next day.

That afternoon a general court-martial administered five years' penal servitude to one of the runaways of the morning; but the proceedings were subsequently quashed at home for some unexplained reason. It was supposed afterwards, when a worse runaway was suffered to go unpunished, that this man could not in justice be brought to book. Others said that it had been forgotten to send out a warrant to South Africa empowering the Officer commanding the Forces to assemble general and district courts-martial. Few know the truth to this day.

On the 7th the Headquarter Staff left for Fort Pearson *en route* for Durban, for the transports with troops were arriving there daily, and it was then the busiest place in South Africa. We made an early start, and riding rather nearer the coast so as to pass Dunn's house between the Inyoni and the Tugela, reached Fort Pearson at noon.

Dunn's house (or rather houses) was a sorry sight. Everything had been looted or pitched outside: some things had been burned; but what vexed him most was the destruction of all his journals. He took it very stoically, merely observing, "I have not done with the Zulus yet." I only saw John Dunn once again, at Durban; and though invited, I never had a chance of visiting him at his home. Rough things have often been said against one who has "turned Zulu"; but the account I have given of him will show, I hope, that he was a genuine man, brave, generous, warm-hearted, and to us on this expedition certainly a host in himself.

CHAPTER 7

The Prince Imperial

We were at Durban on the 9th of April and found the place full of the new arrivals, and gay as a fair with "brass hats," gold lace, and patent leather. Very spick and span they all looked, and a startling contrast they certainly made to our battered and shabby appearance. It was amusing to hear their remarks, which were sometimes the reverse of complimentary; but, as I told one of them whom I knew, their turn would come soon enough.

I was right glad to be with Gosset again. His arm was still like a bent bow; but it was mending fast, and he had had the Prince Imperial of France with him to keep him busy. The prince had arrived on March 31st, and had been staying with Captain and Mrs. Baynton. The day after our arrival he came with Gosset to see the general, and was delighted when the chief attached him to his personal staff, asking him to act as an extra *aide-de-camp*. The prince then and afterwards always wore the uniform of the Royal Artillery; he was not very well at the time, with a slight touch of fever.

On his arrival the chief thought it would be as well to have a medical officer attached to the Headquarter Staff, and Surgeon-Major F. B. Scott was accordingly appointed to the post. The prince was a charming young fellow, burning to distinguish himself, a capital rider and swordsman; but of course, like all high-spirited young men, a little difficult to manage, and I think the fever never quite left him while he lived.

The staff, special-service officers and troops, fresh from England, had now to be told off to their respective posts. Colonel R. Harrison, R.E., was to take over the quartermaster-general's work at Headquarters, which hitherto had been done by the deputy-adjutant-general, and he was given as Deputy-Assistant Lieutenant Carey, 98th Regiment. Cap-

LORD CHELMSFORD

tain Ernest Buller, A.D.C., was made Commandant of Headquarters. Those not included in the accompanying field-state were detailed as station and railway staff-officers, commandants of posts and garrisons on the line of communications, transport-officers, etc.

The earlier in the field were christened *aasvogels* (vultures) by those who came at the eleventh hour, because they had eaten up everything; and the latter were familiarly known as *boomvogels*, because they were "up a tree," there being nothing but transport-work for them. The Headquarter Staff were very sorry to lose Gosset from their mess; but he was too good a man to be kept on as *aide-de-camp*, and since the staff of the second division had not a man with them who knew the country, he was appointed to it as Assistant-Quartermaster-General. This left to me the business of senior *aide-de-camp* and caterer; I was generally known as Minister of the Interior.

The troops had all arrived from England by April 11th. Three of the battalions, as we have seen, had been in time for the relief of Echowe, and they with the 88th were to remain with the First Division on the Lower Tugela. The 21st, 58th, and 94th were sent to the Second Division, while the 80th from Luneberg reinforced the headquarters of the Flying Column. Fifteen officers and over five hundred old soldiers, volunteers from regiments at home, had replaced the casualties of the 24th.

The entire force under the command of Lord Chelmsford was as follows:

CAVALRY BRIGADE....Major-General Marshall. *Brigade-Major*, Major Herbert Stewart, 3rd Dragoon Guards.
    1st Dragoon Guards.
    17th Lancers.
[The cavalry, less two squadrons left on the lines of communications, marched with the Second Division. The two regiments mustered about 1,000 horses, and 100 mounted natives were attached to them.]

ARTILLERY..............Colonel Reilly, C.B. *Brigade-Major*, Captain Poole.
[These officers had to look after parts of five batteries, a Gatling battery, and an ammunition-column, apportioned between three divisions whose extremities were three hundred miles apart. They might perhaps as well have stayed at home.]

FIRST DIVISION.........Major-General Hope-Crealock, C.B.
Staff, Major Walker, 99th, Captain Cardew, 82nd. *Brigadiers,* Colonel Pearson, 2nd batt. 3rd Buffs, Colonel Clarke, 57th.

Artillery .....10 guns.
Engineers ...One company.
Infantry ......3rd Buffs.
57th.
3rd batt. 60th Rifles.
88th (six companies).
91st.
99th.
Irregulars.—Barrow's mounted men, 500.
Dunn's Scouts, 100.
Two native battalions .... 9,414 men

SECOND DIVISION ...Major-General Newdigate. *Staff*: Major Robinson, Rifle Brigade ; Major Gosset, 54th. *Brigadiers*: Colonel Glyn, 24th ; Colonel Collingwood, 21st.

Artillery .....12 guns.
Engineers ...One company.
Infantry ......2nd batt. 21st (six companies).
1st batt. 24th (seven companies).
58th (six companies).
94th (six companies).
Irregulars ...Mounted men under Bettington and Shepstone, 200.
One native battalion .... 4,822 men.

FLYING COLUMN ......Colonel Evelyn Wood, V.C., C.B.
Principal Staff Officer, Major Clery, 32nd.

Artillery :...Four guns and a Gatling battery.
Engineers ...One company.
Infantry ......1st batt. 13th.
80th.
90th.

110

Irregulars ...Redvers Buller's
mounted men,700
Natives, chiefly
Swazis, 500 ...... 3,849 men.

Base and Lines of { Major-General Clifford, V.C., C.B.
Communication. { *Staff:* Major Butler,69th; Captain
Fox, R.A.
Cavalry ......1st Dragoon Guards
(two squadrons).
Infantry ......21st (two companies).
58th (two companies).
94th (two companies).
Irregulars ...Two native battalions.

Transport was, as usual, the great difficulty. At one time, besides other vehicles, there were about seventeen hundred waggons and twenty-six thousand oxen employed. The government waggons cost £100 and the oxen £17 a-piece; while the hire of a waggon and span of sixteen oxen was £90 a month. I had bought a new horse at Durban, for Poll Evil had gone the way of poor Lampas; and I telegraphed to the remount depot at Maritzburg to secure two more and a pack-horse. The sorriest cripples were selling now for £30 at the port; everything, in short, with four legs was worth money, and of course the newspaper correspondents, who were now arriving in crowds, would give any price for a really good beast.

On April 17th we left Durban by rail for the north, and heartily glad we all were to be on the move once more. At Maritzburg the Prince Imperial, whose health had not bettered by the rough travelling (for the rail did not run all the way), met with an accident, which necessitated his being left behind for a time. We were all saddled up ready for a start on the morning of the 22nd, when the horse ridden by Longcast the interpreter bucked him clean over its head. The prince, who was standing by, caught the beast, rearranged its bridle, and, before we could stop him, vaulted on to its back. He was still weak from the fever, but regardless of that and of having no stirrups, he stuck to it for some time, till in the end he also was shot over its head, and unfortunately landed on a heap of stones.

This so knocked him out of time that the general had to insist on his stopping behind with Dr. Scott until better. With a salute, and a sorrowful face, he said "As it is your wish, sir," and shook us all by the hand as we rode off. However, he was able to join us again at Lady-smith on the 27th, having driven up in the lieutenant-governor's carriage. He looked better, but we could see at meals that he was hardly yet up to the mark to face our rough fare.

On May 6th we were at Utrecht, one hundred and fifty-six miles from Durban; and here the chief resolved to fix his headquarters for a time. Mr. Rudolph the *landrost* lived here, and there was much to be learned from him and others.

Colonel Lanyon, the administrator, and Colonel Rowlands, commanding in the Transvaal, were to be consulted on the subject of the malcontent Boers. There was Uhamu also, Cetewayo's brother, who with a portion of his tribe, chiefly women, had been induced by Wood to leave Zululand and remain neutral in some *kraals* near Utrecht. The staff had to get into working order. Milne was down with fever at Ladysmith; Lieutenant Bartle Frere, of the Rifle Brigade, was coming up to replace Ernest Buller (now *Commandant* at Headquarters) as *aide-de-camp*; Colonel Harrison was busy reconnoitring across the Blood River, and comparing accounts of the country with Redvers Buller. The columns could not advance till the Second Division had got its supplies, fuel, and transport. At Utrecht therefore we remained till May 24th.

The halt was not unwelcome to me. I, in common with many others, had to get a new packhorse; my sick nag had to be sent up from Maritzburg; the mess had to be reorganised and stores collected for the campaign. This last business, by the way, proved a somewhat costly process; beer was selling at four shillings a bottle, brandy or champagne at the comparatively moderate figure of twenty shillings. Then I had to find the variation of my compass, rate my watch, fix the latitude, and draw maps. But Utrecht is certainly not a very pleasant place of residence, being built along the edge of a marsh, its altitude, three thousand five hundred feet above the sea, alone preventing malaria. It is liable also to Indian "devils" on hot days; to whirlwinds, that is to say, of black dust spinning through the camp and covering everything with filth.

Colonel Harrison and the prince were making maps, and on one occasion were away at the Blood River for a week. The prince was much better now, and was in excellent spirits; being a gunner he and Colonel Reilly were great friends, and had always some joke on hand. One day the chief, with a large party of us, visited Uhamu's people, who were at some distance from Utrecht in a bit of country intersected with *dongas*. On our way back Colonel Reilly could not get his English horse up a steep bank, and as we helped him out the prince said: "How would you have liked it, colonel, if we had ridden away and left you to the mercies of those savage ladies?" It was a curious coincidence, considering that within a fortnight some of our people rode away and left the poor boy to his fate in another *donga*.

One day, when the general had gone to Newcastle, I was asked by a friendly Boer to come out shooting on the morrow; there were a lot of buck, he said, on the Elandsberg, north-east of us. Next morning accordingly, I took a rifle and a bag of cartridges, and attended by Noot and two horses set out for the place. When I met my friend, he said: "What have you got in that bag; your dinner?"

"No," I answered, "cartridges"; whereat he roared with laughter.

"You Englishmen must be very rich; they cost sixpence a-piece here."

"Where are yours?" I asked, not seeing the joke.

"In this," he said, tapping his double-barrelled rifle.

"You don't intend to shoot much."

"Two springbuck are as much as I can carry."

"Suppose you miss?"

"Nobody misses when a cartridge costs sixpence."

That was the conversation, and it taught me much; it may perhaps teach us all why we were beaten by the Boers in 1881. The Boer does not waste his ammunition. He will aim and take down his rifle a dozen times, until he is satisfied that he is going to get something for his cartridge. An Englishman shoots for sport, the Boer only for the pot; and the notion of one of them going out snipe-shooting is absurd. He will stalk a *pauw* (great bustard) and get it; it will feed his family for two days; a *koraan* (lesser bustard) is not worth powder and shot to him. In places where there is game this shooting goes on from the time a boy is old enough to be trusted with a rifle, for the more game killed the less the need to kill from the flocks and herds.

No wonder the men become such perfect shots; they have been born in the country and can judge distances infallibly. My friend got his two bucks: I fired five shots and got one; and then we off-saddled for a rest. He did not think much of my Martini, wanting to file off the foresight and put a bit of white bone in its place; but government arms are precious things, and I would not have it.

In 1881, after Majuba and the surrender, the 14th Hussars had some practice at the targets at Ladysmith, some Boers also competing; the latter were easily beaten at known distances. This clearly shows that their superior marksmanship in the field is due to their being

THE PRINCE IMPERIAL

better judges of distance, and to their being accustomed from earliest youth not to throw a single shot away.

On May 20th Lieutenant Frere arrived from Gibraltar and took up his duties as *aide-de-camp*; being a rifleman, he was housed with Ernest Buller. Milne came up from Ladysmith on the 23rd, and lived in a tent with me; and the staff was now complete. We started on the 24th with packhorses for Landman's Drift, where Gosset met us with news of the Second Division. It was estimated that all would be ready in three days, and the chief therefore arranged with General Newdigate to move his division to Koppje Allein (Lone Hill) on May 28th.

The delay was utilised by daily reconnoitres into Zululand. It was then that I first noticed what an unhandy lot as a rule our cavalry were. One day we were reconnoitring some fifteen miles over the border with a squadron of our own men and about as many Irregulars, and while the party were offsaddled on an open down, I was sent with two troopers to make a report on a neighbouring valley.

We rode to the top of a hill overlooking it and all the country for miles round, where I gave my horse to one man, telling him to hold the three and let them feed, while the other kept his eyes open in every direction. My sketch took me, I suppose, half an hour, and on my return, there were my two men, both mounted and both looking the same way, as rigid as rocks; they had never stirred from their saddles, nor let the horses have a bite at the grass. "Why did you not dismount and let your horses graze, as I told you?"

"Beg pardon, sir; regimental standing orders say vedettes are not to dismount; and if the horses graze, they busts their breastplates."

The last remark is quite true enough, provided you have not sense to slacken the breastplate. English horses are bred from generations of ancestors who have been accustomed to feed out of mangers and nosebags; it is a positive exertion to the leggy ones of sixteen hands to bite at short grass, as you may see from their trembling knees when they try it; and with a breastplate naturally the exertion is greater. This did not look well for the future condition of our nags, for they will not thrive on oats alone. But the men only wanted a little experience in the field to fall into the way of active service; and I fancy most of them got it before they had done with us.

As we rode home that day, the Prince Imperial and I were walking our horses a little behind the rest, talking over all sorts of things, while half a mile away in all directions were scouting parties of Irregulars. Some days before, when out with Colonel Harrison and Bettington's men, the prince had gone straight for some Zulus on a hill, who luckily had bolted. Reverting to this, I asked him why he had risked his life, when the death of one, or even of a dozen Zulus would not affect the success of the campaign.

"You are right, I suppose," he said; "but I could not help it. I feel I must do something."

Just at this moment a shot was fired on our left. I looked across, and saw the man who had fired riding on quietly, reloading. If he had fired at a Zulu, he had killed him; if he had fired at a buck, he had missed it; he was neither hurrying nor dismounting; the conclusions were plain enough. Yet there was the prince, going, sword drawn, at full gallop for the man; I could have no chance of catching him, and in the dusk, he might break his neck in the wild ride.

"Prince, I must order you to come back! I shouted. He pulled up at once, saluted, returned his sword, and said nothing for a minute; then he broke out, "It seems I am never to be without a nurse"; and a moment after, "Oh, forgive me; but don't you think you are a little phlegmatic?"

I reminded him what he had just owned about the affair with Bettington's men, and he laughed, saying that I had answered him rather neatly. "Someday," he added, "in Paris, I hope, I will be *your* guide, philosopher, and friend."

How could one help loving a boy like that—brave, daring to rashness, and determined to make a name for himself to add to the records of his race? But with all our love we were terribly anxious about him.

The Second Division moved from Landman's Drift to Koppje Allein (fifteen miles) on the 28th as arranged, with a train of three hundred and fifty waggons, which, on a single track without intervals, and without troops, took six miles to itself. The Flying Column had already moved to Munhla Hill, to converge with the Second Division until they met toward the Ibabanango Mountain. The cavalry were given a free hand to cover our front and explore the country.

Both brigades were across the Blood River by the first of June, and our first camp was formed on the neck between the Incenci and Itelezi Hills. Three *laagers* were formed, in plan something like the "three of diamonds"; an infantry brigade in each of the outside squares, and the cavalry, oxen, and natives in the centre one. It did not answer, in consequence of the stupidity of the *foreloopers*, and afterwards an oblong of two hundred and eighty yards by one hundred and forty was adopted to contain the whole of the Second Division and the cavalry;

this was easier formed, and covered less ground.

I was assisting at the *laager*-making this day, and did not think of much beyond it, except that I had seen the cavalry doing some very pretty parade drill about two miles off over the *nek*, and had wondered why on earth they were not ten miles to the front. That evening, as I was in my tent, working out the distances for the next day's *laager*, Ernest Buller came in.

"The prince is killed," he said. "A colonial has brought in his horse; the near wallet is torn half-way down. Carey, who was with him, has gone to tell the general."

It was so; the torn wallet on the near side was the awful proof that the horse had got away from him when trying to mount; and we knew that if dismounted, disabled, and abandoned, there was no chance of mercy from the Zulus.

There was not much to say; there was too much to think about—of the terrible luck that pursued our dear chief—of the empress, whose love and ambition were centred in her only son—of what they would say in England to Englishmen leaving a Napoleon to his fate—of what they might think of English officers in France after such a proof of our chivalry—of the loss we all had sustained in our bright young comrade. It was useless to attempt anything then; the night was too dark for any chance of finding the body, and that the prince might still be alive no man dared to hope after hearing Carey's report. But it was decided that the cavalry, with the mounted irregulars, should start the first thing next morning for the scene of the tragedy.

Dr. Scott and myself were to go with them to represent the general, with Frere to represent his father, the High Commissioner. On the next morning accordingly, so soon as it was light enough to see, the party moved out of camp on its melancholy errand. Lieutenant Carey rode with us to show the way; and with Scott, Frere, and me came the prince's two English servants, Uhlmann, his French valet, having been left behind at Durban.

The march was very slow, with much trumpeting. After about an hour of it our little party rode ahead on its own account, and guided by a trooper who had been with the prince, soon reached the *kraal*, which was only eight miles from camp between the junction of the Tombokala and Ityotyozi Rivers, tributaries of the White Umvolosi. The scouts of the Flying Column had now joined us, and we searched the ground together. The bodies of the two men of the Natal Horse were soon found; and then Captain Cochrane, 32nd Light Infantry (at that time commanding the troop of Natal Basutos), called the attention of Scott and myself to another body at the bottom of a *donga*, which, on being reached, was discovered to be that we were in search of.

It lay about two hundred yards north-east of the *kraal*, and about half a mile south-south-west of the junction of the streams. It was stripped, with the exception of a gold chain with medallions attached, which was still round the neck; the sword, revolver, helmet, and clothes were gone, but in the grass, we discovered his spurs with straps attached, and one sock marked *N*. His sword and boots were recovered later. The body had seventeen wounds, all of them in front, and the marks on the ground, and on the spurs, we found, indicated a desperate resistance.

As soon as the cavalry arrived, a stretcher was made with lances and horse-blankets, and the body carried from the *donga* up the hill homewards by Major-General Marshall, Captain Stewart, Colonel Drury Lowe, and three officers of the 17th Lancers, Scott, Bartle Frere, and myself, with M. Deléage, correspondent of the *Figaro*, who expressed a wish to assist, which was immediately granted. It was not long before we met the ambulance, in which the body was then laid and escorted back to camp by officers' parties of the Dragoon Guards and lancers.

The prince, Colonel Buller, Colonel Harrison, Captain Carey, and even I, had been farther into Zululand, and on this track too, on previous occasions. If any one of us had been asked to point out a death-trap within twenty miles, he could hardly have avoided choosing this very *kraal*. It was on low ground overlooked by high hills on the south, and by low hills on the west; there was an intricate system of *dongas* to the north, a river and impracticable hills to the south, with mealie-fields and tall grass to the east and west. To the north-east, over the *dongas*, was open rising ground. When the party had watered their horses, why they did not go there to off-saddle was what everyone was asking; that was the route by which the survivors rode away, and it was in the *donga* between the open ground and the *kraal* that the prince was overtaken.

The escort consisted of six of Bettington's men and a friendly Zulu, all mounted; the party that surprised them numbered forty, of whom only eight followed the prince. A gallop of two hundred yards took Lieutenant Carey and a trooper to and over the *donga* to open ground. Had they even then considered and halted they might have saved the prince, who was only overtaken and overpowered after a most desperate resistance at that point; but they went on, assuming that because his horse was loose, he had already been killed; and that is the whole sad story.

Lieutenant Carey, after riding four miles northwestward fell in with two officers of the Flying Column, who were reconnoitring the road for the morrow; and if report speaks true, he did not hear very friendly words. Officers do not ride about alone; escorts have ears, and the conversation that ensued was rumoured to have been somewhat as follows. It may have been true, and it may not; at any rate it was the talk of our camp afterwards.

Fugitive. "Look out! The Zulus, the Zulus!"

1st Officer. "What are you shouting about? Come here!"

F. "The Zulus are coming!"

1st O. "Nonsense! I can see two miles, and there is not a soul in sight."

F. "I tell you they have killed the prince, and are following me."

1st O. "Then why are you not with him? Why are you here? You ought to be shot!"

2nd O. "Hush, old man! he has not been tried yet." (To F.) "Go and report what you have to say to the general at once; and try and collect your wits."

Fugitive rides away as ordered.

Officers (together). "May the Lord have mercy on his soul!"

What happened afterwards is common knowledge. Lieutenant Carey was tried by a general court-martial on June 12th, and found guilty on the charge of misbehaviour before the enemy. He was sent home, where the sentence was subsequently quashed and he was permitted to rejoin his regiment. We could only surmise that the personage most injured had in her mercy interceded on his behalf.

We got back to camp soon after two; and at five the whole force paraded for a funeral service. The body was brought out on a gun-carriage covered with the tricolour of France, the pall-bearers and carriers being officers of the Royal Artillery: the general, followed by his Staff, was chief mourner; and the Reverend Mr. Bellord, Roman Catholic chaplain, was the officiating priest.

It was received by the assembled force with a royal salute, and after the service was moved to the field-hospital and placed in Dr. Scott's care for preservation, a guard being posted over the tent. Early next morning, it was laid in a tin-lined coffin and with all the prince's effects placed in an ambulance-waggon; this, accompanied by M. Deléage and the prince's servants, and guarded by a troop of cavalry, proceeded by Koppje Allein, Landman's Drift, and Dundee to Maritzburg.

At Maritzburg and Durban the remains were received with all possible honour. H.M.S. *Boadicea*, the new flag-ship, carried them down to Simon's Bay, whence they sailed for England in H.M.S. *Orontes*. On July 12th they reached Camden Place, Chislehurst, in the charge of Lieutenant-Colonel Pemberton, 60th Rifles. In England the young prince was given a soldier's funeral amid every token of love and regret, with our sovereign's four sons as supporters for "him who lived the most spotless of lives, and died a soldier's death, fighting for our cause." He now rests at Farnborough. The spot where he fell in Zululand is marked by a cross bearing the following inscription:

> This Cross is erected by Queen Victoria, in affectionate remembrance of Napoleon Eugene Louis Jean Joseph, Prince Imperial, to mark the spot where, while assisting in a reconnaissance with the British troops on the 1st of June, 1879, he was attacked by a party of Zulus, and fell with his face to the foe.

On June 3rd the Division resumed its march, the Flying Column being one day ahead beyond the Ityotyozi River. We crossed the river next day, and on the 5th the Cavalry Brigade passed on to the front of the Flying Column, which had now moved southward across the Nondweni, and, joining Buller's mounted men, reconnoitred the road and the Upoko River Valley. Buller's men soon were at work with some three or four hundred Zulus round the Uzulaneni Kraal, across the Upoko towards the Ezungayan Hill. We heard of the skirmish when at breakfast about five miles on the road, and all set off at once to Stony Hill to watch the fight.

The ground was bad for mounted men, for at the back of the *kraals* was thick bush and in front deep *dongas*; but the *kraals* were burned, and on the enemy getting into the bush Buller retired, covered by the cavalry. The irregulars had two men wounded, and the lancers lost their adjutant, Lieutenant Frith, who was shot through the heart.

That evening there was a long palaver with the three messengers who had come in from the Zulu king on the previous day. You may know a Zulu gentleman by his long fingernails, a token of not having to work, just as it is in China and Japan. They said that Cetewayo wanted peace, to which the general replied that there should be peace on the following conditions: (1) restoration of the two guns captured

at Isandhlwana, and of such oxen captured there as were now at Ulundi. (2) A promise that all arms captured should be surrendered. (3)
One Zulu regiment to come in and lay down its arms. They were also
entrusted with a message asking that the Prince Imperial's sword and
clothes might be returned, and promising a reward for them.

These messengers, by the way, must have been reassured by one
curious sight. That day an old Zulu woman, in the last stage of decrep-
itude, had been found in a deserted *kraal*; some men hearing moans
proceeding from a bundle that looked like a chrysalis, had in the kindness of their hearts brought the nuisance into camp. She had been
wrapped up tightly in a fresh hide, raw side inwards, put out in the sun
to harden (so that the skin might protect her from the dogs), and then
deserted. Our men had cut a peep-hole for the old naked skeleton,
and were feeding her with green mealies, which was all she would eat;
but her great joy was snuff made out of Cavendish tobacco.

Perhaps her sons could hardly have been expected to take her with
them on the war-path; but to be buried alive in a hide was rather hard
measure even for a Zulu mother. Our fellows did what they could for
her till she died, which fortunately for all sakes was in a day or two,
and then gave her decent burial.

It was now determined to build two stone forts at opposite angles
of our *laager* on the Nondweni River for a depot of stores. Two companies of regulars, one squadron, and one company of the Native Contingent were to be left as guard; and the post was named Fort Newdigate
after the general of the Second Division. The stores were unloaded
from as many waggons as possible, for the division was to move to the
Upoko Valley for woodcutting, while the Flying Column, reinforced
by three squadrons and four companies from our division, was to escort
all the empty waggons back to Conference Hill or Landman's Drift for
fresh supplies. Buller's men, however, were to remain at the front.

This night, the 6th, was a lively one in our *laager*. Some groups of
natives were posted with the outlying pickets, and one of these began
firing at about eight o'clock; whereupon the pickets retired into the
unfinished forts, the tents outside the trench and *laager* were struck,
and the men fell in to resist an attack. Now the camp-kettles had been
left on their tripods at the usual cooking-places on the outer side of
the tents, and presumably this deceived the men of one regiment, for
they gave them a warm independent fire, and even the artillery assisted with two rounds of case. Horses and oxen galloped round the
interior like mad things: all who were not firing shouted to all those

who were, to cease; and the din was tremendous.

When quiet was restored it was found that the enemy consisted of a stray ox or so; that two sergeants and three men of the outposts had been hit; and that all the camp-kettles, tents, and kit left outside one face were perforated. Fort Newdigate got the slang name of Fort Funk, and one regiment did most of its cooking in mess-tins afterwards. This was rather a disreputable affair, as showing what exaggerated ideas the new troops from home had of their foes, and how easily a panic increases at night. There was a bright moon with fleeting clouds; so there was really no excuse for a stray bullock, or even the shadow of a cloud, being mistaken for an *impi*.

On June 7th Colonel Wood with the Flying Column marched back from his camp to Fort Newdigate, picked up the empty waggons, and started for the Blood River to reprovision; and on the same day the Second Division, leaving the garrison as stated at the fort, moved on seven miles to the Upoko River Valley, and there formed a *laager* to wait for Wood's return. The men were employed in wood-cutting, improving the road in advance, and the cavalry in reconnoitring and in feeding up their horses, which were getting in a sorry state, for their masters did not take kindly to colonial ways. The valley had very good grass, and if the horses had only been allowed to eat it, they would have fared sufficiently on that and their eight pounds of oats daily; with some mealies in addition they would have done well.

Now the Zulus keep their mealies in pits, which are holes shaped like Eastern oil-jars, dug in the ground below the cattle-*kraals*; a stone is placed over the hole, covered with the *kraal* "*mest*" which the cattle stamp down firmly, and you would never dream there was anything below at all. But our native allies knew better. They went stamping round all over the ground, and where it sounded hollow, in went a pointed stick, or, if they had one, an iron rod.

Two or three taps would tell, if a stone was reached, whether it was hollow below or not, and if hollow it meant mealies. Our cavalry had mounted natives who knew the trick, and the country was full of deserted *kraals*; but one regiment took a week to learn it, and the other never learned it at all, but kept on reporting that the horses were being starved, while just across the Upoko were cattle-*kraals* that would have supplied all their needs.

From the 7th to the 17th, we lay at the Upoko River, waiting for the return of the convoy before we could continue the advance. On the 7th Major Black, of the 24th, with a cavalry squadron, came

122

right through from Rorke's Drift by Isandhlwana to the camp; he was not molested then nor on returning on the following day. Buller was working the country in our line of advance and collecting cattle. The Zulus in response made one or two attempts from the bush to get our cattle; and on one occasion some shells were required to disperse them. Many things from Isandhlwana were found in the various *kraals*, including the folding mess-table of the Headquarter Staff.

On the 14th a cavalry patrol started from our camp for that battlefield, and I went with them to see the country. On our way we crossed the route of the Zulu Army that had marched from Ulundi to the attack. Even after nearly five months the track was as plain as it lately made, the long grass all trodden down in one direction into the mud, just as if a huge roller had been passed over it.

On another day, when out with Longcast reconnoitring, we came on a small patch of Kafir corn (millet); out came our knives, and we soon had a large bundle of the heads for our horses. Suddenly from a rock half a mile away came shrill screams, and behold a very old woman reviling us.

"What is the old thing saying?"

"*Umfazi nzulu* (wicked old woman), why this noise?"

"Oh, the corn, the beautiful corn! Enemies on all sides; black enemies, white enemies! Black enemies take away my sons to the war; white enemies take away the corn."

"Stop screaming; we must have some for the horses."

"Oh, the corn, the beautiful corn; it is not for wild beasts to eat the corn! Enemies on all sides! The wild beasts to live, and the mother of warriors to die for want of corn! Oh, wicked white man to kill an old woman!"

And so the poor old thing went on screaming till we were out of hearing. I told Longcast not to mention the patch of millet to any of our mounted natives; it would not have been a mouthful for each horse of a troop, and the old woman would have starved, or, if her tongue went as fast at them as it had at us, she might get beaten, for the native cure for a female scold is stick, or *knobkerrie*.

While at Upoko a horse belonging to Lord William Beresford (who had come to Natal from India after Isandhlwana, and was now staff-officer to Colonel Buller) apparently went mad. It galloped about with rolling eyes, savaging every horse or man it could reach, and at last collapsed and died in great agony. The case was so curious that a veterinary surgeon made a post-mortem examination, when its stomach was found full of tea-leaves. The animal had got loose in the night, broken into a store-tent containing an open chest of tea, and eaten some pounds of it. Theine, or some such alkaloid, had first attacked the poor brute's brain, and the leaves swelling inside had killed it.

After one of Buller's raids, he gave the Headquarter Staff a milch cow and calf. In Zululand a calf is allowed to run with the cow for a long time, or she will not give milk at all. Our cows in England are artificial in giving milk for nearly the whole year; the Zulu cow is natural; she gives milk when there is a calf to require it, and when the calf is removed, she gives no more. Our cow was very savage and our calf very noisy. Longcast was the only man who could induce the mother to yield us milk, and then the calf wanted first turn.

Zulu cattle are very small, smaller than the Jersey breed; but they are very stout, healthy, and strong in draught, and do not want so much food as the big Afrikander ox. Later on, we got two more cows and calves, the three couples following our baggage until a fortnight after the battle of Ulundi, when we made a present of them to the other staff-officers on leaving for home. I was not sorry to secure such a luxury, for the time was coming when every man's voice would be against the caterer, when every man's appetite would be unappeasable, and when nothing but food would turn away wrath.

The Second Division was now reorganised. A fort was to be built at the source of the Upoko, where the Rorke's Drift and Landman's Drift tracks to Ulundi meet; it was to be garrisoned by four companies and two guns, and named Fort Marshall, after General Marshall who was given command of the line of communications. Colonel Collingwood was put in charge of Fort Newdigate, and the remainder of his brigade (now broken up) was to join the First Brigade under Colonel Glyn. Two squadrons of the 17th Lancers and a troop of the 1st Dragoon Guards were to continue on towards Ulundi under Colonel Drury Lowe, and the rest of the cavalry were to guard the line of communications.

About this time a telegram was received from home to the effect that Lieutenant-General Sir Garnet Wolseley had been appointed High Commissioner for Natal, Transvaal, and Zululand, thus relieving Sir Bartle Frere of the management of that part of South Africa.

On June 17th the Flying Column returned from the Blood River with its huge convoy of stores, and *laagered* about a mile ahead of the Upoko Camp; and on the following day we resumed our march on Ulundi, carrying supplies for six weeks.

CHAPTER 8

Battle of Ulundi

From the 18th to the 24th of June the march proceeded, without any signs of the enemy, and with no particular events worth recording. There was the usual daily allowance of hard work, the usual *laagering* at night, and there was some loss among the oxen. There is probably no human being on earth so blind to animal-suffering as the African native; and the Afrikander does not often check him. There is a saying among transport-riders that an ox in draught can only lie down twice; the third time it is to die. The first time they let him rest awhile, and then goad him up; the second time they twist his tail and bite the bend; the third time, if you are not looking, they loose the yoke-strop, light some grass under his nose to make him get up and out of the way, and go on without him. He falls and dies, food for the vultures.

It was very difficult to teach these fellows that they must get the waggons along, and yet that they must not use what they consider the most efficient means. We thought them brutes; they thought us idiots; where a man's life was worth so little, why take such care of an ox? They would not cast an ox loose the first time he fell, for fear they might be sent back for him after they had got to camp, and the conductor that can see everything that goes on over a quarter of a mile in a bad place is a remarkably sharp man. There was much cruelty that could not be prevented: one could only lay a whip across the driver's own shoulders, or tell him you would stop his food; and until well into Zululand, you could not even do that, for fear the fellow should run away.

The Umhlatoosi was crossed on the 22nd, and a fort (called Fort Evelyn) built four miles beyond it, on the neck which forms the water-parting between the Mpembene and Amanzimpofu Rivers. It was garrisoned with two companies of infantry, two guns, and some natives. On this day Lieutenant-Colonel East arrived from England and took up the duties of deputy-quartermaster-general, Colonel Harrison reverting to the command of the Royal Engineers.

As the *laagers* were being formed on the evening of the 24th, some Zulu messengers arrived from Maritzburg, whither they had gone by order of the king, and been despatched after us by General Clifford. They were kept a day, well fed, and then sent off to Ulundi, under escort, at their own request, of a sergeant and six men of the 17th Lancers to protect them from the Irregulars (Swazis), whom they held in much greater hatred than us. It was agreed that when they considered themselves in safety, they should wave the escort back. The sergeant afterwards reported that when in a place between two patches of bush the messengers gave the arranged signal, a Zulu regiment rose suddenly and would have surrounded them; whereupon the messengers called out, the regiment opened, and let the lancers return the way they had come. Will anyone call Zulus savages after that? They were foemen worthy of our steel.

From the Umhlatoosi River to Entonjaneni (Little Springs), the point overlooking Ulundi, is about five and twenty miles. We reached it on the 27th, and on the next day both columns halted while *laagers* were formed of the waggons to be left behind. Five hundred waggons and eight thousand oxen, with three companies of the 1st Batt. 24th and details of about five hundred soldiers besides natives, were to remain at Entonjaneni; the rest of the force, taking with them two hundred waggons with ten days' supplies, besides carts and between three and four thousand oxen, were to move on the 29th down towards the Mhlabatini Plain, for the enemy were observed from the northern spurs of the ridge to be massing at Ulundi.

That afternoon more messengers arrived from Cetewayo with some elephants' tusks and a herd of cattle. They brought the chief a letter written by Cornelius Vijn, a Hollander who had gone into Zululand to trade at the end of 1878, and who had been detained by Cetewayo during the war. It was an answer to the message given to the Zulu deputation at Fort Newdigate on June 5th, and was to the effect that the cattle sent (one hundred and fifty) were all that remained of those taken at Isandhlwana; that the king had not got the small arms and so could not surrender them; that the two seven-pounder guns were on their way, and that the troops must now retire.

The chief replied, in writing, that the tusks were returned to show that the advance would be continued as the conditions had not been complied with, but that, as he was ready to make peace so soon as they should be, the cattle were retained; that the army would continue to the Umvolosi River but not cross before the 29th; that a thousand Zulus (instead of a regiment as at first stipulated) must lay down their arms; and that, if we were opposed, the cattle would be returned and all previous agreements cancelled.

While we were working at the *laagers* on the 28th, the chief received a despatch from Sir Garnet Wolseley who had now landed in Natal, ordering him to fall back on General Crealock's column, and informing him that he was in command of the Second Division and Flying Column only. This of course meant that a new Commander of Forces had been appointed; whereas the telegram received from England at the Upoko River had, to the best of my knowledge, stated that there was to be no supersession. The order to fall back on General Crealock, I am afraid, made us all laugh, considering that the chief had long been unsuccessfully plying General Clifford to find out where Crealock was.

We afterwards discovered that he was on the Umhlalazi River, about twenty miles east of Ginghilovo, and that he had taken over two months to get there. To fall back now, when in actual sight of the king's forces, would of course have been a grave military error; and as the one on the spot who knew most of the game, the chief wisely declined to alter his plans, except to give the Zulus a little more respite, but pushed on steadily to the goal.

No tents were taken beyond Entonjaneni and no mule-transport. Ox-waggons carried the commissariat and reserve ammunition: oxen drew the carts with ammunition and entrenching-tools; and the staff carried their kits and food on pack-horses.

Shortly after we had moved off on the 30th (for we had found it impossible to finish the work by the 29th) more messengers from the king met us. They brought the Prince Imperial's sword, and a letter dated that morning from the Hollander Vijn, announcing that "the two seven-pounder guns and a lot of oxen will leave tomorrow morning to bring at Your Worship's feet." There were also two postscripts; the first asking to be taken out of the country and excusing himself for being there; the second to the effect that the king and people wanted to fight, but that the king's brothers wanted peace; and in pencil on the envelope was written a third postscript:

Be strong; if the king send in his army, they are about twenty thousand.

Highlanders in the square at Ginghilovo

The messengers were sent back to the king with the answer that we must now go on to the Umvolosi for water, which was scarce at Amakeni, but that we would not cross it before noon on July 3rd, so as to give the king time to fulfil the conditions. These were again modified; one thousand rifles taken at Isandhlwana would be accepted, without the submission of any Zulus, and if there was no opposition, no more *kraals* would be burned. A telegram was at the same time despatched to Sir Garnet Wolseley, explaining the situation, the terms offered, and again asking for news of the First Division. That night we bivouacked at Amakeni, a six-mile march from Entonjaneni, but only three miles as the crow flies from that *laager*, which was in sight on the top of the hill.

On July 1st we continued our march to the Umvolosi. It was a very trying day, the atmosphere in the dense bush being oppressive after that on the highlands, and water only to be found by digging in the beds of dry *sluits*. The transmission of messages and reports was slow because of the narrow path; many parties of Zulus were reported by our scouts in front, and yet the bush prevented us knowing which way they were moving. It was seven miles to the river, and very thankful we all were that it was downhill. About three in the afternoon, when the Flying Column was *laagering*, a report came in from the front that the Zulus were advancing. There was an open space at the head of the Second Division, in which the waggons belonging to it were rapidly parked; but on the report proving unfounded, they were formed into a *laager* half a mile in rear of that of the Flying Column.

That night was a noisy one in both *laagers*. In that of the Second Division an officer of the Native Contingent was fired at by a sentry when visiting his pickets. In a minute the whole of our natives outside made a wild rush at the abattis and *laager*, and it says much for the discipline of the soldiers opposite them that they were not shot down and bayoneted, as occurred near Ginghilovo. The soldiers were driven back by the rush to the waggons, and the natives came clean over both into the interior. Headquarters were in bivouac just inside the waggons, and we were all lying about in various positions when the black avalanche came down. For a minute we could not tell what was up; but the noise tended to reassure us.

The rush of panic-stricken feet only requires to be heard once to be remembered: no enemy attacks with such velocity as the frightened attain in running away; and so, the jumpers were given blows from sticks and fists instead of cuts from swords and shots from pistols.

A burly native landed full on the adjutant-general's prostrate form, who at once forgot all about his published work on *The Treatment of Natives*. He forgot to call them "*Abantu* (people)," "*Amadoda* (men)," or "*Amabuti* (soldiers)": he did not recollect to tell them that they were behaving like "*Amakafula* (common Kafirs)"; but he called them a very insulting word (with the addition of an adjective) and other things; and he beat them till we regained our good temper, which had been temporarily lost with the disturbance of our beauty-sleep.

Next day a fort was built on a knoll between the two *laagers*, and then the waggons of the Second Division were moved down and formed into two lines, one end of each line resting on a side of Wood's *laager* and the other ends converging on the fort. Throughout the day the Zulu marksmen, posted in the rocks on a high hill over the Umvolosi just below the *drift*, fired at our watering-parties and wounded several men and horses. Large bodies of them were seen moving about over the river during the day. Our men were employed felling the bush for one hundred yards round the *laagers* and making a huge abattis of the thorny stuff round the waggons. I got a welcome present from home that day by a friend of the Engineers who arrived at night, bringing me two silk pocket-handkerchiefs in a letter. All mine had been stolen, and a towel cut in four pieces had been their substitutes for some time; so, they were useful presents indeed.

On the 3rd the Zulus were still firing on us. This was clearly a breach of the agreement. Accordingly, when noon came and the time allowed the king had expired, the cattle sent to us at Entonjaneni were driven across the Umvolosi as a sign that negotiations were at an end. An hour later Buller crossed the river with his mounted men, drove the Zulus from the hill, and pursued them over the open towards Nodwengn Kraal. From the waggons at the highest point of the *laager* we could see with our glasses most of what was going on.

When Buller reached the Imbilane Stream a large force of Zulus appeared suddenly in front of him, while at the same time other large forces rose out of the valleys on his right and left. It looked as if he must be cut off, or would at least have to fight his way through, as the Zulu wings were closing behind him. It was an exciting moment, and right glad we were to see him retiring. Two nine-pounders were got into position and some infantry sent to the *drift* to cover his retreat. Some of his men left on the hill checked the pursuit, and he got back with a loss of only three killed and four wounded.

It was a most successful affair. He had noted an excellent position

BATTLE OF ULUNDI

for the next day's fight: he had shown us where the Zulus were in force, and that they were posted in horseshoe form ready for us to enter the trap; and he had returned, when nearly surrounded by many thousand men, with a very small loss indeed.

On this day a further telegram was received from Sir Garnet Wolseley, dated from Durban on July 1st, the drift of which was that he wished the force to be united with the First Division, and that therefore, if compelled to fall back, it was to move by way of Kwamagwasa and St. Paul's Mission Station. The chief replied, giving his proposed movements for the 4th, and said that afterwards he would march by the route ordered.

The night of the 3rd was rendered hideous by the war-songs which proclaimed the enemy's intention of fighting next day; by "*Umlungu wahlab' inkosi* (the white man struck at the king)" among others. We could gather from the volume of sound that there was a goodly host assembled, and between the roars of the men came the shrill cries of the women, which told the old hands that they had got hold of the three bodies of the troopers killed that day and were mutilating them. Perhaps it was well that they made a night of it, for they were very late rising next morning. They said afterwards that, seeing our *laager* standing, they thought we should not move that day; but I doubt whether they could see it for the fog, though they might have listened for the rumbling of the waggons, and not hearing that thought we were not moving.

We were up next morning at five, to find everything shrouded in a thick white mist. Five companies of the 1st Batt. 24th, one company of Royal Engineers, with detachments from other corps, some six hundred men in all, were left to defend the *laager* under Colonel Bellairs, Deputy-Adjutant-General. At six the rest of the force advanced to the Umvolosi in the following strength:

Cavalry (17th Lancers and Irregulars)	1,344
Infantry (1st Batt. 13th; and 2nd Batt. 21st; 58th,	
80th, 90th, and 94th)	2,840
Native Contingent	958
	_____
	5142

With twelve guns and two Gatlings.

Buller's mounted men were to lead: the infantry, with the guns, were to follow in a rectangle, natives, ammunition and tool carts, and bearer-company in the centre; and the 17th Lancers were to bring up the rear. We were all across the river by seven, and at half-past eight had reached the knoll selected by Buller on the previous day for our position. The chief now took personal command of the united force, wheeled the rectangle half-right, so as to face Ulundi Kraal, halted it, faced the men outwards, and ordered the ranks to be dressed, and the ammunition-carts to be placed handy and opened. Wood proposed to entrench, but the chief refused. "No," he said, "they will be satisfied if we beat them fairly in the open. We have been called ant-bears long enough."

The Zulus did not keep us waiting long. The ranks were scarcely dressed before our mounted men on the right commenced firing at the back of Nodwengu Kraal, and almost immediately it was taken up all along the line of scouts. Buller and Drury Lowe brought in the Irregulars and 17th Lancers at a gallop, so as to clear the infantry front. "Volleys by companies" was the order when the square was closed again. The chief refused to dismount, so all staff-officers, including Newdigate's and Wood's, remained on horseback throughout the action; and a very fine view we had of the whole battle.

The Zulus had remained in the horseshoe formation of the previous day, and now joining the two horns, they came with a tremendous rush at our rear face. This was held by two companies of the 2nd Batt. 21st, and two of the 94th, the greatest rush coming at the right rear-angle held by the 21st. There was a patch of bush and long grass thirty yards off it behind which the enemy were assembling; so, the chief brought the 5th company Royal Engineers up behind the 21st to help them in case of need; but company volleys and case from two nine-pounders scattered the Zulus at this point and stopped a closer rush. The guns this day were in action in line with the infantry; the two Gatlings in the centre of the front face, and the others, two together, either at the angles or at the intervals between the regiments.

The flank and front faces were the next engaged, and it seemed to me, from horseback, that the Zulus killed many of their own men. At one time I was watching the enemy opposite the left face. They were in a hollow, and our men, being unable to see them, were not at that moment firing; yet two or three threw up their arms and fell, which could only have been from shots fired by their friends opposite, who were attacking our right face and whose bullets had passed over our heads and hit them.

Shortly after nine o'clock a dense black mass of Zulus emerged

133

from Ulundi Kraal and moved down the slope, east of the Imbilane Stream and towards us; it was the reserve, or the "Loins" of the Zulu Army, consisting of the royal regiments of the Undi corps at least five thousand strong. Two nine-pounders had been moved from the left rear to the left front angle, and they had taken the range to a solitary euphorbia tree on this slope about two thousand yards off. Down the slope came the Zulus in a wide rectangle, fifty deep, beating their white shields and shouting their war-cry.

The two Gatlings in the centre of our front face, after playing havoc in the black ranks, had now jammed and were out of action; but the nine-pounders were equal to the occasion. Loading with shrapnel they fired, both shells bursting in the centre of the front of this mass which at once opened out into two wings; two more shells followed, one into the heart of each wing; they hesitated, then closed again; two more shells sent them all to the right about, and we saw no more of Cetewayo's reserve that day. It had at no time been within a mile of us.

After three quarters of an hour the foremost Zulus began to waver. Seeing this the chief told Colonel Drury Lowe to take his lancers out and disperse them. Just as he had mounted, a spent bullet hit him on the spine and benumbed him, so Major Boulderson took command. Leaving by the left face, where a company of infantry was wheeled back to form a gateway, he took his men out towards Nodwengu Kraal, and then, wheeling into line to the right, charged the still unbroken part of the Zulu right horn. Poor Wyatt Edgell was shot dead almost before the lancers had cleared the square. One Zulu regiment stood firm and even gave the cavalry a volley; the fire was wild, however, and the ensuing shock when horse met foot could even be heard by us.

The Zulus broke and fled, followed fast by the lancers; but some rallied on the rocky hills to the north-west where the cavalry could not follow, and they were dispersed by shrapnel shells. The lance-pennons were a sight that night; there was not one that had not done its work. Buller's mounted men, who had left the square after the lancers, dispersed several other parties of the enemy; and within an hour there was not a Zulu to be seen.

So ended the fight at Ulundi. We all at once crowded round to congratulate the chief; the soldiers cheered their generals, and every one rejoiced. Of the chief's staff Milne only was wounded, but General Newdigate had both his *aides-de-camp* hit. Our total loss was one officer and ten men killed, nineteen officers and sixty-nine men wounded, twenty-eight horses killed and forty-five wounded. The

Zulus, whose total strength that day was certainly over twenty thousand, were estimated to have lost fifteen hundred. Cetewayo did not witness the fight, having left Ulundi the day before; the commanders were Mnyamane Tshingwayo and Dabulamanzi.

We halted till half-past eleven to bury our dead and attend to the wounded, and then moved forward to the Imbilane stream, where the men dined.

There was a tremendous cloud of smoke all over the country, for Ulundi and all the smaller *kraals* near the Mhlabatini Plain were fired that day. I got leave to ride on, reached Ulundi before it was quite destroyed, and got some of the white shields out of a shield-house. The *kraal* was an enormous place in the form of an oval, one diameter being about seven hundred yards and the other five hundred. There were seven rows of beehive huts round it, facing inwards; but the heat was so intense from the burning mass that little looting could be done before it was all destroyed.

The troops now returned by the way they had marched, slowly, for all the wounded were carried in litters. Our Basutos (who were Christians) held a most elaborate musical service over the grave of one of their men who had been killed; their hymns could be heard quite a mile away. They have the most splendid voices, and every morning and night on the campaign they used to sing a hymn in their own musical tongue. We were back again in our *laager* by half-past three, and then commenced the drudgery of writing. But it was nothing now; we all felt so light-hearted at having completed the business without interference.

All the Zulus that were questioned declared the war over. Our *inkos* was Bayete now instead of Cetewayo; the men on horses with the long *assegais* were terrible; they had been fairly beaten, for this time we did not make a *laager*, and did not dig like ant-bears. Amazulu and Abalungu would now be friends. Umbyembyee had been seen at Maizekanye. Years ago, when the Zulus, working at the wharf at Durban, first saw a field-gun they asked its name. The men landing it said, "We will tell you bye-and-bye," and the natives ever since have called them *umbyembyee*. They call a penny *ipeni*, and a pound *umpondwe* as a matter of course; but the derivation of *umbyembyee* is curious.

On July 5th we broke up the *laagers* on the Umvolosi, and moved back up the hill to Entonjaneni. There we found that some enterprising traders had arrived from the Transvaal with three huge tent-waggons, loaded with jam, matches, tobacco, potted meats, and tins of

Normandy butter. As soon as our waggons were parked and the tents up, everyone clustered round the strangers like bees. The prices were four shillings for a pot of jam or a pound of butter, threepence for a box of matches, and so on; but if they had charged double, they would have been sold out, and those traders must have made an uncommonly good thing of the venture.

That night a letter came in by native runners from General Crealock, endeavouring to explain Sir Garnet Wolseley's wishes; but it was in cipher, and must have been composed hurriedly, for the key made it into a curious mixture. The sense, however, evidently was that supplies were being brought to Port Durnford north of Umhlalazi River by land and sea, for the force which was to be concentrated there; and a reply notifying our proposed movements in that direction was sent off next day.

It was very cold at Entonjaneni after the heat of the plain. There was a strong wind all day on the 6th, heavy mist, and then rain at night; fog and rain continued on the 7th, followed by another stormy night, and next day was no better. The oxen were now dying by hundreds. The rain brought enormous black worms out of the ground four feet long, and when contracted as thick as a broom-handle. All our kit was wet through, and life was not worth living. No movement was possible till the 9th, when the Flying Column returned to Icibe Ridge on its way towards Kwamagwasa. It would have been impossible to have moved the whole force down towards the sea, for supplies were running short; and the Second Division accordingly returned to the Upoko River for food, wood for fuel, and grass for the oxen.

After visiting the wounded and bidding goodbye to our friends of the Second Division, we joined the Flying Column on the 10th, and reaching Kwamagwasa mission station on the following day, encamped half a mile beyond. Two of John Dunn's men came through from General Crealock, who reported that he had had his little bonfires too, having burnt Emangwane and Old Ondine Kraals on the 4th and 6th of July.

During this day's march the scouts found the bodies of Lieutenant Scott-Douglas of the 2nd Batt. 21st, and Corporal Cotter of the 17th Lancers. The former had been in charge of the signalling on the line between Fort Evelyn and Entonjaneni, and some ten days before had ridden out with the corporal to carry a message which a heavy fog made it impossible to flash. On the return journey they missed the way, took the Kwamagwasa track instead of that to Entonjaneni, and losing themselves wandered about hopelessly till they were killed by the Zulus about two miles east of the mission station. We buried them side by side under two euphorbia trees on the ridge, the chaplains of the English and Roman Churches officiating, and crosses were afterwards erected over their graves.

A small fort was built here, and garrisoned by two companies and two guns (detached from the Second Division) which had accompanied the Flying Column, one hundred of Buller's mounted men, and a company of natives. It was called Fort Robertson, after the missionary who had formerly resided here.

On the 14th, while again on the march, the chief received a letter from Sir Garnet Wolseley with a copy of general orders issued by the latter on the 6th, congratulating the troops on the victory at Ulundi; and about an hour later a second letter followed, dated July 12th. Both were understood to refer to the change of command. The next day came yet a third letter saying he would be at St. Paul's that day, and requesting an escort might be sent to meet him. The chief therefore took Buller's men for an escort, as requested, rode ahead five miles to the Umhlatoosi River and three miles beyond it; but as, after waiting for several hours, no one had arrived, he returned, and on our way back we hit off the *spoor* of Barrow's men who were escorting Sir Garnet, and who had come in by a side track through the bush. We galloped back and found them just arrived in camp.

It appeared now that, in addition to a commission constituting Sir Garnet Wolseley High Commissioner for Natal, the Transvaal, and Zululand, he had been given another as Commanding the Forces. The despatch received at the Upoko River had made, I believe, no mention of this. "Will you ask for leave or resign?" was, of course, all Sir Garnet had to suggest; and of course, our chief chose the latter alternative. Colonels Wood and Buller got leave at the same time, so much the same party that came out together at the beginning of 1878, with the additions of Milne and Frere, and Ernest Buller in Gosset's place, were now homeward bound together.

On July 16th the new Commander of the Forces reviewed the Flying Column and presented Lieutenant Chard, Royal Engineers, with the Victoria Cross for the defence at Rorke's Drift on January 22nd. There was a flogging-parade after to teach three of Wood's Swazis that they must not now murder Zulus. We then got rid of superfluous stores, packed a mule-waggon, and on the 17th started for the Lower Tugela, which we reached two days later, none of us perhaps very sorry to find ourselves once more in Natal.

It was curious on this run of over fifty miles to notice how rapidly the people had settled down again after Ulundi. Those *kraals* that had not been destroyed were full of people at their old avocations. In one would be the lord and master lying on a sheepskin in the sun, taking snuff and calling to the women and girls, hoeing in the mealie-patch, to get on with their business and not chatter; or giving them stick when, fondly imagining him to be asleep, they had knocked off work. In another the old man was absent after some cattle, and the field full of men, women, boys, and girls, busier at play than work. A woman with a dozen little children was sitting round a fire on which simmered a three-legged iron pot. Nobody seemed in the least afraid of us. Mealie porridge was being ladled out of the pot in a long wooden spoon, and the youngsters were opening their mouths for it in turn like a lot of young birds.

"That is what the soldiers would call 'orderly man,'" said Longcast. "Ask her which of that lot are her own children."

He did so, and back came the reply, "They are all my husband's children."

Polygamy here had not done much harm at any rate. The marital relations and rules among the Zulus are so different from those of other people, that the men must either remain bachelors or have a plurality of wives.

One large *kraal* I visited on the 18th was full of wounded men, who were as friendly as possible. Thirty-one miles is a long trek, and by the middle of the day we had grown rather thirsty. Longcast knew this part of the country well, and many of the people, as he had lived at Kwamagwasa for years. "I should like a good pot of Kafir beer," said he; "and I think they will give us some at that *kraal*."

I had never tasted the Zulu brew, and willingly joined him. At the gateway stood a sentry with a bundle of *kerries*.

"It is peace, oh people!" cried Longcast.

"Peace in the land again," said the sentry, who was thereupon asked to call the chief. A fine-looking, old, ringed Zulu came out and asked us in.

"Leave your sword and revolver with the sentry," said Longcast, giving up his carbine. "It is the rule, and you will be quite safe, for I know the head of the *kraal* well."

So, I gave up my weapons, but with some reluctance.

When we were inside, they all crowded round us, and Longcast introduced me to the headman as an *Induna* of the *Amangesi* (English). They gave us beer, drinking out of the basket themselves first, and then offered us a bleeding piece of goat just killed, while I emptied my tobacco-pouch in the headman's hand. The beer is kept in gourd-shaped baskets, so beautifully made that, when wetted, the material swells and the vessel is water-tight.

There were a lot of wounded, all as merry as could be. One had lost two brothers at Isandhlwana, and had been wounded at Ulundi himself; his regiment was the *Nkobamakosi* (the bender of kings), commanded by Usicwelecwele. How he had got home in a fortnight he scarcely knew; it was very hard work, for he had been wounded in the thigh, but the other boys had helped him. He had been one of the Eyes of the King, but that was all over now. I asked Longcast what the Eyes of the King might be.

"Oh, you see, sir, the king has detectives, like white kings and queens. They keep him informed of what is going on all over his country. No one knows if there may not be a spy in his own *kraal*. It is against the law for men to fight unless permitted by the king; but as there may be men of many regiments in one small *kraal*, they will fight at times. Then some man will rise and say, 'Beware, I am the Eye of the King'; and then all those who have been quarrelling will cease, and slink away into the bush so as not to be recognised."

The floors of two of the huts in this *kraal* were beautifully polished and coloured like mahogany. The fireplace is always in the middle, and there is no chimney, so as a rule you are too much blinded by the wood-smoke to see much; but on this coastline it is hotter, and there were no fires burning within, the cooking being done outside. I was almost ashamed to crawl in with my boots on, but did so on invitation, and the floor-making was explained. The white ant-hills furnish the material; this is pounded, wetted, and then beaten down mixed with cow-dung, after which, when dry, it is polished with bullock's blood rubbed in with charred sticks. It is smeared over with cow-dung and water, and polished again, from time to time.

Always carefully swept by the women, it looks a model dwelling, till you sleep in an old one, when the various insects come out of the thatch and make your nights uneasy. All over South Africa the earthen floors are smeared with the same mixture to fix the dust; and the best way to be comfortable in camp is to get your boy to treat the floor of your tent to a dressing of it.

An old man, who had lost half his right arm, owned Dabulamanzi, the king's brother, as his chief. He did not, however, belong to the *Tulwana* regiment, of which the latter was commanding-officer, but to the *Ngulubi* (pigs) of the *Udhlambedhlu* (ill-tempered) corps. Being old now, he had fought in the district, at Inyezane and at Ginghilovo, and at the latter place the bone of his arm had been smashed by a bullet below the elbow; but he had cut the loose part off, and the wound had healed now.

The many little mounds outside, covered with stones, told how many poor fellows had crawled home merely to die. One could not help being sorry that such a generous, brave race had undergone so much suffering in supporting their peculiar military system. We left with mutual salutes, and found our arms outside the *kraal*, untouched, as the interpreter had promised.

Now that we had no cares except for ourselves, our horses, and our baggage, there was time to talk with Longcast, who had lived so long among the Zulus. He spoke the ordinary language of the race perfectly; so well, in fact, that in the darkness of a hut they would not know him from one of themselves. He had a great respect for Cetewayo, whom he described as every inch a king. When asked if the king killed many of his people, he answered:

"Only to keep up his authority when they have done very wrong. It is an old law that anyone meeting one of the king's wives must turn out of the path and not look at her on pain of death; but I have never heard of any one being killed if he looked at one by accident."

"Is not his will the law?"

"Oh no; he has councillors, and they sometimes speak what they think. Two years ago, at the *Umkosi* (feast of first-fruits) the Nkobamakosi regiment set upon the *Tulwana* regiment, though four times their strength, with sticks, and beat it soundly. The *Tulwana* went back to their huts and, by order of Uhamu, their commanding officer, took their *assegais* and killed so many of the Nkobamakosi that Ulundi streamed with blood. Cetewayo wanted to punish them for killing his favourite boys; but the Council said that the king ought to be punished for putting such numbers of a young regiment into the same *kraal* with the old warriors of Panda, and that these were not to blame for taking up the *assegai* against such hordes. So, the Nkobamakosi were moved to Old Ondine Kraal, towards the coast on the south of the Umhlatoosi, and the *Tulwana* were praised. But Uhamu feared the king, and that is why he came to Colonel Wood rather than go to the war with his regiment."

"You have been talking to a lot of Zulus; what do they think of the war?"

"They are quite satisfied since Ulundi that they have been fairly beaten, and are glad that there is peace again so that they can go on with the planting, for food is short now; but before Ulundi they thought that they could beat the white men in the open. They beat the Boers in 1838 when they had left their waggons: they beat the English at Isandhlwana under the same conditions; and at the In-hlobane Mountain they beat a force that fought like the Boers, all on horses. But at Kambula and at Ginghilovo, when they attacked *laagers*, they own to having been very badly beaten. At Ulundi, when they saw that there were no waggons and that the soldiers were out in the open, they made sure of killing them all; but not even the young regiments who were fighting for wives could face such swarms of bullets as met them that day. If the white *inkos* would let them marry, there was no use fighting anymore; they had had enough now; we had fought them fairly, and not dug like ant-bears."

It was the same cry throughout. With a remodelled system, and an army led by Englishmen, these men would have followed us any-where. We might have had Southern Africa up to the Zambesi, and beyond it; but it was fated that the Zulu country was to be parcelled out among thirteen petty chiefs, so many tempting baits for the fili-bustering Boers, after the latter had beaten us two years later and we had made that shameful surrender of the Transvaal. It is well said that soldiers build up empires for statesmen to pull down.

On the 18th July we tried hard to reach the Tugela Punt, but night fell at six o'clock, when we were four miles short of it; so, we outspanned, pitched our tents, tied the horses to the waggon, turned the mules, knee-haltered, out to graze all night after their thirty-one miles' run, and slept the sleep of the just. Next morning Crealock rose at dawn to stir the servants up; just as he got outside the tent, he asked me to give him his watch which he had left under his pillow. My blankets were on the ground alongside his, and I was pulling on my boots, so I jerked his pillow over, and there coiled round his watch was a big puff-adder!

As it began to crawl away, I flattened its wide head still more with a tent-mallet; but it was a near thing for us both, for they are most deadly brutes. Had he not forgotten his watch, but felt for it as usual; or had I slipped my hand under the pillow instead of jerking it off! It seemed like a reminder that Providence watched over us to the last day in Zululand. The tent had been pitched in the dark over a foot-path. This should never be done; in wet weather it is a little river, and on cold nights snakes travel along it for warmth, as the dew does not condense there as on the grass. Our snake had been travelling along it from his spoor, and had been induced to lie up by the warmth of the blankets.

We reached Durban at six o'clock on the evening of the 20th. The town had turned out to meet us, with a guard of honour and a regular ovation. There was a great dinner at the club, with much speechify-ing, and so, as Pepys says, to bed. It *was* a bed too, and one was glad to feel, for the first time for three months, that there need be no more rising before day-break. Maritzburg was no less demonstrative; and that Durban had by no means exhausted its welcome we discovered on our return there on the 26th for a public ball which the chief had promised the commodore to attend.

On the road between Botha's Hill and Maritzburg a rather curi-ous incident occurred. I was travelling ahead with the staff clerk, the others following later, and had got two seats in the omnibus, having engaged the post-cart for the general's party. When I started for the thirty-two miles' drive, I found one of my fellow-travellers was Bishop Colenso.

Now the bishop had all along held the view that the English, and not the Zulus, had been the wrongdoers from the first, and not being one whit afraid of his opinions, he had lost no opportunity of airing them in the newspapers. This view had not been generally popular in Natal, and at that particular time His Lordship was not very much honoured in his own country. When we were three miles from Mar-itzburg a strong party of men rushed at us, took the horses out of the omnibus, cheered like maniacs, and began to drag us towards the town. The bishop knew the general was following later, saw at once the mistake, and could not bear the notion of being mixed up in any way with a demonstration in favour of the victor of Ulundi. "I am not the general!" he shouted.

We were bowling along at a fine rate; the horses had been turned adrift and had galloped off down the road; if the men found out their mistake, we should be left stranded on the *veldt*. I tried, therefore, to pacify His Lordship, but in vain; he would not listen to reason as a mathematician should.

"I am the bishop! I am not the general!" he yelled again.

"By Jingo, it is the old bloke of a bishop!" said one of the crowd;

and at once, as I had foreseen, we were left ignominiously to cool our heels on the road. A quarter of an hour later the post-cart with the general and his party galloped madly past us to avoid the demonstrators.

"Send back our horses!" I screamed.

A wave of the hand was the only response. At last, I induced some of the fellows to buckle-to again, and myself getting out to help, we moved slowly along.

But at last, all the feasting was over, and on the 28th we embarked in the *Queen Margaret* transport for Capetown. There we stayed five days, till August 5th. Again, there were official receptions in honour of the chief, and now, being a free agent, he gave, in his reply to an address, his opinions of the evils that might be caused by writers to the Press. He pointed out that if, while active operations are actually going on, persistent attempts to lower the general in the estimation of those he is commanding are to be considered as not exceeding the licence granted to the correspondents who are allowed to accompany our armies in the field, the gravest consequences might ensue, and the proper conduct of a campaign would become almost impossible.

He might have gone on to mention the ill-informed and biased utterances of some Members of Parliament as likely also to contribute to the demoralization of armies. We are a silly people! Wellington even was constantly censured for delay, when he had not been provided with the means to advance. It did not do much harm then: the ministers at home might grow nervous about their places, and so be frightened into changing their plans; but the soldiers in the field did not get newspapers by every mail then, and discipline did not suffer.

It is otherwise now, and a man who speaks in the House, or writes to a newspaper anything against the skill of a general commanding in the field, should be liable to be tried for creating false alarms and "causing fear and despondency." Let them say what they please at the end, when all the evidence is before them; but let them hold their tongues while the only evidence is to be obtained from party newspapers.

On Sunday I went to call on my old friend Von Linsingen, who was now governor of the gaol at the breakwater. He hailed me warmly, introduced me to *Madame* as his Imperial Staff-Officer at the Intaba Ka'ndoda fight in 1878, and then asked me to attend his church-parade in the prison-yard. Four warders with loaded rifles occupied the angles on the top of the walls: there was a wooden platform, like a scaffold, in the middle, which we reached by a ladder; and then a gate was opened, the convicts marched in, and the service began. Linsingen was a wise man and gave them plenty of hymns, and the singing was excellent. In the middle of the first hymn a Kafir came up the ladder, and said, "May I offer you a hymn-book, sir?" and there stood Edmund Sandilli, son of the late chief of the Gaikas, formerly magistrate's clerk at Middle-Drift, in a convict's dress dotted over with broad arrows.

When the service was over, I asked permission of Linsingen to speak to the fellow. Matanzima, his brother, was there too, the handsomest man of all the Gaika race. He was rather irreconcilable, and did not seem to care much about talking to the white man; but Edmund was quite ready to expound his views on things in general. The chiefs, he said, had simply followed their supreme chief, as was right in their eyes. The supreme chief had been killed, and the tribe scattered; that was the fortune of war, and they, the minor chiefs, recognised the justice of their sentences, for they had led the tribe and fought to the last. But the people generally could not so understand matters.

In the beginning of the war some had been taken prisoners who had only fought for a short time. When the judge was driving from Grahamstown to King William's Town, to hold the assizes, some of their people had shot at him and his escort; the prisoners, who had only fought a short time, were tried by him and sentenced to penal servitude. When the war began to subside, and the white men grew less frightened, the prisoners received much lighter sentences, though they had fought longer. Finally, when the great chief was killed, an amnesty was granted, and the men who had fought right through the war got no punishment at all.

I know the white man's law, but most of the tribe say that they cannot see its justice. They only say the more the white man is frightened, the more punishment the Kafir gets. That's no law; Xosa law is better—big wrong, big fine.

Dear old Von Linsingen had been longing all this year to be on the war-path again. He was given the gaol to keep him quiet, and later on, much to his surprise, received the order of St. Michael and St. George. But the following year, when the Tambookies rebelled, he left for the front, and lost his life in trying to save that of his son. A fine old fighting man of the Hanoverian race died in him; the stamp of man that loves the battle, a leader of the pioneers that lay the foundations of empires, valuing nothing but a good name, and when the fighting is

144

GUARDING ZULU PRISONERS

over returning to their farms without desire for other reward.

On August 5th we sailed in the mail-steamer *German* for England, and arrived at Plymouth on the 26th. I must end my account of Zululand by a story that shows the generosity of the British soldier to perfection. After the war, the company of the 24th that had defended Rorke's Drift was marching into Maritzburg amidst a perfect ovation. Among those cheering them was Mr. Dalton, who, as a conductor, had been severely wounded there. "Why, there's Mr. Dalton cheering us! We ought to be cheering him; he was the best man there," said the men, who forthwith fetched him out of the crowd, and made him march with them.

No one knew better the value of this spontaneous act than that old soldier. The men are not supposed to know anything about strategy, and not much about tactics, except *Fire low, fire slow, and obey orders*; but they do know when a man has got his heart in the right place, and if they have a chance, they will show him that they know it. Mr. Dalton must have felt a proud man that day.

CHAPTER 9

Departure for Egypt

In January, 1880, I was appointed brigade-major to General Peyton then commanding the Third Infantry Brigade at Aldershot. In the summer of that year Sir Daniel Lysons took over the command of the division from Sir Thomas Steele, and the Duke of Connaught, who had been commanding the 1st Batt. Rifle Brigade in the North Camp, succeeded General Peyton.

My time was now fully occupied with staff-duties, in the course of which it was my fortune to see much of the volunteers; indeed, I think I may say that during about ten years at Aldershot, and as a staff-officer at six volunteer reviews, I have seen as much of the volunteer forces of England and Scotland as most regular soldiers.

The regiments of course vary in efficiency; how can provincial corps, with their companies scattered over a whole county, be as efficient as those that belong to the great cities, and that can be exercised in battalion drill and often in brigade? But I have seen a Volunteer battalion at Aldershot, from St. Martin's-le-Grand, of which the men were almost as soldierlike, and much more intelligent than men of the line. I have seen a battalion from Bloomsbury detrain at Lewes, entrain at Brighton, and work in the long day's interval as smartly as could be wished. Again, I have seen a battalion, that came all the way from Manchester for a week's drill with the Regulars, excel the latter in physique, and not fall far short of them in manoeuvring.

I have seen a company of a Wiltshire battalion, and a smart one too, that could have built a railway engine if we had given them the tools and materials. The force is now subject to the provisions of the Army Act when exercised with, or attached to, the regular forces or militia, or when on actual military service. It is worthy of all praise from its patriotism alone; and its members' emoluments are absolutely noth-

147

ing, for the capitation grants allowed each efficient go to the credit of the corps funds, not to the officers and men personally. *Salus patriae prima lex* is the principle both officers and men go on. For this they toil, in the time they can spare from their regular professions, at the qualifying drills and target practices; and, for their reward, they get at best but very meagre thanks, and too often ungenerous and spiteful criticism. In my humble opinion the Volunteer decoration of 1892 was a gracious recognition thoroughly well deserved.

It is certainly in no captious spirit that I tell the following anecdote. In 1882 there was the usual Volunteer review on Easter Monday. Twenty thousand men were assembled at Portsmouth under Prince Edward of Saxe Weimar, then commanding the Southern District; and there were brigaded with them for the first time columns under the Home District Staff, which marched there from Petersfield. Unfortunately, I was not present at the operations that year, which was my loss. Everyone who went was delighted, except, so the story goes, a certain subaltern of a regular rifle regiment, employed as railway staff-officer at a detraining station, who was thus addressed by the first arrivals from London: "You before us! When did your regiment leave Waterloo?"

Drawing himself up majestically, the subaltern replied, "We left Waterloo in 1815." He got much applause for his smartness; and certainly, if it was not exactly the answer to turn away wrath, it was an uncommonly ready one.

The year 1881 was a disastrous one for the British Army. It witnessed our defeats by the rebels in the Transvaal, and the surrender of that country to the Boers before we had retrieved our reputation. The Zulus being broken up into thirteen tribes, and Sekukuni's stronghold captured by Sir Garnet Wolseley, the Dutchmen were left with no enemies but ourselves, and they made the most of their opportunity, when we had a weak government in office, by waylaying the 94th on December 20th, 1880, on the march, and breaking out into open rebellion.

The only officer not wounded at the surprise at Bronker's Spruit was Captain J. M. L. Elliot, who had been a combatant officer in the regiment, and was then its paymaster. He was an old schoolfellow of mine at Cheltenham and a comrade at Aldershot. I knew all the 94th well: they had been one of the battalions of the "Elephant and Castle" brigade in Zululand; but Elliot I knew best. We had been friends for twenty years, and I think no apology will be necessary for recalling the fate he suffered at the hands of the Boers, a people who within less than a month were granted belligerent rights by our Colonial Office. It should be remembered not only by soldiers, who, indeed, are little likely to forget it, but by all Englishmen.

Captain Elliot was taken prisoner with some forty men of the 94th, and conducted to Heidelberg, where he found Captain R. H. Lambart of the 21st Fusiliers also a prisoner. The latter had been to the Orange Free State on duty, buying horses, and, on returning, was captured by the Boers and his horses stolen. On December 24th, the two officers were offered the choice of remaining prisoners or of giving their word of honour that, if conducted to the Orange Free State under escort and then released, they would not bear arms again during the war.

They chose the latter alternative, and were informed by Mr. Bok, Secretary to the South African Republic, in the presence of Mr. P. Joubert, Commandant-General, that on the 27th they, with their private property, would be escorted by two Boers to the nearest drift over the Vaal River, twenty-five miles off. The Boers led them astray to a drift at the junction of the Vaal and Klip Rivers; here was a punt capable of holding two persons only, into which they were ordered to get, leaving the carriage behind and swimming the horses. They asked rather to be taken back to the Boer camp, than to be put across with no means of conveyance further. The escort then disappeared, and the officers drove along the river-bank towards the proper crossing at Spencer's drift.

On the way they were met by two other armed Boers who gave them an official letter from Mr. Bok, which stated that they had broken their parole and must be guided by the escort. The local *commandant*, on their arrival, ordered them to start at once, in the darkness, for Spencer's Drift. The officers, who knew the way, soon saw they were again being misled, and protested; whereupon, the escort being now suddenly increased to eight men, they were ordered to cross the river where they then stood. As it was pitch dark, with occasional flashes of lightning, and the river in flood, they asked at least to be allowed to wait till morning. "Cross at once," was the reply of the Boer *commandant*.

They entered the water; the horses fell, were got up, and then fell again, turning the cart over on its side. The officers struck out for the farther bank, when the Boers fired a volley at them. Poor Elliot was shot dead; a second volley was fired at Lambart, but he, after a hard

149

struggle, managed to reach the opposite bank, and, though frequently fired at, escaped untouched in the darkness. (I have taken the substance of this summary from Captain Lambart's official report, published in a Blue Book.)

When the Spaniards cut off Jenkins's ears within historical times, he had merely to say in England, "I recommended my soul to God and my cause to my country," and Spain paid dearly for her brutality. It was left to the Prime Minister of England in 1881 to applaud these Boers under the description of a "people rightly struggling to be free," to surrender the Transvaal without reasserting our rights, and to exact no reparation whatsoever for this foul murder.

I do not profess to understand the ways of statesmen; I will merely give two maxims by great soldiers. When the Transvaal was annexed in 1877 the treasury was practically empty, the Boers did not pay their taxes, their commanders had been beaten by Sekukuni; it may be said, in short, that there was no government worthy of the name. Three years previously Von Moltke, speaking in the Reichstag, had said:

> A weak government is a misfortune for any country, and a source of danger to its neighbours.

Speaking as a soldier, we were, therefore, right in annexing the Transvaal. In 1880 Her Majesty's High Commissioner for the Transvaal had informed the Boers, who were then simmering into rebellion, that as long as the sun should shine so long should the country be held for Great Britain. What followed in 1881 all England knows. When Napoleon heard of the capitulation of Baylen in 1808 he exclaimed:

> That an army should make a shameful surrender is a blot on the French name and a stain upon its glory. It would have been better that they had all perished. We can find more soldiers, but national honour, once lost, is never recovered.

Comment on these two maxims must surely be superfluous.

Nor was this the only incident of that year that the army had to endure; in the autumn came the severest shock it had suffered since Mr. Cardwell's in 1871. It came this time from the hand of Mr. Childers, then Secretary of State for War. This was the relocalisation of the forces into Territorial Regiments. A revision of the Forces Acts became necessary, terms of enlistment were altered, long or short service was introduced, the whole of Section VI. of the Queen's Regulations had to be rewritten. All the numbers of regiments were abolished; nearly all the uniforms were changed; officers were made more interchangeable still; the old corps generally got new names, and the Infantry of the line was in a perfect uproar. But enough of this ancient history. I will resume my own story.

★★★★★★★★★★★★

In the year 1882 the summer manoeuvres were to be on a larger scale than usual. Camps were to be established in July at Chobham and Aldershot for two army corps, each of fifteen thousand men, to be commanded by Lieut.-Generals G. H. S. Willis and Sir Edward Hamley respectively. The Duke of Connaught was to command a division of the southern corps, and Sir Daniel Lysons was to be umpire-in-chief. Affairs, however, were now looking so black in the Mediterranean, that the orders for the manoeuvres were cancelled on July 8th. Everyone, of course, at once volunteered for active service, in the event of troops being required for Egypt.

Through the Duke of Connaught's good offices, I was appointed Deputy-Assistant-Adjutant-and-Quartermaster-General to the First Division, which was to be commanded by General Willis, with Colonel Gillespie, late 106th, as his Assistant-Adjutant-General. His Royal Highness was to command the First (Guards) Brigade of that Division, and he chose Captain Herbert of the Grenadier Guards as his brigade-major, and Major Lane of the Rifle Brigade as his *aide-de-camp*.

We all sailed together on July 30th in the *Orient*, taking with us a troop of the 19th Hussars and the 1st Batt. Scots Guards. The latter came down to the docks by river, in three steamers, to avoid the crowd in the city; and Sir John Astley and Colonel Farquharson of Invercauld, Crimean veterans of the regiment, brought down a large party in a special steamer to see them off. The Duke of Connaught came down by river also, with the Duchess, the Prince and Princess of Wales, the Duke of Edinburgh, the Commander-in-Chief, and the Duke of Teck. The *Orient* cast off her moorings at one p.m. amid a scene of great enthusiasm.

We reached Gibraltar on August 4th, Malta on the 7th, and Alexandria on the 10th. At Gibraltar we only stopped an hour to call for orders; at Malta we stayed nine hours to coal, and nearly drowned thirteen subalterns of the Guards who, in undress uniforms with swords, were all upset out of one boat when on the way to pay their respects to the governor. Before leaving England, the staff had been liberally supplied with maps, blue-books, and a report on Egypt, and we all

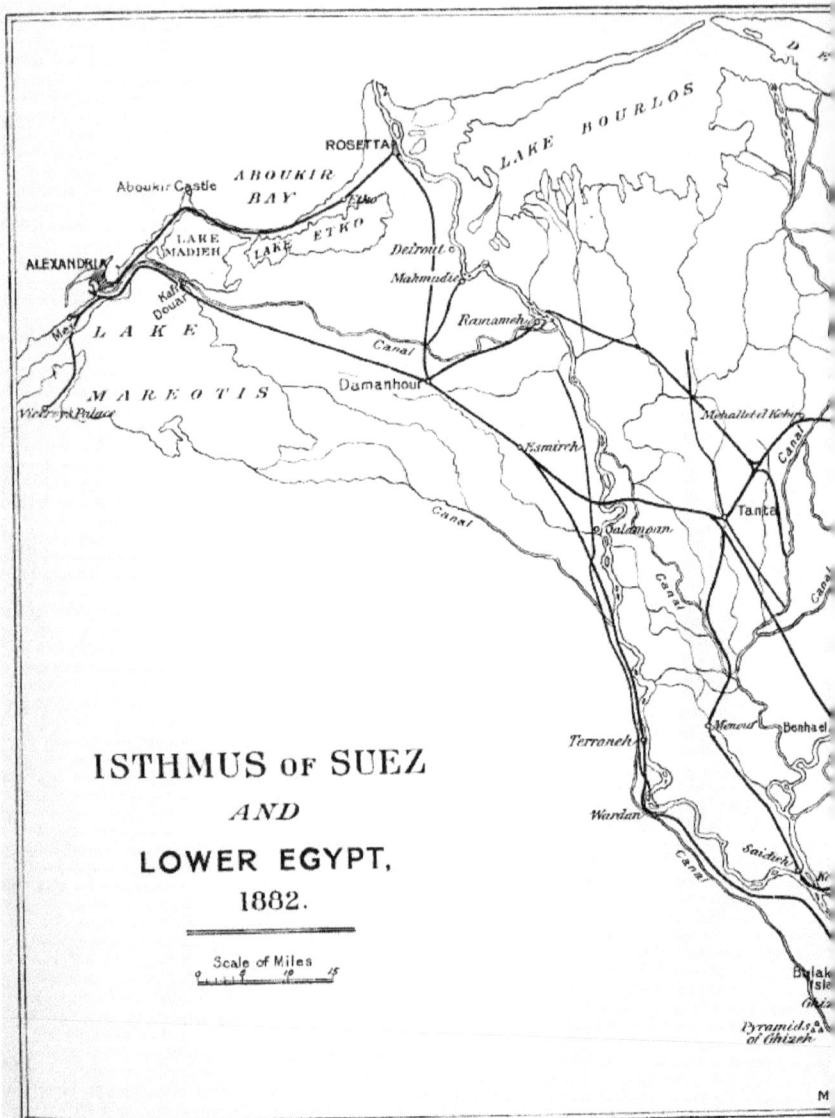

ISTHMUS of SUEZ
AND
LOWER EGYPT,
1882.

Scale of Miles

DAMIETTA

Bay of Dibeh

LAKE   MENZALEH

PORT
SAID

Bay of Pelusium

Menzaleh

Canal

Mansurah

Canal

amanhoud

Canal

Kantara

oSalahieh

Abey.Kebir

Canal

Canal

Canal

M
A
R
I
T
I
M
E

Kassassin
Mahsameh   Tel el Mahuta
El Magfar   Plateau of el Guisr

ISMAILIA

Zagazig

Tel el Kebir

SWEET

LAKE TIMSAH

Tel Basta

Nefiche

WATER

Tel Mirh

LAND   OF   GOSHEN

Plateau   Serepeum

CANAL

BELBEIS

GEBEL GENEFFE

B
I
T
T
E
R

L
A
K
E

C
A
N
A
L

Canal

Great   Hadj   Route

Canal

Abbasoych

CAIRO

GEBEL MOKATTAM

GEBEL ATTAKA   Port Ibrahim

SUEZ

RED
SEA

Baths

R. & R. Clark, Limited, Printers, Edinburgh.

now set to work to study the reasons of our being ordered off to spoil the Egyptians. These reasons may be thus briefly stated.

The Suez Canal is our highroad to India, and should be neutralised by international agreement, or held by a friendly power. To England therefore a stable and friendly government in Egypt is of vital importance, and that must be secured at all hazards. In August, 1879, Ismail Pasha, the first *Khedive*, or Viceroy, of Egypt (his predecessors having held the title of *vali*, or governor, only) was forced by the British and French Governments, in consequence of his misrule, to abdicate in favour of his son Mohamed Tewfik. In September, 1880, the Egyptian Army, led by Colonel Ahmed Arabi Bey, compelled the new *khedive* to grant certain concessions.

By the beginning of 1882 Arabi was a *pasha* and Minister of War, his assumed mission being the removal of abuses, and his motto *Egypt for the Egyptians*. Within a few months he was to all intents and purposes ruler of Egypt. Now there were nearly one hundred thousand Europeans in the country, and, rightly or wrongly, England and France had, in January of this year, agreed that the maintenance of the *khedive* on the throne was the sole guarantee for its future good order and prosperity, and that they would accordingly unite to support him. In May, therefore, the allied fleets entered the harbour of Alexandria to protect the foreigners' interests and to give the *khedive* an assurance of their governments' support.

The *sultan* sent Dervish Pasha as his representative to restore order in Egypt; but while the *khedive*, Dervish, and Arabi Pasha were in Cairo, serious riots between the Mahomedans and Christians broke out in Alexandria on June 11th. A wave of religious excitement now spread throughout the country, and the Christians fled almost *en masse*. On June 24th the English and French Controllers were told they could no longer be allowed to sit in council with the Egyptian Ministry; Arabi proclaimed that no forces would be permitted to land to restore order; fortifications were constructed near Aboukir Bay, and the Bedouins were reported to be assembling along the Suez Canal.

The *sultan* took this opportunity of decorating Arabi with a high Turkish order, there having always existed a jealousy between the Porte and its Egyptian vassal since the latter was accorded the dignity of viceroy. The fleets at Alexandria soon found that heavy guns were being mounted to oppose them, that attempts were being made to block the entrance to the harbour, and that in fact their safety was threatened. The Egyptians were warned that they were ignoring the *khedive's* or-

COLONEL AHMED ARABI BEY

ders; whereupon they worked at night and, being detected by the electric light, complained of the foreigners' discourtesy in using it. Certain forts were accordingly demanded for occupation, and this not being complied with, on July 11th the bombardment of Alexandria began.

The French fleet put out to sea and took no part in it. On the 13th the forts were found to have been evacuated, and, as the mob was pillaging and burning the city, seamen and marines were landed and took charge of Alexandria till Sir Archibald Alison, with the first detachment of troops, arrived on July 17th. These were the 1st Batt. South Staffordshire (38th), the 3rd Batt. King's Royal (60th) Rifles, the 17th company of Royal Engineers from Cyprus, and a battalion of marines from Malta. The rebel Egyptian troops retreated along the Cairo railway about nine miles, and took up a position on the neck of land between Lake Mariût and Lake Aboukir, which they strongly fortified west of Kafr Dauar. The English troops being reinforced by the 2nd Batt. Duke of Cornwall's Light Infantry (46th), and half the 1st Batt. Royal Sussex (35th), moved out on July 24th along the Mahmudiyeh Canal to Ramleh to observe them. We thus secured the Ramleh waterworks but as Arabi had dammed the canal behind his works, water was scarce.

At home, on July 25th, the men of the reserve, who had left the colours within the two previous years, were now called out. On the 27th the House of Commons voted a credit of over two millions for the expedition. The French Chambers refused to vote a credit, and England had to act alone. She did not hesitate. A division was ordered from India to Egypt, including two batteries of Royal Artillery and two regiments of the line, 1st Batt. Manchester (63rd) and 1st Batt. Seaforth Highlanders (72nd). Four regiments of cavalry, two batteries of horse artillery, six of field and two of garrison artillery, four companies of Royal Engineers, three battalions of Guards and seven of the Line, with the necessary complement of commissariat, transport, hospital, and other duties, were furnished from home. Sixty-one steamers were engaged to transport the force from England, and we in the Orient had the honour of being the first to start. The Mediterranean garrisons supplied nine battalions, and, as already stated, some of these had reached Alexandria as early as July 17th.

★★★★★★

The following is the return of the forces employed after the "Redistribution of Troops" on the 7th Sept, (inclusive of the Indian Contingent but exclusive of those left at Alexandria).

FIRST DIVISION.
Lieut.-General G. H. S. Willis.

First Brigade ....
- 2nd Grenadier Guards.
- 2nd Coldstream Guards.
- 1st Scots Guards.
- Naval Brigade.

Second Brigade.........
- 2nd Royal Irish (18th).
- 1st Royal West Kent (50th).
- Royal Marine Light Infantry.
- 2nd York and Lancaster (84th).
- 1st Royal Irish Fusiliers (87th).

Divisional Troops ...
- 19th Hussars (two squadrons).
- 2nd Duke of Cornwall's Light Infantry 46th).
- A—1 Royal Artillery.
- D—1 „ „
- 24th Company Royal Engineers
- 12th Company Commissariat and Transport.
- ½ No. 1 Bearer Company.
- No. 3 Field Hospital.

SECOND DIVISION.
Lieut.-General Sir Edward Hamley.

Third Brigade ....
- 1st Royal Highlanders (42nd).
- 1st Gordon „ (75th).
- 1st Cameron „ (79th).
- 2nd Highland Light Infantry (74th).

Indian Contingent (attached) ....
- 7—1 (Mountain Battery)
- 1st Manchester (63rd).
- 1st Seaforth Highlanders (72nd).
- 7th Bengal Infantry.
- 20th Punjaub Infantry.
- 29th Beloochees.
- Medical Department, Ambulance, &c.
- Transport.
- Commissariat.
- R.E. Field Park.
- Ordnance Department.

Divisional Troops ...
- 19th Hussars (two squadrons).
- 3rd King's Royal Rifles (60th).
- I—2 Royal Artillery.
- N—2 „ „
- 26th Company Royal Engineers.
- 11th Company Commissariat and Transp
- ½ No. 2 Bearer Company.
- Nos. 4 and 5 Field Hospitals.'
- No. 2 Field Hospital (attached).

CAVALRY DIVISION.

Major-General D. C. Drury Lowe.

First Brigade ....
- Household Cavalry (three squadrons).
- 4th Dragoon Guards.
- 7th   „   „
- 17th Company Commissariat and Transport (part of).
- ½ No. 1 Bearer Company.

Second Brigade.........
- 2nd Bengal Cavalry.
- 6th   „   „
- 13th Bengal Lancers.

Divisional Troops ...
- N—A Royal Horse Artillery.
- Mounted Infantry.
- Detachment Royal Engineers.
- 17th Company Commissariat and Transport (part of).
- No. 6 Field Hospital.

CORPS TROOPS.

(Commanding Royal Artillery, Colonel Goodenough.)

Corps Artillery.........
- G—B Royal Horse Artillery.
- H—1 Royal Artillery.
- C—3   „   „
- J—3   „   „
- F—1   „   „   (ammunition column).
- Royal Marine Artillery.

Siege Train ....
- 1st London.
- 5th Scottish.
- 6th   „

(Commanding Royal Engineers, Colonel Nugent.)

Corps Engineers ......
- " A " (Pontoon) Troop.
- " C " (Telegraph) Troop.
- Field Park.
- 8th, 17th, and 18th Companies.
- Railway Staff.
- Queen's Own Sappers and Miners (A and I Companies).

- Commissariat and Transport (8, 15, and Auxiliary Companies).
- Ordnance Store Department.
- ½ No. 2 Bearer Company.
- Nos. 1, 7, and 8 Field Hospitals.

******

Now although it is about a hundred miles away, Cairo is really the key to the Suez Canal; for Suez, Ismailia, Port Said, and all the stations along the Canal are supplied with fresh water from the Nile at Cairo through the Ismailia Sweetwater Canal, and the supply can therefore be cut off at the will of the ruling power. The Egyptian capital therefore was our natural objective.

In 1882 the sea had been practically brought within a hundred miles of Cairo by the construction of the Maritime Canal. From Ismailia to Cairo there was fresh water and a railway all the way, if an attacking force could be quick enough to secure them. The desert alongside the north bank of the Sweet-water Canal was hard until the irrigated Delta was reached; it was known that the principal military station was at Tel-el-Kebir, just short of the Delta, along this line, and that the rebels would probably stand there; if the Maritime Canal could be seized before it was injured, the English and Indian contingents could concentrate on Lake Timsah, and, once taken, the canal could be protected by our fleet. Secrecy was above all things necessary, or the canal would have been blocked; and the secret was indeed so well maintained by contradictory orders, that we all began to wonder, when we were detained at Alexandria, if in deference to politics, the Porte, or the High Contracting Parties, our leaders had been warned not to use the International Waterway.

In furtherance of this design the Guards Brigade, which had all arrived by August 12th, was landed at Alexandria and moved out to camp at Ramleh. The Household Cavalry (formed of a squadron from each of the three regiments), on arriving two days later, was also landed, and the horses picketed at Gabarri, the terminus of the Cairo railway, as was the first field-battery that had arrived on the same day; while Sir Archibald Alison, at Ramleh, made constant reconnaissances of the position at Kafr Dauar, and in this his force was assisted by an armour-clad train, rigged up by the navy, which carried a 40-pounder Armstrong gun.

It was necessary to distract Arabi's attention, for on July 27th the *Orion*, on the *khedive's* authority, moved through the canal to Ismailia, the Indian squadron had arrived off Suez, and three ships of the Mediterranean fleet lay off Port Said ready to seize important points if necessary. The effect of the constant reconnaissances of Kafr Dauar was splendid: the Egyptians could be observed each night, when their works were illuminated by the sailors' electric search-light on Fort Kum-ed-Dik, working away at their entrenchments; and, whatever we knew or suspected, they certainly thought we were coming by that road to Cairo.

On the 14th Major Hildyard, the other Deputy-Assistant Adjutant and Quartermaster-General of the division, arrived from Gibraltar, and General Willis's Staff was now complete. On the next day Sir Garnet Wolseley, our commander-in-chief, arrived, and took up his quarters on board H.M.S. *Salamis*. We utilised some part of our time of waiting by an inspection of the damage done by the bombardment on July 11th. The fleet that took part in it, under the command of Admiral Sir Beauchamp Seymour (afterwards Lord Alcester), consisted of eight armoured ships, *Inflexible, Monarch, Temeraire, Alexandra, Superb, Sultan, Invincible,* and *Penelope,* besides six gun-boats and despatch-vessels. They may be said to have mounted eighty-four heavy guns, while the battery of the forts opposed to them included thirty-seven rifled, one hundred and eighty-two smooth-bore guns, and thirty-one mortars.

With the exception of those at Fort Pharos, which had casemates, all these guns were in open batteries. The parapets were all of sand, revetted inside with stone, and the superior and exterior slopes protected from the action of the wind by a coating of cement about an inch thick.

There was no doubt of the accuracy of our fire, but it is extraordinary how little effect the heaviest shell-fire produces on a soft sand parapet. It may be estimated that the ships fired three thousand heavy shells. Port Pharos suffered much, for the stone casemates offered sufficient resistance to explode all the shells which hit them, and Fort Adda was destroyed by a lucky shot which blew up the magazine; but Ras-el-Tin, which came under the heaviest fire, suffered comparatively little, for many shells lodged in the parapet and did not explode. I saw several of our missiles in the various works standing up on their bases on the superior slopes; they had struck the slopes, and after plunging through the sand in a curve, had come up like a diver. There were a good many blind shells, sixteen and ten inch, which apparently wanted something harder than a sandbed to set up the powder and explode it.

Most of the guns, and nearly all the torpedoes, found at Meks had been rendered useless by our landing-parties by bulging with slabs of gun-cotton. Some people said this was a needless waste, but they forgot that at the time there was no force available for landing except the marines of the fleet; and, for all the admiral knew, Arabi might recapture the city with larger forces, and give him all the trouble of silencing the forts again.

The rabble of Alexandria had destroyed the best part of the city by fire, and plundered as much as they could. The square, or *Place des Consuls* as the French called it, was one heap of ruins; and it says much for the energy of our navy that they had managed to clear roads through it so soon.

★★★★★★★★★★★★

Thus, between business and pleasure, affairs went on till August 18th, when the Guards Brigade was brought in from Ramleh and all the horses and equipment embarked. The secrecy now became rather a nuisance. It was given out that the fleet was to bombard the forts, and then that a force was to be landed at Aboukir Bay, as Sir Ralph Abercromby had done in 1801. My orders that day were to go the Salamis at four in the afternoon for the final orders for the division. I did so, and was told that the orders would be issued as usual at the office at Moharem Bey Gate. Off I went accordingly on foot, my horse having been shipped, only to find, after tramping a mile and a half, that the office was deserted, and that we were the victims of a rather superfluous practical joke.

I say we, because the deputy-adjutant-general, the officer commanding the Royal Engineers, and several other officers had been deceived with me. Frederick the Great is believed to have said that if his left hand knew what his right hand was going to write he would cut it off; but with all due respect to the memory of that illustrious soldier, I cannot believe that the arrival of a lot of officers clamouring for orders at Moharem Bey Gate on the afternoon of August 18th, was necessary to confirm Arabi's spies in the belief that Aboukir was our destination and not Port Said.

By the time we were back at our respective wharves, our ships had sailed. I tried to get a launch from the Poonah, to hire a *dahabiyeh*, to get a boat of any sort, but all in vain. At last, I found that the *Calabria* was going on next morning, and a friend on board gave me dinner and a berth for the night. Next morning I found that H.M.S. *Cygnet* was leaving for Aboukir Bay, and boarding her, found an old friend in Captain Dudley-Ryder commanding. He had other applicants for a passage, Colonel Dormer and Brigadier-General Nugent among them, and he welcomed us all and promised us a close view of Fort Aboukir. We passed between it and Nelson Island about three hundred yards from the former.

The fort hoisted a large white flag, but the Egyptians stood to their

161

guns. We could see the men traversing them, covering us as we moved, but they never fired; if they had, and had hit us, we should have been rather mauled by a ten-inch shell through a wooden gun-vessel. But as our commander put it:

> They know me; I always come this way, as there is water enough for me, and it is so much shorter.

We had pretty nearly hemmed the fort in by sea and land, and so I suppose the garrison thought it as well to be civil.

We reached the fleet, which was anchored in Aboukir Bay, about half-past five, and the *Cygnet's* boats took us off to our various ships. At seven a gun was fired and the whole fleet sailed for Port Said, except the gun-boats and gun-vessels which, moving close in, opened fire on the shore to hide our movements. We arrived off Port Said at daybreak on the 20th, dropped anchor, and waited in suspense.

Now under the orders of Sir Beauchamp Seymour, the Naval Commander-in-Chief, Admiral Hoskins at Port Said, Admiral Hewett at Suez, and Captain Fitz-Roy at Ismailia, had seized those points before daybreak of the 20th, and the men-of-war in the Gulf of Suez had stopped all ships entering the canal from the south on the 19th. The garrison of Port Said, completely surprised, surrendered at once; at Suez and Ismailia there was some opposition, but the whole of the Maritime Canal was soon in our hands, the telegraph lines to Syria cut, and those to Cairo secured; in fact, the seamen and marines carried all before them, and when some contumacious and belated merchantmen had cleared out of the canal at Port Said on the 20th, the course was open for the transports.

The First Division (less two battalions), half the cavalry with two batteries of artillery, and seventy men of the Mounted Infantry and Departmental Corps, were with the commander-in-chief. The remainder of the First Division and of the Cavalry Brigade were still at sea *en route* for the canal; and the Second Division was left for the present at Alexandria to detain part of the Egyptians at Kafr Dauar. Even Sir Edward Hamley, who commanded it, was not informed before the morning of the 20th of the move to the canal, and up to this time even he had imagined that the force from Ramleh was to co-operate with the First Division from Aboukir in an attack on the position at Kafr Dauar. I need hardly add that this treatment did not please him.

When the ships of the First Division sailed eastward from Aboukir Bay on the evening of the 19th, we on board all knew that Ismailia must be our landing-place, and everybody applied to the printed report for information about it and the Sweetwater Canal. We found that, if the lock connecting this canal with Lake Timsah could be protected, a volume of water nearly a mile long, twenty-five yards broad, and six feet deep, would be preserved for us. To seize it was the business of Captain Fitz-Roy of the *Orion* and his men, and in fine style they did it. On the Sweetwater Canal, which would of course have to be secured by the army, there was a lock about nineteen miles from Ismailia at Kassassin, and if this could be seized before it was damaged, all difficulties about fresh water would be settled. It was clear that the troops first landed would be hurried up to the front at all costs, provisioned or not.

Port Said, at this time, seemed to be the rendezvous for all foreign war-vessels on the Mediterranean station. Frenchmen, Turks, Italians, Egyptians, and even Americans, were there, moored in the eastern basin, side by side, bows towards the line of the canal. The fleet that had convoyed us to Alexandria consisted of eight ironclads; there were three already at Port Said, and so, even if there had been discourtesy, there could not have been obstruction for long. On the 20th, so soon as the contumacious merchantmen had cleared the north end of the canal, the expedition entered.

Four men-of-war and two transports with fifteen hundred marines led; three transports with four battalions and the staff of the Second Brigade followed; next came three transports with the brigade of Guards, half a battery of artillery, and the Staffs of the First Division and First Brigade, one transport with Headquarters Staff, commissariat and hospital, cavalry and mounted infantry, a battery of horse artillery and one of field artillery, lighters with railway-plant, and gunboats. It was a stately sight, and might have done some of the grumblers at home good to see. The Frenchmen were mute, and so of course were the Turks and Egyptians; but the Italians gave us a cheer, and when we got abreast of the Americans blood proved itself thicker than water, and they gave us such ringing rounds of applause that it seemed as if it would not have taken much to make them join us.

The *Orient* was the tenth in order and entered the canal at five p.m. The *Catalonia* with the 1st Batt. Royal West Kent, one of the few ships with a pilot (who were nearly all Frenchmen), took the ground about eight miles inside the canal. She was two ahead of the *Orient*, so the latter had to be moored for the night to the eastern bank after a very short voyage. During the night, however, the stern of the *Catalonia* had been warped over towards the bank, and there was now room to pass with a few inches to spare. On we went therefore, reached Lake Timsah at half-past three, with as little delay as possible slung the horses into an iron lighter, and, towed by the gunboat *Dee*, got to the wharf, made a ramp of planks covered with dunnage, and landed them with difficulty. I and one *aide-de-camp* bivouacked by them for the night.

Ismailia had been seized as described on the 20th. When the Catalonia had run aground Major-General Graham had gone on in a torpedo-boat with half the Royal West Kent to assist the marines there. By noon on the 21st he had reached Nefisheh, and was holding the point where the Sweet-water Canal branches to Suez. The disembarkment of the marines, the regiments of the First Division, and the cavalry had therefore to be hurried on as quickly as possible, for Arabi had twelve thousand men at Tel-el-Kebir already, besides three thousand Bedouins. The railway was destroyed in many places, and the canal was evidently dammed above Nefisheh for no water was coming down.

At Ismailia, close to the wharf, was an establishment, called by our soldiers Bain's Hotel, but by most other folk Hotel des Bains, which boasted a real French waiter. Some six months before one of our officers had been staying there, ostensibly for snipe-shooting, and Francois used to wonder why he brought in so few birds. When the man now caught sight of him, he approached, pointed to the soldiers and said, "*Bonjour, monsieur, voilà les bécassines!*"

Francois gave me some excellent coffee at four o'clock on the morning of the 22nd, and we then set to work, got the horses to the *khedive's* new palace, and then went back to the ship to superintend the disembarkation of men and baggage. That day and the next every one worked like a slave, and by the night of the 23rd nine thousand men were on shore; but to clear the small wharf of their baggage alone was very hard work; and of the cavalry, only the Household regiment, the *Orient's* detachment of the 19th Hussars, the Mounted Infantry, and two horse artillery guns were on shore.

On the 24th the Household Cavalry with two guns were ordered to move to Nefisheh and reconnoitre beyond it to the westward, and General Willis decided to go with them. The 2nd Batt. Duke of Cornwall's Light Infantry was ordered to follow to Nefisheh, and the force there, consisting of the 2nd Batt. York and Lancaster and the Royal Marine Artillery, were to push on if possible and clear the dam at El-Magfar. We were off soon after four in the morning. The desert here-

Fighting at Tel-el-Kebir

abouts was a series of sand-drifts mixed with brackish lakes, and the railway-track, heavy as it was, proved the better road. The staff of the First Division had intended to see a bit of the country and then return to Ismailia to clear out the details of the division. We started therefore with one horse apiece, no kits, servants, or clerks, a tin of beef and some biscuits in our wallets, and a great coat strapped over them; but as luck would have it, it was a full week before any of us saw Ismailia again, and most never saw it again at all.

Just before reaching El-Magfar we came on the Egyptian outposts, and soon drove them back; but nearer Tel-el-Mahuta the cavalry found the Egyptian infantry in force, and on their report, we sent back to Nefisheh to hurry up some of ours; later on, as the enemy threatened to attack, we sent back for the Guards. The ground was so heavy that none of our reinforcements could arrive before nine, and meanwhile the cavalry and mounted infantry had enough to do to keep the Egyptians back.

Before one of their movements to the front against the enemy's skirmishers, the cavalry had disencumbered themselves of their hay nets; these lay on the desert four hundred yards ahead of the line our infantry took up, all in a row, two and two, looking in the mirage for all the world like an extended battalion of soldiers, and so deceived the Egyptians that many a volley was fired at them. By nine o'clock the 2nd Batt. York and Lancaster with the Marine Artillery had arrived, a welcome addition of nearly eight hundred rifles and carbines to our little force. The enemy now opened fire on our infantry, which lay still without replying. His fire with shell was very accurate, but he only had percussion-fuses, and the shells generally burst under the sand; our two horse artillery guns on a knoll were his chief target, but only three men and seven horses were killed in that division.

We could see that there was a strong fort between the railway and canal at Tel-el-Mahuta, and some twelve or fourteen battalions with field-guns and cavalry were advancing; we could not therefore move, and had indeed some difficulty in holding our ground. At half-past eleven our mounted infantry on the extreme right had been obliged to fall back, and sent down to say their ammunition was running short. The York and Lancaster lent me a mule and some two thousand rounds of ammunition, which I took across to the right flank. On my way I found Captain Parr, who commanded the mounted infantry, sheltered behind a mud wall, with a bullet through his leg and vainly endeavouring to get his long boot off; I helped him, promised to call on my way back, and went on.

Lord Melgund (now Earl of Minto) was now in command of the little body of seventy men, and as I was talking to him, after handing over the ammunition, smash came a Remington bullet through his hand. With the new supplies he said he could hold his own, and I returned to Parr, told him the news, and then left to send a stretcher for him. Shortly before two, the 2nd Batt. Duke of Cornwall's Light Infantry arrived, six hundred strong, a welcome reinforcement, as also were two Gatlings from the *Orion* manned by sailors, but they had to be dragged up the last two miles by two pairs from our horse artillery teams, so heavy was the sand. Our gunners were now so hotly engaged with six times their number of field-guns, besides those in the fort at Tel-el-Mahuta, that men of the Royal Marine Artillery were sent to help them serve their pieces.

The heat was tremendous, and everyone was clamouring for water; the canal was on our left flank, but men could not be sent from their posts to fill their bottles, the water-carts were mostly stuck in the sand two miles back, and so the artillery-buckets were in great request. The enemy was evidently being strongly reinforced by train, for we could see the smoke of engines at Tel-el-Mahuta; and as he was now endeavouring to turn both our flanks, one Gatling was sent to each of them. Shortly after five the 4th and 7th Dragoon Guards arrived, followed within an hour by the Guards Brigade and the remaining four guns of the horse artillery. After sunset it looked for a moment as if the enemy meant coming on again; but we were strong enough now, and they only made a feint.

Sir Garnet Wolseley returned to Ismailia at sunset, leaving General Willis in command, with orders to hold his own during the night and attack at daybreak. Before leaving he complimented all the corps that had been engaged, telling them that few troops had had greater odds to contend with than they had that day; and he was right, for had the Egyptians pressed on in the early hours, we must have retreated or been overwhelmed. This gave the men a great idea of their superiority; which was well, for large bodies could not be pushed to the front till their supply was secured, and the leading battalions had therefore to fight, almost unsupported, whatever force was opposed to them.

General Willis formed the force which bivouacked at El-Magfar in a semicircle towards the north with its flanks resting on the canal. The 2nd Batt. York and Lancaster and the sailors with two Gatlings were on the left nearest the enemy; then came the Marine Artillery, the

THE BAYONET CHARGE AT TEL-EL-KEBIR

2nd. batt. Duke of Cornwall's Light Infantry, the 7th Dragoon Guards, the Guards Brigade, and the remainder of the cavalry, in that order round to the right flank. The canal water was like pea-soup, but we all drank our fill of it without waiting to try our pocket-filters, which in fact clogged almost immediately and needed to be constantly blown through to clear them; then, having foraged a bit for the horses, the Staff reposed on the sand on their faces with their arms through their bridle-reins. In the middle of the night another field-battery of artillery joined us from Ismailia with six 16-pounders, and the Royal Marine Light Infantry with the 3rd Batt. 60th Rifles arrived early in the morning. We had now, therefore, twelve guns, part of three cavalry regiments, and eight battalions for the morrow's fight.

At five o'clock next morning the force was formed up to the westward and advanced towards Tel-el-Mahuta in the following order: Cavalry and Horse-Artillery on the extreme right; the Guards Brigade in direct echelon of battalions from the right on the high ground; after an interval the Duke of Cornwall's, the Marine Artillery, and the York and Lancaster in attack formation, their left resting on the canal; the Royal Marine Light Infantry and the 60th Rifles formed the second line.

Four field-guns remained at first on the sand-hill occupied by the two horse artillery guns on the previous day, the other two guns of that battery being now on the right of the Guards; our right was thus much thrown forward so as to manoeuvre the Egyptians out of their works. Just as we had started Sir Garnet Wolseley arrived; and soon after the guns left on the sand-hill were ordered to advance into the interval between the two brigades.

It soon became evident that the enemy was evacuating his position, and the infantry pushed on to occupy it, while the cavalry and horse artillery, after attempting to intercept a train, continued on to Mahsameh, where they captured seven Krupp guns and over seventy railway-waggons containing a lot of ammunition and stores. Meanwhile the infantry at Tel-el-Mahuta had captured Mahmoud Fehmi Pasha, Arabi's chief of Engineers, who was in plain clothes, nearly escaping thereby, and after being caught, nearly being shot by accident.

On these two days our losses were five men and twenty-one horses killed, with three officers, twenty-five men, and six horses wounded; there were also forty-two cases of sunstroke among the men and twenty-one among the horses; as all the latter died, it will be seen that the Egyptian sun in August is as fatal to English horses as Remington bullets fired by Egyptian soldiers.

The Marine Artillery and Light Infantry battalions were now sent on to Mahsameh, for General Drury Lowe reported that they need not return, having captured sufficient corn and biscuits to feed his horses and men. The remainder of the infantry were bivouacked on either side of the canal at Tel-el-Mahuta, and were at once set to work to remove the enormous dams which the Egyptians had made across both canal and railway.

The Egyptian is a splendid worker with hoe and basket, and is born to dam the banks of canals and to confine the waters from the high Nile to their proper channels. He had made a dam across the canal at Tel-el-Mahuta about thirty feet broad with alternate courses of bulrushes and sand. We had no hoes and no baskets, and when we tried our entrenching shovels on the wet sand and rushes, it was like digging into a mattress. The railway passed here through a cutting twenty feet deep, and thirty yards of this was filled to the top with dry sand. It was no use attempting to remove this till a truck or two could be brought up into the cutting, and the line had been so damaged by the affair at El-Magfar that this could not be done for some days. In the meantime, we attacked the canal dam; and a queer sight it was to see battalions of the Guards, with nothing on but helmets and shirts, in the water dragging out the rushes and bailing away at the sand.

At seven that night our grooms had arrived with our spare horses, and I was glad to be relieved of some of my duties as forager, groom, cook, etc.; but we did not get a tent to sleep in till August 30th, and no kits or clerks till the 1st of September. On this night my dinner was some unleavened bread taken out of a dead Egyptian's haversack. The canal supplied our drinking water; and as there were already a good many dead Egyptians and camels in it, all bathing was forbidden out of regard for those down at Ismailia. Those who wanted to wash pulled off their clothes and joined the working-party in the water.

But in hot weather the thing to keep you in health in the desert is a sand-bath. You strip just before sunset, spread your clothes on the desert, rub yourself all over with the hot sand, jump into your clothes again (which are now well dried), put on a great coat, and there you are, ready for the great change of temperature which takes place at sunset.

We were a motley lot. The staff-officer had two patrol jackets, red for fighting and blue for office-work, with a quilted pad down the spine and lots of roomy pockets, a light brown helmet with a *puggaree* coloured according to his Division, smoked glass spectacles, blue veils, and high-lows and *putties* instead of jack-boots. Only experience can teach the difference colour makes as regards heat. In the scarlet jacket one was comfortable even in the fiercest sun, while the blue one was simply unbearable. No doubt, too, there is a good deal in imagination: put on your smoked glasses, the day turns to dusk and you feel cool; take them off for a minute and the heat seems terrible; perhaps it is the reflected heat from the sand to your brain through the eyes.

Flies were the greatest plague, particularly when writing. They crawled about your eyes, neck, and nose, defying tobacco, and with an insatiable thirst for ink. The only thing was to wear glasses, keep your mouth shut, and let them crawl. It was rather nasty, for every second Egyptian you see has ophthalmia or at least weak eyes, and in 1801 two thirds of the French Army had been affected with the disease. The filthy habits of the people cause the plague of flies, and these convey the contagion. *Putties* are capital things in hot weather for men who have "good legs for top-boots"; but any one afflicted with a sixteen-inch calf had better eschew them, or he will shed two long flannel streamers for his horse to tread on, even though he be bandaged scientifically by a hospital-dresser.

By the evening of the 25th a boat had been lifted over the dam at El-Magfar, and it was determined to send back the wounded by it. Each regiment or battalion had its surgeon, but we could not spare them to accompany the casualties, and I was accordingly sent off that night to tell a doctor, who was posted at the El-Magfar dam, to join the boat. At ten o'clock I started off down the line on foot, and as I passed the pickets warned the sentries that I was coming back that way. It was bright moonlight, and all along the line one could see the dead camels, each with its crowd of jackals making merry over the remains.

Suddenly a horseman approached and shouted; I answered and continued on my way. "Stand and give your name, or I fire," was the reply, and, regardless of the fact that I was talking English to him, the stranger kept me covered with his revolver, refusing to be satisfied for a long time. The young gentleman had brought a message from Ismailia for General Willis to send on the rest of the Second Brigade towards Kassassin. He went on to deliver it, and I proceeded to El-Magfar. As I did not find my doctor till after twelve there was not much sleep for me that night.

Early on the 26th the York and Lancaster and Duke of Cornwall's moved to Mahsameh. When they arrived, the cavalry had reconnoitred as far as Kassassin Lock and found it undamaged and deserted; General Graham therefore marched his regiments on there, while the cavalry remained near the captured grain at Mahsameh. Thus, within five days after landing we had covered the nineteen miles from Ismailia and secured the water-supply as recommended by the report; but the bulk of the First Division had to remain at Tel-el-Mahuta to facilitate supply and remove the obstructions on the canal and railway.

From this time, until after the Battle of Tel-el-Kebir, the British public thought it did not get sufficient news, and that we must all have gone to sleep. The water had been secured at tremendous exertion and risk, and now food and ammunition for the whole force had to be collected; but *paterfamilias* cared for none of these things. He does not remember that there are a hundred days' marching to one of fighting in most campaigns: he likes to have a real good fight to read and lecture over, propped against the toast-rack while he chips his egg each morning at breakfast; and between August 25th and September 13th the poor fellow was only relieved by the news of the two actions at Kassassin. It seemed hard, and he let us know it.

On the evening of the 26th we, at Tel-el-Mahuta, got a post-boat service started for El-Magfar dam and on to Ismailia. On the 27th, after great exertion, we got three boats full of ammunition for the horse artillery and cavalry above the dam, and had them towed by horses up-stream to Mahsameh, while a detachment of cavalry kept at bay some brigands on the south of the canal. I don't think I ever performed more manual labour than on those two days; and as the hip injured by the aftereffects of fever in 1878 began to give me warning, I was sincerely glad when, on the 28th, General Willis sent me off at noon to find out what some heavy firing to the westward might mean.

Our detachment of the 19th Hussars had joined us the night before, and I took two of the troopers as orderlies. We rode out north to the hard desert, and then turned west towards the sound of the firing. The heat that day was tremendous and the mirage most deceiving. When we reached the right of the cavalry vedette line, which was facing west between Mahsameh and Kassassin, it was impossible to say whether they were Bedouins or our people. Huge figures seemed to be dancing about in the air, and whether riding horses or camels it was impossible to say. We must have presented much the same appearance, too, for we heard a voice say, "Try a shot at them," after which we thought it time to proclaim our identity.

It is a curious thing that horses do not seem to be deceived by mirage. No matter how thirsty they may be, they never rush wildly to what you imagine to be a lake; and if you know your horse well, after a time in the desert you can always tell by his behaviour whether the four-legged dancing thing you are approaching is a horse or a camel. They can neigh of course, and so talk to a comrade of their own race; and if they get a reply you know as well as they do that it is a horse, and you can infer that it is probably not mounted by a Bedouin.

Apropos of Bedouins: if you want to surprise them, let it be between the hours of twelve and three; day or night you are sure then to find them asleep. In the daytime they are enjoying a *siesta*; and at night they do not turn in early, but "sit at the door of their tent in the cool of the eve" and gossip.

On reaching the right of the cavalry vedettes I rode along their line southwards, and soon came on the main body with General Drury Lowe and Sir Baker Russell; they were all dismounted, most of the men sitting under their horses to get some shade. They had been out for some hours that morning, by request of General Graham, who had signalled that the enemy's cavalry was reported to the north of Kassassin. The Egyptians kept up an artillery-fire, but did nothing more. Hildyard from Tel-el-Mahuta came out at two, and returned to tell General Willis how things were. I sent back an orderly at three with similar news; and then, as General Lowe decided to return to Mahsameh to water and feed, I went on to Kassassin to tell General Graham, whose force I found had already withdrawn into camp, that the cavalry would retire to Mahsameh but would turn out again directly he wished them to do so.

I watered and fed my horse at Kassassin, and was sharing a frugal meal with a friend, when the mounted infantry, who were out to the north and west, reported that the enemy's infantry was advancing, and immediately after a shell plumped into the sand close to us from the north-west. General Graham turned out his force at once, while I, at his request, rode off to Mahsameh, to ask General Lowe to send on the battalion of marines as soon as possible, and to move the cavalry to the north-west to watch for an opportunity to attack the enemy's left flank. I then went on to tell General Willis what was up.

General Graham had with him two horse artillery guns and two guns of a field-battery, some marine artillery, the Duke of Cornwall's and the York and Lancaster regiments; but the ammunition we had sent on by boat from Tel-el-Mahuta had not yet arrived, and the limber-ammunition was all the four guns possessed, for the waggons were back, delayed by the heavy sand. He also had a captured Krupp gun which was mounted in a railway-truck and manned by the marines.

I was riding a nearly thoroughbred horse that day, and I strongly recommend every officer to have as well bred a charger as he can secure. I could not go up into the hard desert, for the enemy's cavalry were already all along the skyline; the only thing to be done was to keep to the sandy low ground near the canal and get over it as best one could. It was four miles and three quarters as the crow flies to Mahsameh, and about five miles beyond that was Tel-el-Mahuta. I sent the good horse along as fast as I dared, for I had one orderly still with me and his animal was not a flier.

The bullets told us that the enemy was within range before I left, and as cavalry, artillery, and infantry were all attacking our small force at Kassassin, a little determination on the enemy's part might have made matters extremely hot for it before the supports could arrive. Five-and-twenty minutes brought me to Mahsameh, where I met General Drury Lowe and Herbert Stewart at the station, and gave General Graham's message. The marines and four 16-pounders were sent off at once, and orders given for the cavalry and horse artillery to follow. We were all old friends of Zululand, and while I was resting my horse, Stewart chaffed me for being the bearer of a "scare"; they had had one already that day, he said, and as all their horses had their nose-bags full of the *khedive's* best beans, I ought really to have known better. I bid him listen to the guns, and wished I had the chance of staying with him.

I left Mahsameh at half-past five, telling the orderly to come on easily, and covered the five miles in forty minutes. My horse lay down on arrival, and had to be fed and watered from a bucket till the third day. He had done the ten miles in an hour and twenty minutes, including the quarter of an hour's halt.

This may not sound much at home; but considering the heat, that the sand was over fetlock-deep for the greater part of the way, and that he had thirteen stone on his back, it was blood alone that brought him through in the time.

General Willis ordered the 60th Rifles off at once to replace the marines at Mahsameh, while I put my report in writing for transmission to Ismailia. Heavy firing was soon heard from the westward, and about half-past seven a trooper arrived asking for immediate aid. General Willis thereupon ordered the whole of his force, except a battery of artillery and half a battalion of the Guards, to march on to the high ground to the north and thence westwards. Reaching a point north-east of Mahsameh a little before midnight, we found all quiet, so the force was halted, while the staff with the detachment of the 19th Hussars proceeded cautiously forwards. On arrival at Mahsameh we found that the last report had been too highly coloured, and that in fact we were not required. Our cavalry had got well home on the Egyptian left flank, and General Graham had repulsed the attack on his camp, though not till his artillery had fired off all their ammunition.

The cavalry staff were carousing over an immense brass bowl full of boiling coffee, and we joined them, after sending off to tell our force to retire at their leisure to Tel-el-Mahuta. Everybody was jubilant.

"Oh, if you had only stopped with us! We got fairly home this time," said Stewart to me.

"You were the man that said I was a 'scaremonger,'" was my reply. "You had better show us where to sleep, and where to get some coffee in the morning."

My bed was a railway-truck half full of bags of lentils, with my horse tied to a buffer. I never was in a place with so many bugs, fleas, and mosquitoes; if you struck a match you could see swarms of them running, jumping, and flying away in all directions. My horse was evidently of the same opinion, for he broke his headstall, walked away to the sand, and rolled all night.

We were up at four next morning, and with the detachment of the 19th Hussars rode out to view the scene of the cavalry charge. It was about two and a quarter miles north-west of Kassassin, and some seven from Mahsameh. The Bedouins were already on the ground, looting friends and foes alike, and had to be driven back by our Hussars. I counted fifty-eight Egyptian dead, besides many wounded. Our loss was one officer and eight men killed, one officer and seventeen men wounded, twenty horses killed and twenty-one wounded.

Stewart was right; the Household Cavalry had got home with a vengeance, and if only there had been light they would have captured a lot of guns besides completely routing the enemy. At Kassassin Lock General Graham had lost one officer and seven men killed, ten officers and fifty-one men wounded.

General Willis now returned to Tel-el-Mahuta, and we resumed our labours on the line of communications.

CHAPTER 10

Conclusion

The railway between Tel-el-Mahuta and Ismailia was now being gradually got into working-order; but it was a laborious job and constantly needed renewing. The line had in fact been damaged not only by the Egyptians, but by our own artillery in this way: the Egyptians had removed the rails; we had replaced them; our artillery had used the track as a road. The sleepers are cast-iron bowls, "potsleepers" is the ordinary name; they are fashioned so as to hold the sand like a camel's foot, and between the two there is a wrought-iron band which holds them together at the right gauge. The 16-pounder gun and limber filled would weigh, I suppose, a ton and a half, and the waggon for the same two tons.

The horses, moving along the track, kick up the sand and leave the ties exposed; along come the limber and gun, and the waggon, each wheel of either giving a blow to the exposed tie of, say, half a ton going at the rate of a walk; the ties, thereby getting knocked out of shape or smashed, draw the iron pots together, or leave them unsupported laterally, with the inevitable result that the gauge is either tightened or widened, and the wheels either run on their flanges or down between the rails on the sand. Add to all this that the foot-traffic levels the sand up to the rails, and it will be clear that an Egyptian railway in war-time needs a regular army of gangers and navvies to keep it clear.

There was a line of telegraph-posts from Ismailia by Tel-el-Kebir to Cairo, but the Egyptians, besides breaking down the wires, had removed the instruments, except a few at Mahsameh, where we had been too quick for them. Our telegraphers were not disembarked in time to save the advanced parties the trouble of sending their messages by officers or orderlies, and in consequence there was at first great trouble and uncertainty in communication.

The corps of signallers were no use at all. This was due to no fault of theirs, but to the mirage. South Africa is the country of all others for signalling. The frequent hills and mountains render only a few posts necessary, and the mirage is rare, but in Egypt, besides this nuisance, the signallers must be stationed at short intervals, owing to the flatness of the country, and consequently are of little use.

The Post-Office Corps, I am afraid it must be agreed, was not very successful. They were undermanned from the first, and the few men there were tried to do too much.

The cavalry used to water their horses a quarter of a mile below the Tel-el-Mahuta dam, and to reach the canal had to cross the railway. Four or five times a day the place where they crossed had to be cleared of sand and set in order, or there would be an engine or truck off the line. The men hated this job. They did not mind the mud-larking at the dam; every rush pulled out or shovelful of sand thrown up the bank helped to clear the way; but as soon as the railway-line had been made good, over would come a lot of carts or horses and throw it all into disorder again.

I am still undecided whether it is discipline or superior physique that makes the Guards the best workers we have; but no one who was a week at Tel-el-Mahuta would deny the fact. Officers and men, all alike worked without grumbling. After the first day or two we learned from the sick-reports that in Egypt you cannot allow men, who may have to fight at any moment, to work between the hours of ten and four during the month of August; from six to ten in the morning, and from four to six in the afternoon were accordingly fixed for the working-hours.

The troops that had hurried up from Ismailia on August 24th, when we were hard pressed at El-Magfar, had left the desert between that place and Nefisheh littered with carts and all sorts of articles; and the discarded hay-nets still lay on the desert, for no corps had had time or transport to bring them on, their own beasts scarcely sufficing for their own needs. On September 2nd, therefore, as the infantry at Tel-el-Mahuta were to be employed in constructing a fort there, I got leave to show a wing of the 4th Dragoon Guards, who were in camp, where the nets lay. We started at four in the morning, recovered them, still tightly packed with hay, and were back in time for breakfast.

I then got together twelve carts and all the spare horses of a transport company, and returned to collect the other things at El-Magfar. We brought back six abandoned Maltese carts, over ten thousand rounds of ammunition, cooking-pots, shovels—all sorts of odds and ends. It proved to me more than anything else how great had been the stress on the men marching to our assistance on the day of the fight, through the heavy sand in the noontide heat.

An engine and trucks were now working above the obstructions at Tel-el-Mahuta; but what with empty water-tanks, scarcity of coal, and inexperienced drivers, interruptions were frequent. Sir Garnet and his staff were the victims on one occasion. They were returning from a visit to Mahsameh when the train broke down; they had to walk in to Tel-el-Mahuta, and go on by canal to Ismailia in a pinnace, and must, I should think, have seen daylight before they got there. Still, it went on somehow, pushing food, ammunition, and equipment to the front. The 2nd Batt. Royal Irish had arrived on September 1st, and we were able to send them on by the 3rd.

On the 4th the troops at Tel-el-Mahuta were inspected by General Willis; a wing of the 4th Dragoon Guards, the Guards Brigade, two batteries of artillery (both 16-pounders), half a bearer company, the 12th company Commissariat and Transport Corps, and a field hospital. On the 5th the Indian Cavalry began to arrive, one regiment mightily astounding us from England by bringing twelve hundred pack-ponies with them. On the 6th we sent the 17th company Commissariat and Transport Corps through to Kassassin; and on the 7th we were told that we might go on there ourselves, which we accordingly did with great delight and expedition.

On September 8th a reconnaissance was ordered to move across the canal to some sand-hills across the Wady Tumilat, from whence the lines of Tel-el-Kebir could be seen. It consisted of the Mounted Infantry, a regiment of Indian Cavalry, two guns of horse artillery, two screw guns from an Indian mountain battery, and the 2nd Batt. Duke of Cornwall's Light Infantry. Generals Graham and Wilkinson, and Colonel Redvers Buller (who had arrived from England on the 5th) went with it, and Hildyard and myself got leave to accompany them. We started at four in the morning, moving in a south-westerly direction three miles across the cultivated ground of the *wady*; after reaching the desert on its south side, we turned west and moved on to some high sand-hills south of El Korein-el-Gedid about three and a half miles from the point where Arabi's entrenchments touched the canal.

At daylight the enemy sent out his scouts mounted on camels as usual, and we kept quiet hoping to catch them; but when we tried to surround them their camels walked away from our cavalry as if we had been standing still, for in the deep sand a horse could only trot. The enemy then deployed all his infantry south of the canal, and came on to turn us out. We accordingly retired on Kassassin, having had a fair view of the enemy's position.

The force at Kassassin was now as follows:

Cavalry	Detachment of 4th Dragoon Guards.
	Half 19th Hussars.
	Mounted Infantry.
Artillery	G—B Royal Horse Artillery.
	A—1 Royal Artillery.
	D—1 „ „
	½ 5—1 Scottish Division Royal Artillery.
	Royal Marine Artillery.
Infantry	2nd Royal Irish.
	2nd Duke of Cornwall's Light Infantry.
	1st Royal West Kent.
	3rd King's Royal Rifle Corps.
	2nd York and Lancaster.
	Royal Marine Light Infantry.
	Naval Brigade.
Engineers	Detachment of A and C Troops Royal Engineers.
	Detachment of 17th Company „ „
	24th Company Royal Engineers.
Details............	Commissariat and Transport Company.
	Bearer Company.
	Field Hospital.
	Signallers.

The total strength amounted to 6,045 men, 1,247 horses, and 20 guns.

The bulk of the cavalry was still back at Mahsameh, while the Guards and two batteries held Tel-el-Mahuta. The railway was now able to supply sufficient stores for the whole army, so the Highland Brigade of the Second Division (which had been now brought round from Alexandria to Lake Timsah), the Indian contingent, and the remainder of the artillery were ordered to the front from Ismailia.

When Sir Edward Hamley brought on Sir Archibald Alison's Highland Brigade, he left Sir Evelyn Wood with the Manchester and Derbyshire regiments, one thousand men of drafts, a garrison-battery and the Malta Fencible Artillery, to hold Alexandria and the position at Ramleh.

In the meantime, Arabi had developed a plan for crushing; our six thousand men at Kassassin, and he applied it, as if out of revenge for our reconnaissance of the 8th, on the very next day, attacking us with two columns, one from Tel-el-Kebir on the west and the other across the desert from Es-Salihiyeh on the north, and employing some twenty battalions in addition to cavalry and artillery. We were up early that morning, and shortly after daybreak there was a stir along the skyline. It was soon made out to be some Indian troopers going full speed to turn out the cavalry at Mahsameh.

About the hour of dawn some of the vedettes of the 13th Bengal Lancers had found themselves the wrong side of one of the enemy's cavalry regiments which had advanced past them in the dark, and rallying together had charged the Egyptians, spearing their way through back to us with the loss of only one man. Our infantry were at once turned out, and at seven o'clock the enemy's infantry advanced against us.

He had a hard nut to crack. South of the canal, facing west, were the Marine Artillery, a detachment of Royal Artillery with two 25-pounder guns, and five companies of the West Kent; north of the canal, facing west, were the Rifles, the York and Lancaster, and the Marine Light Infantry; then two 16-pounder batteries at the angle, and the Royal Irish and the Duke of Cornwall's Light Infantry facing north. The force at Mahsameh consisted now of six cavalry regiments in two brigades (an English and an Indian), with a battery of horse artillery to each brigade.

When our cavalry got out into the desert, they could plainly see the two distinct forces coming against us from the west and the north. It was promptly driven in like a wedge between them and kept them apart throughout the day by threatening their inward flanks; while the Guards from Tel-el-Mahuta moved out into the hard desert and threatened the left flank of the force from Es-Salihiyeh; the enemies from the north accordingly gave very little trouble and retired without much fighting. But those from Tel-el-Kebir looked more formidable; there was such a lot of them, and they were using the railway to bring up more troops. General Willis, therefore, to get a more favourable position, moved the infantry that were facing west forward, and those who had been facing north were moved westward in echelon with their right refused, as supports.

At about ten the marines and Rifles found themselves opposite some Egyptian guns which were near enough to fire case at them. I happened to be close to the interval between the two battalions, and it was curious to listen to the conversation of the men. They were all old soldiers, as times went; not of twenty-one years' service, but on the average, say, of five. It is common to talk of Inkerman as a "soldier's battle;" but almost every fight the English troops are engaged in must be a soldier's battle. Our troops are as a rule so few that, until the officer can feel how the men's pulses throb, he dare not order an offensive movement: he holds on, repels attacks, and wearies out his enemy; that is the best he can generally do with his small means.

On this occasion the men were using rather strong language about the battery that had come into action against them, and also about the order to lie down. They were not far from the canal: the desert slope was undulating, and the Egyptians had got good cover; and our men could only see the muzzles, for the gunners could load the Krupps without getting off their knees. There was a deal of noise, and an officer may have given the command and I not have heard it. All I know is that the men of two adjacent companies, marines and Rifles, suddenly jumped to their feet, rushed three hundred yards to the front, and captured three guns before you could wink. Perhaps rivalry did it; who knows? At all events the guns were ours, and the rest of the line had to conform.

The enemy did not seem to like this, for the firing lulled. We moved slowly on to within three miles of his lines, halting just out of range of the guns mounted there; our guns set the Egyptians on the run, and there seemed little order in their ranks as they re-entered their entrenchments. There is no doubt that General Willis could have captured the lines then and there with heavy loss, but that was not the game; we should merely have driven Arabi back on the Delta, without completely crushing him; in fact, there would have been a lot more desultory fighting, instead of one general action and a rapid march on Cairo.

Sir Garnet Wolseley arrived at noon, having come by train from Ismailia. He approved of all that had been done, acknowledging that an attempt on the lines would have spoiled the plan. Two battalions and a mountain battery were now left in observation, while the rest of the force retired to camp. The former were ordered to retire at dusk, while a fresh force of one battery and five companies of infantry were to hold a hill closer in at night. The force from Es-Salihiyeh had retreated too quickly to allow the Guards to take them in flank. The latter camped this night at Kassassin, so the end of our troubles was evidently approaching. Our losses this day were three men killed, two officers and seventy-five men wounded, five horses killed, and ten wounded.

On the 10th, Captain Fitz-Roy arrived with the Naval Brigade of fifteen officers, one hundred and ninety-nine men, and six Gatlings. On the 11th the 1st Seaforth Highlanders and the Indian Infantry began to arrive, and at noon on the 12th the 1st Royal Irish Fusiliers came in, thus completing the First Division. By this day, too, Sir Edward Hamley, Sir Archibald Alison, and the Highland Brigade of the Second Division were at the front.

At four on the morning of September 12th all the generals, with one staff-officer each, were ordered to meet Sir Garnet Wolseley on the ground where the fight had taken place on the 9th. He then and there explained his plan for attacking the lines before daybreak on September 13th. Colonel Gillespie being ill, Major Hildyard went with General Willis while I looked after the incoming troops.

I never saw this plan till it was published, "as distributed to general officers." The First and Second Divisions were to be north of the Sweet-water Canal, the Indian Contingent on the south of it, each facing due west and each in two lines. The railway, which is on the north of and fairly parallel with the canal, intersected Arabi's entrenchments, and the left of the Highlanders was to be two thousand yards north of it, with General Graham's Second Brigade of the First Division on their right at an interval of twelve hundred yards.

A thousand yards in rear came the second line, Colonel Ashburnham's Brigade (temporarily formed of the Duke of Cornwall's Light Infantry and the Rifles) in rear of the Highlanders; the Guards Brigade in rear of General Graham's; and in the interval which would thus be left in the middle of the second line, were placed Brigadier-General Goodenough's forty-two guns. To the right rear of the Guards was the Cavalry Division, with twelve horse artillery guns. To the left rear of Colonel Ashburnham's Brigade, and on the railway, came the Naval Brigade with a 40-pounder gun mounted on a truck, and its Gatlings.

On the south of the canal the Seaforth Highlanders formed the first line of the Indian Contingent, and the Native Infantry the second line. Headquarters had as escort the Marine Artillery and 19th Hussars; and one company of the West Kent escorted the reserve ammunition-column, the remainder of this regiment guarding the posts along the line of communications. The Indian Contingent and Naval Brigade were to start one hour later than the troops north of the railway, so as not to disturb the villagers in the *wady*, who might give the alarm.

Sir Garnet purposely placed the two divisions apart so that any repulse of one might not affect the other, while the guns between the brigades in the second line could assist either if driven back. The front then was composed of two horns, and each horn had to steer by the stars, for it was naturally forbidden to strike a light to look at a compass.

In furtherance of this plan, we struck camp just after sunset, stacking all the baggage in heaps alongside the railway, and leaving one non-commissioned officer and two men to look after each regiment's effects. Besides tents, there was the officers' light baggage with the men's valises and blankets in the heap; the regimental carts were packed with rations, cooking-kettles, fuel, etc., ready to come on in the morning after the ammunition-mules. Each man carried one hundred rounds of ammunition, one and a half days' rations (except meat), and filled water-bottles; the water-carts and stretchers were to accompany the battalions.

The men fell in at seven, were formed in brigades and marched out north-west into the desert, taking up, after a deal of searching, the positions marked for them by posts which had been set up by the Engineers. By eleven we were all aligned on the pole star, and lay down to rest. Shortly after that hour Sir Garnet Wolseley visited the brigades. It was very dark, and he had a large mounted escort; as they came along at a trot, some men of the First Division at once sprang to their feet, ready to give any Bedouins a warm reception. "Lie down, it's all right," was passed quietly along, and the Headquarter Staff escaped injury.

The idea had been for the brigades to advance in line of columns at deploying intervals, each battalion having four companies in front and four in rear. An hour after midnight the march began. The distance from our bivouac to the entrenchments had been estimated at three miles and three quarters, and as our pace was calculated at one mile an hour, with halts, we should have arrived at the lines at a quarter to five, about an hour before sunrise. But it is impossible to say what may happen at night, and as it turned out, both the leading brigades were from a quarter to half an hour later in delivering their attack. General Willis, or General Graham, I do not know which, thought it better to move in line of half battalion quarter-columns by the left; it was easier for the guides to see the next body towards the directing flank.

At two o'clock we halted for twenty minutes, and on advancing again deployed into line; this was, of course, as wavy as a whiplash; then we advanced by fours from the right of companies, and so the long night wore on. For night-attacks in open ground, I am persuaded that the best way is to move by double column from the centre.

The left of the leading brigade dropped connecting files to show the left of the Guards Brigade the proper direction. My business being to see that the leading brigade did not overlap, or get too wide away from the line of guns to its left rear, I had to move frequently for a thousand yards or more steering south-east or north-west by a star. Mounted men at night, where silence is necessary, should always go in pairs; for a horse alone on the desert in the dark will neigh enough to waken the dead, and you cannot stop him. The rumble of the artillery-wheels seemed that night to be very loud, in contrast, I suppose, to the impressive silence elsewhere.

We heard afterwards that there had been delay also among the Highlanders. They were marching by the centre, and when the order to halt and rest was given in the middle of the night, it was not passed along the line quickly enough to reach the flanks at once, so that these, feeling inwards, naturally wheeled and halted in a semicircle. When they again advanced the flank battalions almost met in front of the centre, and good discipline alone kept them from a serious scrimmage. To re-form the line in the dark took, however, nearly half an hour.

Just before dawn a bright light was seen in the east right behind us. It proved to be the tail of a comet, of which the nucleus was below the horizon, first seen then, but most conspicuous at night afterwards during our sojourn in Egypt. That the comet was a big one is proved by the fact that in the early morning of October 10th I measured it with a pocket-sextant when at Cairo, and found that from the nucleus to the end of the tail was 14°.

Returning from one of my trips to the right flank of the artillery (the course of the right gun of which was like the track of a snake), I found the Second Brigade again in line; the companies advancing in fours having been formed to the front once more.

About this time a few shots were heard to our left front, and short-ly afterwards some Egyptian cavalry on white horses rode right up to our advancing line. Two companies opened out, and the enemy only too gladly rode through and disappeared in the darkness. Our men had been ordered not to fire, but to take the works at the point of the bayonet. The first Egyptian troop therefore went in peace, but its support followed; some of our men must have had time to push in a cartridge unseen; for when the support came through, they again opened out and gave them a volley as they passed.

Strong language from the officers was the result, but their words were drowned and all our eyes for a moment dazzled by a perfect sheet of flame a mile long, and a roar of musketry away to our left front; then across the desert came the ringing cheers of the Highland Brigade, for they had got within charging distance while we were still half a mile from our portion of the lines.

The Second Brigade was, as stated, in line, the battalions standing in the following order from right to left, Royal Irish, York and Lancaster, Royal Irish Fusiliers, Royal Marine Light Infantry. We had to change front-about-quarter-left on the left company of the marines so as to face the sheet of flame; and as each battalion got into the new alignment, it went at the works in attack-formation without waiting; for the next on its right. The Royal Irish was the exception; Colonel Gregorie, who commanded it, having been shown a weak point of the parapet by Major Hart of the Intelligence Department, he took his battalion intact into the works, and outflanked the retiring Egyptians who were opposing the other three regiments of the brigade.

The result of the battalions advancing from the left in succession was that the marines reached the works first, then the Irish Fusiliers, and so on to the right; the marines undoubtedly had the toughest job as their total losses of eighty proved, against thirty-nine of the next battalion, and twelve of the third, the latter losing less than the outflanking battalion. In fact, the Marine Light Infantry suffered more in the total of killed, wounded, and missing than any battalion in the corps that day.

General Willis told me, when the whole of the Second Brigade were started, to order the Guards to close up and be ready for a rush to the front in case of accident. When I reached them, I found that they had suffered a bit, and that the Duke of Connaught's bugler had been shot while at his side. They were all impatient for the order to charge the works; but it did not become necessary, as the Second Brigade got in without needing assistance. On returning to the front, I found General Willis all alone.

As we were talking, slap came a bullet on to his left shoulder; it cut through his tunic and shirt, making a scar four inches long, fell on to the case of his field-glass, and thence on to the sand, where he secured it as a memento. It was a very narrow escape, for though the ball was spent, a touch on the spine would have paralysed my chief. As it was, he was black and blue for a fortnight. We now went on and joined the Second Brigade; the parapet was already carried, but there was a tremendous scrimmage going on inside it and around the high detached forts, of which there were two, one hundred yards within the lines, each armed with artillery.

It is impossible to describe a fight when it comes to close work. What seems ten minutes may turn out to have been an hour on looking at a watch.

I know that there were some entrenchments on our left at which the Highland Brigade was still hammering. I found myself with a staff-officer of the Second Division, and men of both divisions shooting down Soudanese gunners in one of the detached forts within the lines, who were still firing at our second line with their Krupps, till we, entering at the gorge, drew off their attention. They tried to slew their guns round to give us a turn, but were foiled and fell like men, using their gun-rammers as clubs to the last. I remember finding my horse pawing at a goat-skin full of water, and my ripping it open, and his drinking every drop of its contents; and then, when the Second Brigade was re-formed within the lines and the Guards were up in support, a shell coming from the east, bursting over our heads and knocking down some of our own men.

Next, we saw the cavalry galloping across our right front towards the railway; and then we pressed on till we found ourselves on a knoll north-west of Tel-el-Kebir station, alongside a battery of horse artillery, which was shelling the departing trains. Somebody now said, "Why, it is six o'clock;" and then we rode down into Arabi's camp, I and the *aides-de-camp* taking possession of his own tent for our General, and soon breakfasting off the Egyptians' provisions—Turkish delight and all sorts of rubbish—when the order came:

"Cavalry cross the canal, march by Belbeis on Cairo—Indian Contingent seize Zagazig—Guards to go to Cairo by train—Second Brigade remain and bury the dead and look after the wounded—Second Division seize Benha, Tanta, and towns in Lower Egypt."

It all seemed like a dream, as neither self, horses, nor servants had got so much even as a scratch.

Apropos of horses, I had two out that night, the thoroughbred and a powerful half-bred horse fit to draw a brougham. The latter was all right during the darkness, except that he would neigh; but directly the shooting commenced he began to sweat and shake all over, though he had enjoyed several seasons with blank cartridge at Aldershot. I therefore mounted the other, upon which the soft-hearted one lay down. He would have been a splendid nag for the Islington tournaments. The animal's instinct must have told him that there was danger in the whistling things around us, for there was not a scratch on him; perhaps he did not like the smell of blood. The well-bred one seemed to revel in the uproar; and again, I advise everyone to get the best-bred horse he can find for a charger.

While our attack on the lines was going on, we were astonished to hear firing to our left rear; and, except that the sound was too near, it seemed as if the Indian Contingent on the other side of the canal, or the Naval Brigade with the 40-pounder, must be hotly engaged. It turned out afterwards that the Egyptians had a detached redoubt to mount eight guns constructed north of the railway, and twelve hundred yards in advance of their lines, which we had never distinguished as separate from them; and that this work, after the Highland Brigade had passed to the north of it, had been firing at the Headquarter Staff until it was taken in reverse by two of our batteries and silenced by the explosion of a magazine.

Arabi's tent (a gorgeous affair which was afterwards sent to England) contained a curious medley of things. There were three tents joined by canvas passages, a large one for receptions, with beautiful carpets, tables, chairs, and sofas; a smaller contained several excellent French bedsteads, and the smallest a lavatory. Stuck in the sand outside the entrance was the lance of a man of the 13th Bengal Lancers killed on the 9th, probably passed off by Arabi as a captured standard. On the writing-table lay an envelope (unfortunately empty) bearing the London postmark with the stamp of the Oriental Club, and addressed in English, and in a hand-writing known to some of us, *Ahmed Arabi Pasha, Cairo, Egypt.*

I suppose it had arrived by an Austrian-Lloyd boat, *via* Damietta; I forget the exact date it bore, but the year was 1882. Arabi's paper-weights were pillar-fuses for Armstrong 10-inch shells, marked *Elswick Ordnance Company* and dated 1866. They had of course been supplied to the *khedive* in the ordinary way of business, like the guns at Alexandria or the field-guns by Krupp; but they had our broad arrow on them, which was queer. There were large tin boxes full of sweetmeats, sweet biscuits, and rice cakes, but no drinks that our thirsty souls craved for.

There was plenty of cheering by the men as their generals passed; it was more refreshing to hear this than to read some of our old London papers which arrived later in the day. The news of the victory was in the evening papers of the 13th. I looked up the back files in London afterwards, and I will give two specimens of the revulsion of feeling, taken from two morning papers of the 14th.

"The delays and the shortcomings of the past fortnight have now been effectually obliterated"

"The practical reply which Sir Garnet Wolseley has given to his critics, who declared he was throwing away his opportunities by unnecessary delay, is triumphant and complete."

It was to be more complete than they thought. They knew nothing of the rush by our cavalry for Cairo over fifty miles of desert, and the preservation of that famous city from the fate that had befallen Alexandria at the hands of the mob. They did not know that the war was now practically over; we had only to look at our commander-in-chief's face to see that; he was smoking and laughing all day.

There is not the slightest doubt that the hardest task in the assault was that which fell to the lot of the Highland Brigade and the Royal Marine Light Infantry (the left battalion of the First Division). The works in their front had a ditch ten feet wide and four feet and a half deep, with a parapet four feet and a half high; whereas farther from the canal the entrenchment was not quite completed and decreased northwards, to seven feet wide, three deep, and three high. The high forts were all completed, and they had ditches fourteen feet wide and six feet and a half deep, with a six-foot parapet; so, the corps that actually struck on them lost most men.

Our total losses that day were nine officers and forty-eight men killed, twenty-seven officers and three hundred and fifty-five men wounded, and thirty men missing. We captured fifty-eight guns and an immense amount of ammunition. The Egyptian losses were about two thousand killed or died of wounds. We had eight hundred of their wounded in our field-hospital, and of course many more wounded escaped.

The men in the Second Brigade of the First Division must have fired that day nearly twenty-two rounds a man; but I am very much afraid, so strangely improvident and reckless is the British soldier, that, finding themselves encumbered with their hundred rounds, they threw away some on the march; for three or four days afterwards, marking some Bedouins prowling about on the line of our midnight march, I went and found numbers of intact packets lying about on the sand.

There is no doubt that luck is one of the chief factors in war, and Tel-el-Kebir proves it. Put the fact that the two wings of the Highland Brigade did not charge each other in the night down to discipline alone; yet it and the whole force escaped a reverse from another cause by a miracle. Each division steered its own course by the stars, as did the artillery between them. The left of the Highland Brigade started two thousand yards north of the railway, and the order was to march west. Had it marched west it would have passed within four hundred yards of the detached redoubt, which was twelve hundred yards in front of the entrenchments, and must have been discovered by the troops stationed there. Imagine, then, what would have taken place.

In the dark, everyone (of Hamley's Division, at least) would have gone straight for the work even as in daytime at the Alma men of six different battalions converged on and captured the great Russian redoubt of fourteen guns. After the capture of this advanced work, whether the force could have been got into order, started on the right course again for the main lines, and carried them, with Arabi's force there now thoroughly aroused, is an undecided point; but viewing the facts that daylight would have been upon us, and that we should have had to cross twelve hundred yards of level ground under the fire of breech-loaders from behind entrenchments, I think it will be admitted that, to say the least of it, we should have had our hands about as full as they could hold; for even our umpire rules say that to carry an entrenchment you must be in the proportion of three to one, and that even if successful you will lose one fourth of your strength in doing it; whereas our force that day was about one half of the enemy's.

But on that night the stars in their courses fought against Arabi, not as a figure of speech, but literally. Lieutenant Rawson, R. N., steered the Highland Brigade, Brigadier-General Goodenough the artillery, and General Willis the First Division; and not one of them kept the westerly course as directed. After the battle, this was clear to those who rode over the desert by which we had come. A mile from the lines the general course of the advance was 18° north of west. There was no mistaking the tracks of the guns, which were probably distinct for months; while foot-marks and the ominous packets of ammunition showed the advance of the First Division. The left of the Highlanders struck the entrenchments twenty-eight hundred yards from the railway; if they had steered due west their left would have struck the parapet two thousand yards north of the railway.

According to the scheme, therefore, they were eight hundred yards out to the north; and thereby, as I have said, they passed clear of the advanced redoubt, escaping inevitable discovery and all that would have followed. The reason for this drift to the north is plain, when you come to think it out. To march north in the northern hemisphere, above the tropics, is easy enough; you keep your eye on the pole star, which circles only a little; but to keep it on your right hand, looking at it from time to time, will cause you to drift that way, besides being inconvenient, and so you cannot do it, though you may dress your line of men on it when halted.

You therefore take a star as near west as you can calculate, march on it, and as it gets low, take another higher up—also west, if possible—and so on. You have the pole star on your right to guide you in the selection of the star on your front, and when first selected it is probably near enough to west; but unfortunately, none of them set straight down, all moving northwestwards. Take a celestial globe and set it for latitude 30°, 35 N. (where we were); take any star about your zenith—Castor, Pollux, Mirach—you will find it sets about 45° north of west. This is an extreme case, for you cannot march on a star over your head.

Take one, then, say of 45° altitude and west of you—the Pleiades for example; push the sphere on, and it will set 30° north of west. Refraction, haze, dust, make low altitudes uncertain; but take a star at 30° to 20° above the horizon—say Regulus; even that will set 15° north of west, as the other extreme. Now this shows the least drift of a suitable star to the north; so, think how often the lines must have been corrected by alignment on the pole star, and by changing the stars on which we were marching to get the actual total error down to 7°.

It was providence that prevented us reducing our errors still farther. If we had made no mistakes in carrying out orders, there would have been at least (what the umpire rules say is right) one quarter of our force *hors de combat.* We did the best we could; and I repeat once more that the stars themselves fought for us by leading us away northward from that advanced redoubt.

The staff of the base and line of communications had their work cut out for them now. They had been pretty forward, considering that five out of the eight had been present at the battle; one came on with a lot of mules carrying casks of rum, and found himself an amazingly popular man that day. There was a dam across the canal just within the lines, which the Engineers had to remove to let down the water to the posts towards Ismailia.

The Indian Contingent reached Zagazig on the afternoon of the 13th, and captured ten engines with a hundred carriages, which were sent back to Tel-el-Kebir to take the Guards on to Cairo. The Highland Brigade followed the Indian Contingent to Zagazig, and then pushed on to Benha and Tanta, while General Willis was ordered to send a wing of the Royal Irish Fusiliers back to guard Kassassin, and to remain with the rest of his Second Brigade, two field-batteries, and the ammunition-column at Tel-el-Kebir.

On the 14th I took charge of the burial-parties, and a ghastly job it was. How the Highlanders and marines got into the works it was difficult to say, but evidently only by degrees. Between every two Egyptians on the banquette was an open box of Remington cartridges containing twelve hundred rounds when full. Our men were lying chiefly in the ditch, on the superior slope of the parapet, and on the banquette; the Egyptian dead were, as a rule, farther back. There were still heaps of the enemy's wounded whom we had not yet had time to collect. *Acqua* was their incessant cry (learned, I suppose, from Italians), and if you gave them a tin water-bottle off a dead man, the poor wretches would kiss your hand.

One of our Bearer Company was looking after a wounded Bedouin when the brute fired off a pistol in his face, just grazing and singeing his cheek. He was forthwith deprived of his pistols, a beautiful pair of flint-locks inlaid with gold, and the soldier knew their value, for he would not sell them to me. The Bedouin was probably an *emir*.

While on this subject I will mention an instance of native medical practice which came under my notice. Our own surgeons had their hands so full that Sir Garnet Wolseley asked the authorities to send Egyptian surgeons to look after their wounded. Having suffered from the knife somewhat myself in earlier days, and being of an inquiring mind, I was one day in the tent (a large praying-tent which we had utilised as a hospital) watching an amputation by one of our surgeons.

Shortly afterwards I noticed one of the newly arrived Egyptian doctors examining one of the wounded, and as the poor fellow cried out in pain, the Eastern *medico* gave him a good slap in the face. One of the Army Hospital Corps happened to be close by, and without a minute s hesitation he raised his foot and gave the brute a rousing kick. There was a precious clamour, as may be supposed; but the most extraordinary thing was that nobody appeared to have seen the incident, and nothing therefore could be done to avenge the outraged dignity of the *hakim*.

As a proof how surprised the enemy was, we found at the back of one of the forts in the front line attacked by the Highland Brigade, and some hundred yards in rear of it, a tent, in which lay a dead Egyptian *bimbashi* (major) of artillery, shot through the heart; he was only half-dressed with one boot on, and the other still grasped in his hands. He could not have been shot until our men were on the top of the parapet.

The Egyptian soldiers' food was poor stuff; unleavened cakes, unripe dates, and dirty water. The cakes were not bad to eat, but a green date is more acrid than an acorn. They seemed to have plenty of these, but I did not see a single ripe one. Their water-bottles were of tin and very large, holding more than a quart, but what water remained in them was very muddy.

Some books of drill and field-fortification in Arabic were picked up. The latter were illustrated, and the designs not unlike ours and the French; but curiously enough they had no chapter on obstacles. This was well; think what a wire entanglement in front of their lines would have meant to us in the dark!

The interior slopes were riveted with bunches of twisted dry grass and mud, laid alternately; and most effective it was, keeping the slopes as upright as desired. The rest was all sand, the thickness averaging about ten feet, and in one place, near the canal, twenty-four.

We had sixty-four unwounded prisoners, whom we made help to bury their fallen comrades. They were much more particular about touching a dead body than our men; cutting up some canvas tents into slips, they would wrap the slip round the wrist of a corpse and drag it, but would not touch it with the bare hand. Every Remington rifle we found we broke at the lock by hitting the ground with the butt sideways, first, of course, taking care that it was not loaded. All the small-arm ammunition we upset out of the boxes over the parapet into the ditch, put the Egyptian dead on the top of it, and then shovelled down the parapet till they were covered a foot deep. It would have taken a month to fill up the ditch.

The Bedouins, however, made more than one attempt to get at the ammunition by digging up the bodies at night, for our camp was a long way west of the lines. These rascals had become an intolerable nuisance, swarming all over the place after loot, and sometimes even firing at our men it they saw one alone. A troop of the Hussars had to be sent out once to hunt them away.

There were one or two Nubians among the prisoners, and though unaccustomed to our English spades, were worth all the rest together. One fellow, whom I watched closely, worked all day like a slave. When too far away from the ditch to drag a man to it, he would scrape a shallow trench, lay the body in, stretch the left arm down by the side, cross the right forearm across the breast, put a bit of rag over the face, mumble some words, and shovel the sand over it. This was all right for the time, but on the third day the bodies had swelled, and over each little mound was a hand which had been pushed up through the sand. I gave my friend some tobacco, and from the look of astonishment with which he took it, grinning and saluting, I suppose he had never had anything from an officer but the whip before.

On the morning after the assault, riding near the ground where the Egyptians had entrained, an officer of marines took me to a Milner's Safe which he had found on the desert, and guarded with two men. It was locked, but if tilted over the rattle of coin could be heard; and as treasure must always be guarded by two sentries, a non-commissioned officer and six men as a guard were mounted over the chest till, we left for Cairo, when we took it in state on its own truck, surrounded by its guard, to Abdin Palace, and handed it over to the chief paymaster.

A day or two after a Board was assembled to see the chest broken open by our armourers, and take stock of its contents, which, after all this trouble, were found to consist of a box of cigarettes and a lot of loose *piastres* (twopence-halfpenny apiece); not a jot of gold or silver. Arabi the Egyptian, even in his hurried flight, had managed to save the money.

At last, on the 18th orders came for us to move as soon as able to Cairo. That day two battalions were despatched by train with the Egyptian wounded; next day the guns, carriages, and gunners of the two batteries were sent off also by train, while the horses and drivers marched by the desert to Abbassiyeh. We ourselves got into the city on the 20th.

The quarters for the Staff of the First Division and both its Brigades were to have been Abdin Palace School, for the Guards Abdin Palace Barracks, and for the Second Brigade Kasr-en-Nil Barracks.

When we arrived, however, the school was full, the various departments having slipped past us during our week at Tel-el-Kebir and appropriated the rooms; so off we went to Kasr-en-Nil and seized on Arabi's old quarters—the War Ministry, a very splendid place, but not central. There was room in the barracks for any number of men, and as the Second Brigade arrived, we collected them there. But the place was in such a disgusting state, already tenanted by such numbers and varieties of insects, that on the 21st the Marine Artillery, with much carbolic acid and lime, were left to take charge, and the whole of the Second Brigade moved across the Iron Bridge to ground near the

Gezireh Palace on Bulak Island, and encamped there.

During our detention at Tel-el-Kebir there had been some exciting scenes. After an exhausting march the cavalry, moving across the desert by Belbeis, had reached Abbassiyeh, on the outskirts of Cairo, on the 14th. The citadel, garrisoned by Ali Bey Yousif and five thousand men, surrendered at once; and on the evening of that day the Egyptians marched out before Captain Watson, R. E., and a force of one hundred and fifty men composed of two squadrons of the 4th Dragoon Guards and a party of Mounted Infantry.

On the same date Arabi Pasha and Toulba Pasha surrendered to General Drury Lowe at Abbassiyeh. Tanta, which now contained part of the Salihiyeh force, surrendered to Sir Archibald Alison and three companies of Highlanders on the 17th; the lines of Kafr-Dauar submitted shortly after to Sir Evelyn Wood, commanding the force left at Ramleh near Alexandria, who then proceeded with two battalions and artillery to Damietta, which was surrendered to him by the governor Abd-el-Al. By September 24th the war was over in all parts. On the following day the *khedive* re-entered his capital, the troops lining the streets from the railway station to the palace, while the women screeched their welcome from the house-tops.

The staff of the First Division remained at Gezireh from September 20th till October 8th, when general orders disestablished the staff of both divisions, and we were ordered to proceed to Alexandria and home. The camp-life was rather dull in the interval, except for an occasional shot at our tents at night from across the river, and such petty annoyances as complaints from the servants of the *khedive* that the men picked the grapes growing outside the walls of the *harem*. Not half a dozen bunches had gone, as a fact, and His Highness had been replaced on his throne by the accused, but that was beyond the point; an Eastern servant must grumble, and probably charged the soldiers to cover his own thefts. Nevertheless, we had the trouble of making inquiries into the case and mounting pickets to preserve His Highness's fruit.

On the 28th there was a serious explosion at the station. There was a race-meeting at Abbassiyeh that day, but I, being on duty, had remained in the town. In the afternoon I was riding across Abdin Square, when I felt a concussion, and looking north saw a white pillar of smoke rising up into the sky. I hurried down to the station and found that, on the arrival of the Rifles from Benha, a waggon of powder on an adjoining line of rails had exploded, that shells and small-arm ammunition were going off all over the place, for even buildings were well alight, including one containing tons of our Chicago beef in tins.

Some of the men detraining were killed, and though the explosion was said to be accidental, I met a few who did not think so. The 24th and 26th companies of Royal Engineers were ordered out, but as the people at the Rond Pont de Faghalla began to move their goods, it was occupied by some infantry, for in a panic it is hard to tell whether a mob is looting or peaceable citizens are removing their own goods to a place of safety; besides the sight of disciplined men encourages the timid and keeps the evil-doers in check.

The fire lasted two days, during which thousands of rounds of our own as well as Egyptian ammunition were destroyed, together with provisions and stores of all kinds. It was lucky that the country had been thoroughly overawed; a rising might have been serious before what we wanted could have been replaced.

On the 30th the army marched past the *khedive* at Abdin Palace. It was not a very imposing pageant. The saluting-point was on the wrong flank; the troops had to approach the open place by narrow streets, and regardless of this, the leading corps were started too soon, so that there was loss of distances. Colours were carried for the first time; they had been left on board the *Invincible* at Alexandria, and colour-parties had been sent to Alexandria for them the day before. Review order meant the best you had got; in some cases, full dress was worn with orders and decorations, in others only very shabby "jumpers."

On October 5th the troops took part in the ceremony of the despatch of the *Mahmal*, or holy carpet, to Mecca for the *Kaaba*. The carpet is made yearly in Cairo, and should have been sent off by the pilgrim caravan on September 7th *via* the Wady Tumilat; but the war prevented it; after being started from the square Mahomed Ali and passing through the town, it took train for Ismailia. The *khedive* attended the ceremony, while the Guards lined the square and presented arms, for there were no Egyptian troops to pay the necessary honours; and a strange sight it was to see the Mahomedan symbol being escorted by the hated *infidels*.

There was a report that officers of a certain department, not recognising that we were doing honours to the *khedive* and his religion, protested against the troops presenting arms to the idolatrous thing; and that they were accordingly told afterwards, on the distribution of decorations, that as the Turkish orders carried the Crescent and not the Cross, they would not be insulted by being offered them.

It must not be supposed that the occupation of Cairo meant all work and no play, for wherever a portion of the British Army may be, you will be sure to see some kind of sport going on. There was a gymkhana at Abbassiyeh on the day of the explosion, given by the English mounted troops; and the Indian Brigade showed their mettle on October 5th. We also managed to find time to see all the sights, the pyramids, the *mosques* and the citadel; and from the top of the latter, even on October 3rd, the day on which our signallers were withdrawn from the heliograph stations, you could see the sheen of arms on the western desert, where parties of Egyptian soldiers were returning to their homes up the Nile.

Then there were dinners, levees, and such like comforts, General Willis leading off on October 1st by entertaining all the Staff and commanding officers of his division, who were available, at a dinner at the New Hotel. Twenty-three sat down, and the charge was something like £4 a head, for everything was now at famine-prices. The *khedive* gave a dinner and a garden-party at Gezireh Palace on the night of the 2nd: an Egyptian Colonel, Osman Bey, entertained us on the night of the 3rd with, among other things, a genuine *nautch*; and Sir Garnet Wolseley gave a picnic at Memphis on the 7th, where Baker Pasha in frock coat, tall hat, and large umbrella, as became a *pasha*, amused the company by going clean over his donkey's head on to the sand.

Having been disestablished on the 8th, we settled up business on the 9th, struck camp and handed over equipment on the 10th, and took up our quarters at Shepherd's Hotel for the night. At dinner were Sir Frederick Leighton (President of the Royal Academy), Valentine Baker Pasha, now a Turkish general, and Mr. Plimsoll, M.P. They were the first arrivals after the campaign representing art, war, and commerce.

It was decided that Sir Archibald Alison was to remain in Egypt in command of a force of ten thousand men until a new Native Army could be raised, when the English force was to be gradually reduced. This duty was entrusted to Sir Evelyn Wood with the title of Sirdar, while Baker Pasha set to work to reorganise the *gendarmerie*. The *Mahdi* was already beginning to be heard of in the Soudan, and it was a pity that action was not taken with him at once, for then Khartoum and the more southern provinces would probably never have been lost to Egypt.

We sailed from Alexandria on the 11th in the *Arab* of the Union Line, which also carried Sir Edward Hamley and his diminished staff; and on the 23rd I landed at Portsmouth, after an absence from England of less than three months.

★★★★★★★★★★★★

Here I close this record of my campaigns. To recall experiences with the Bechuanaland Field Force in 1885 might be neither agreeable to myself nor profitable to many readers. There was, as everybody knows, no fighting; and for the rest, most of those concerned in the expedition will, I think, agree with me that silence is best. All it brought me was the revival of an old injury, which eventually sent me to the retired list on the last day of 1887. There is a good saying: "*Never tell your troubles; you only take up the time of the man who is waiting to tell you his.*" Rather will *I* console myself with the words of Prospero:

Let us not burthen our remembrance with
A heaviness that's gone.

The Battle of Tel-el-Kebir

By James Grant

After the concentration of the forces in the camp at Kassassin, the troops were allowed to rest for one entire day.

The correspondent of the *Kölnische Zeitung*, as quoted by Colonel Hermann Vogt, of the German Army, in his work on the Egyptians, gives us a curious description of our camp there, as presenting a great contrast to the regulations of the army in Germany, though he is wrong in some of his details.

Tents are not needed in this climate and under this sky. The troops only pitch tents when they remain some considerable time in the same place; otherwise, the men make themselves comfortable on the bare ground, where the never-failing ants give plenty of trouble. The private soldiers vary much more than ours. There are among them old and young, weak and strong. In general, the strong predominate. Many of them are splendid men, with muscles like those of the 'dying gladiator.' The uniform is the red tunic and Indian mud-coloured helmet The Household Cavalry, Rifles, Marines, and Artillery do not wear red tunics. All, however, wear the sun helmet, which is of a beautiful shape, but an ugly colour. They also wear a flannel shirt and needlessly warm woollen trousers.

The little wooden water-bottle that each soldier carries at his belt appears very practical, as the water keeps cooler than in flasks of tin. The saddlery of the cavalry seemed rather shabby; the stirrups were rusty, and the unpolished leather looked rough. The Life Guards wear red, the Horse Guards blue. They have left their *cuirasses* at home, and are armed with swords and revolvers, carried in a leather holster. The hussars and dragoons are to be distinguished only by their leggings, as they also wear red tunics and helmets. The Indian Cavalry look well in their uniform, which resembles that of the Cossacks. They carry lances; their pointed shoes are in the style of the fifteenth century. All these men have gipsy faces, with beautiful fiery eyes. They move with a catlike softness, peculiar to all southern Asiatics. These Indians know better than anyone else how to forage and steal.

Among the British officers, especially the Guards, are crowds of lords with £10,000 a year and more (?), but without knowing it beforehand, no one would find it out. Lieutenants wear a star on the collar, captains two (?), majors a crown, lieutenant-colonels a crown and star, colonels two crowns, generals two swords crossed. Staff officers wear a pink scarf instead of a white one over their helmets. They have almost unlimited liberty as regards uniform when not on duty. If it is difficult for the continental European to distinguish between German regiments, it is more so when British officers not on duty wear the half military, half civilian costume. (In this he must refer to the camp alone.) They appear in yellow leather lace-boots and gaiters, fancy coats, broad belts, gigantic revolver-pockets, scarfs, &c. Then consider the military tourists, such as members of Parliament and relatives of distinguished officers.

These gentlemen, as well as most of the officers, are pretty men, with white complexion and carefully tended nails. They parade on their arrival in their travel-stained clothes, as though they had already gone through a long campaign. They were fond of dressing in an eccentric manner, but they could not compare with the military appearance of many of the civilians. As far as I was able to judge, they did not trouble themselves much about their men. When they inspect horses, saddlery, &c, they do so in the manner of a merchant inspecting his wares. However, everyone does his duty according to his own fashion.

One effect of the great strictness of our continental discipline is that it is considered sufficient only occasionally to go minutely through the prescribed forms, and without accomplishing anything very thorough. This is not so much the case with the English. Accomplishments of a high order are more rare than with ourselves; but, on the other hand, the total absence of them is more rare also.

The marines and some of our regiments in this campaign entirely abolished the use of pipeclay; it was washed out, and the belts were then stained with tea and tobacco-juice to a brown colour, as were also the helmets, which, being white, in the sun proved a most attractive mark for the enemy's riflemen.

The men in camp had an entire day's rest on the 11th, we have said, but there was no rest for the staff officers. Tel-el-Kebir had to be fully reconnoitred, and the line of the advance considered.

The valley up which the route of our troops to Zagazig would lie is the Wady Tumilat, a depression of the border of the Libyan Desert, asserted by those learned in ancient Egypt to have been, in times prehistoric, once a branch of the Nile, traversing Timsah and the Bitter Lakes to the Red Sea. Under the Pharaohs here lay a canal, by which the river recovered its connection with the latter sea. The line of the valley itself partakes of the nature of the adjacent desert. The soil at Ismailia is mere loose sand, but farther west, towards Kassassin, it becomes firmer, strong, and strewed with pebbles.

Along the shores of the canal are traces of an ancient town of vast extent, and of a once high cultivation that has passed away. At Tel-el-Mahuta there still remains a mighty block of granite, bearing on one side—enthroned between the divinities Thum and Ra—a representation of King Rameses II., the alleged conqueror of Æthiopia, Libya, and Persia, and, according to Pliny, the contemporary of Priam; while Rameses—the railway station—is the site of the Scriptural town of that name in the Land of Goshen

Westward of Tel-el-Kebir lie the ruins of the ancient Pithom, where the Israelites burned bricks, and where, as we are told in Exodus, they had taskmasters set over them "to afflict them with their burdens; and they built for Pharaoh treasure cities, Pithom and Rameses."

Zagazig, which was ere long to echo to the pipes of the Black Watch when seized by that regiment, is the ancient Bubastis—the site of a magnificent temple of Venus—where cats were held in high veneration, because Diana Bubastis transformed herself into a cat when the gods fled from Egypt.

Such was the Biblical and classical ground over which the British troops were now fighting.

The whole welfare of the Wady Tumilat depends on the existence of the fresh-water canal which traverses it, and which the indolent Turks allowed to fill with sand. Since it has been re-opened, under a new regime, great tracts have been made fertile, and it is obvious that the sluices which regulate the water supply could be made most serviceable in a strategical point of view.

Up to the 3rd of September there was no Christian clergyman with the troops at Kassassin, save one Roman Catholic priest, though a large clerical staff had been sent out; and he had to read a burial service over all the dead, after attending them on their death-beds. The Scottish regiments, however, had their Scripture-readers.

On the 11th and 12th of September Sir Garnet Wolseley reconnoitred both sides of the enemy's position, accompanied by the principal officers of his staff, in which there rode Colonels Zohrab and Morice Bey, Lieutenant-Colonels Thurnisen and Abdullah Bey, Dulier Bey and Captain Hussein Bey Ramzy, and Lieutenant Goodrich, of the United States Navy. They saw before them a line of entrenchments some four miles long, extending from the canal towards El Karain, in the desert; on its other bank soft earthworks, with hurdle revetments, which in fortification mean supports outside of a rampart or parapet, to prevent the soil from rolling into the ditch.

These works, on which such numbers of *fellaheen* had toiled for so many weeks, had a frontage of 6,600 yards, and the intended inundation by Arabi south of the position did not seem to have been carried out. At intervals along the line were redoubts armed with cannon, which were so pointed as to deliver alike a front and rear fire, and these redoubts were connected by trenches—all, doubtless, the result of Mahmoud Fehmy's skill as an engineer.

Supporting the front line were other redoubts, which, towards the right centre of the position, were especially strong; alike because they crowned eminences that were natural, and were strengthened by art and skill. Similar works covered the flanks—an entrenched line and armed redoubts. They were supposed to be unassailable by cavalry.

In rear of all these works lay an Egyptian force, which, says the *Times*, can be estimated correctly only by the fact that 18,000 rations were issued the day before for the regular troops, and 7,000 for irregulars:—

> But the strength of the enemy was known only vaguely to Sir Garnet Wolseley, as his despatch admits. The practical facts before him were; the works, the knowledge that they were fully occupied, the knowledge also of a detachment at Salahieh, and the certainty that the enemy would be informed of all his movements by spies.

His experience of an Egyptian sun also told him that although, even while it beat pitilessly on the desert sand, British troops could fight and conquer in the heat of the day, the rough task before them would be better and more easily achieved in the cool dark hours of the early morning.

After Sir Garnet had explained to all his generals and brigadiers the plan of attack, and given each a sketch of the intended operations, he was seen with his staff reconnoitring the position, but the enemy's cavalry issuing from Tel-el-Kebir put an end to the reconnaissance, and he was back to camp by seven a.m. All was quiet there still, and the anxious and curious press correspondents who called at headquarters to glean news were briefly informed there "was none to tell."

There were then with the commissariat only five days' provisions for the whole force, but as the country beyond Tel-el-Kebir was known to be fertile and rich, it was thought subsistence would be found there, though it was but too probable that for miles around it might have been swept by the enemy, in which case it was hoped that a large stock of provisions would be captured together with the entrenchments.

During all that eventful day the enemy's vedettes remained at a long distance from the camp at Kassassin, while our reconnoitring parties reported that they were labouring hard at the earthworks, as if anticipating the event that was to come.

All the troops felt that a move would be most welcome, for, in addition to the discomforts already mentioned elsewhere, the camp was becoming unhealthy, diarrhoea prevailing to a considerable extent, and already many men had been sent rearward to Ismailia.

The pontoons were now all to the front, to enable Graham's force to cross or re-cross the canal at will in the work of turning Arabi's lines.

During the day the advanced guard was pushed forward four miles, while the Indian infantry followed for two miles, and when the evening of the 12th of September came, all knew that the hour of battle was drawing nigh, and that many who saw the red Egyptian sun set might never see it rise again.

The orders were issued for a general advance; they were brief, but significant. By half-past six all tents were struck and packed, and all baggage was piled up along the railway, opposite the camps of the respective corps to which it belonged. At these preliminary duties the soldiers worked hard and cheerfully, while a deep sense of relief pervaded all ranks in the knowledge that a long period of inactivity and comparative inaction, with intense discomfort, was over, and that the beginning of the end was at hand.

No bugles or trumpets were allowed to sound after sunset. The West Kent Regiment, the 19th Hussars, and two companies of the Royal Engineers were detailed to guard the camp and baggage.

No fires were permitted; even smoking was forbidden; and the utmost silence was ordered to be maintained throughout the operations of the night. At half-past one in the morning—after every man had been provided with a hundred rounds of ammunition and two days' rations, including tea in water-bottles (two additional days' supply and thirty more rounds provided for by the regimental transport)—Sir Garnet Wolseley gave the order to advance, and the 1st and 2nd Divisions moved off. His despatch says:—

> The night was very dark, and it was difficult to maintain the desired formation, but by means of connecting files between the battalions and brigades, and between the first and second lines, and through the untiring exertions of the generals and officers of the staff generally, this difficulty was overcome effectually.

The Indian Contingent, consisting of a Royal Artillery Mountain Battery, a battalion made up from three Native Corps and the Seaforth Highlanders, under Major-General Sir Herbert Macpherson, V.C, and the Naval Brigade of 250 men, under Captain Fitzroy, of H.M.S. *Orion*, did not move off till half-past two a.m., as to have done so sooner would have alarmed the villagers among the cultivated land southward of the canal.

Telegraphic communication by means of insulated cable was kept up to Kassassin all through the night, between the Indian Contingent and the south of the canal and the Royal Marine Artillery, with which Sir Garnet Wolseley moved in rear of the 2nd Division.

The total strength thus advancing to the attack was given in the *Times* at 11,000 bayonets, 2,000 sabres, and 60 guns:—

> About half that of the enemy, excluding the Salahieh detachment.

On the extreme right rode the bulk of the cavalry brigade, and two Royal Horse Artillery batteries, with orders to sweep vigorously round in rear of the enemy's line when day broke. Next to them on the left, and forming the right of the infantry, was General Graham's brigade, the 2nd—consisting of the 2nd Battalion of the Royal Irish, Royal Marine Light Infantry, York and Lancaster Regiment, and the

1st Battalion of the Royal Irish Fusiliers, supported by the Duke of Connaught and the Brigade of Guards—the last no longer true to their grand traditions and past history as leading the van—for what reason has never been explained.

Nearer the lines of railway and canal, forty-two guns advanced under Colonel Goodenough, supported by a fourth brigade, made up for the time of the 60th Rifles, the Duke of Cornwall's, and with them, apparently, were the Marine Light Infantry.

On the same line moved the Highland Brigade, consisting of the 1st Battalion of the Black Watch, 1st Cameron Highlanders, and 2nd Highland Light Infantry and Gordon Highlanders, under Sir Archibald Alison, and pioneered, or guided, by the gallant Lieutenant Wyatt Rawson, R.N., of whom more *anon*.

The ironclad train occupied the railway, supported and manned by the Bue-Jackets, who had been drawn from the fleet, and sent to the front to share in the crowning glory. The *Times* says:—

> The Highland Brigade on our left, and Graham's brigade on our right, stole forward through the darkness to the assault of the enemy's position, knowing the effect to be produced by the sudden apparition of a brave enemy, determined to have no preliminary fire, but to trust only to the shadows of night to veil his advance.

In moving over the desert at night there were no landmarks to guide the movements, and their course was directed by the stars, which was well and correctly effected, and the leading brigades of each division both reached the enemy's works within a couple of minutes of each other.

All orders were issued in low tones—almost in whispers; the foot-falls of the marching masses were muffled by the sand amid which they trod. The silence was broken only by the occasional clatter of a steel scabbard or the chain of a guncarriage, while the certainty that a great, bloody, and desperate struggle would commence ere the first ray of dawn shone over the level desert, with the expectation of being challenged at any moment by scouting Bedouin horsemen, combined to make this march amid the darkness of the morning one which those who shared in it never will forget. Thoughts of home must have been in the minds of many, amid the stillness of the time, mingling with those of the stern work in hand; but little was said or heard, save a whispered "Silence there!" as someone asked for a match, or "Put out

COLONEL GOODENOUGH, COMMANDING THE ROYAL
ARTILLERY.

COLONEL NUGENT, COMMANDING THE ROYAL ENGINEERS

LIEUTENANT WYATT RAWSON.

that pipe instantly!" after it had been surreptitiously lit.

There were a few temporary halts, to enable the regiments to maintain touch and cohesion of order, and to allow the guns and waggons, the jarring wheels of which seemed to sound strangely loud, to keep up with the columns.

When dawn was nigh the troops were within 1,000 yards of the enemy, and then a final halt was made for a brief space to enable the fighting line to be perfected, and last preparations to be made.

Deepest silence reigned over the Egyptian desert, and to all who were present it seemed most difficult to realise as a fact that an army of so many thousand men of all arms was now in a vast semicircle round the lines of the enemy, ready to rush at a signal headlong against those who manned the heavily-armed batteries that rose, amid the darkness, in an outline even more opaque than gloom.

The correspondent of the *Standard*, who rode with the Mounted Police, says:—

> The attack began on the left, and nothing finer could be imagined than the advance of the Highland Brigade. Swiftly and silently the Highlanders moved forward to the attack. No word was spoken, no shot was fired until within 300 yards of the enemy's works (a distance since lessened to 200 yards), nor up to that time did a sound in the Egyptian lines betoken that they were aware of the presence of their assailants. Then suddenly a terrific fire flashed along the line of sand-heaps, and a storm of bullets swept over the heads of the advancing troops. A wild cheer broke from the Highlanders in response; the pipes struck shrilly up, bayonets were fixed, and at the double this splendid body of men went steadily forward.
>
> The first line of entrenchments was carried; but from another line of entrenchments, which could scarcely be seen in the dim light, another burst of musketry broke out. For a few minutes the Highlanders poured in a heavy fire in exchange, but it was probably as innocuous as that of the unseen enemy, whose bullets whistled overhead. The brigade again moved rapidly forward. Soon a portion of the force had passed between the enemy's redoubts, and opened a flanking fire upon him.

And here fell that brave sailor, Wyatt Rawson, mortally wounded.

As the Highland Brigade burst like a torrent into Tel-el-Kebir, Private Donald Cameron, of the Cameron Highlanders, is alleged to have

PLAN OF THE BATTLE OF TEL-EL-KEBIR (SEPTEMBER 13, 1882).

been, as his beautiful monument records, "the first man to mount the parapet, and the second to fall."

As, despite the first hasty despatch of this action, the first attack was delivered by the left wing, and, as the *Army and Navy Gazette* has it, "the Highlanders were inside the position long before the right attack," ere proceeding to relate the fighting at other points, we shall quote, in preference to our own, the words of the one-armed veteran who led them. Sir Archibald Alison, who has inherited his father's power of vivid description.

After detailing the impressive nature of the advance amid the darkness of the moonless night, and the dull muffled march of the masses through the desert, he continued thus:—

It exercised upon me a singular fascination, and the words of the Roman gladiators came to my mind, '*Ave, Cæsar Imperator, morituri te salutant.*' The first thin dawn of breaking day was just beginning to lighten the east, when a few shots fired into our men showed that we had touched the Egyptian outposts; the click was heard of fixing bayonets; a deep silence followed; the measured march was resumed, and suddenly out of the darkness there flashed a long blaze of musketry that rolled away on each flank, and by the light of which we saw the swarthy features of the Egyptians, surmounted by their red *tarbooshes*, lining the ramparts in front of us.

I never felt such a relief in my life. I knew that Wolseley's star was bright. A solitary bugle rang out, and then, with a cheer and a bound, the Highlanders rushed in one long wave upon the works. The first line went down into the ditch, but for a time could make no way. Some fell back into the ditch, the majority sprang over the summit, the rest rushed on, and then the battle went raging into the centre of the space behind. While this befell on the centre and right of the Highland Brigade, the Highland Light Infantry on the left had a more chequered fight They came upon a very strong redoubt.

A front attack could not succeed, it would appear; the ditch was too deep, the ramparts too high. Filing off on each side, the Highland Light Infantry endeavoured to force a way in at the flanks of the works, and here one of the bloodiest struggles of the day ensued—a long and stern hand-to-hand fight, which was not ended till Sir Edward Hamley had reinforced that regiment—the old 74th—by part of the Cornwall Regiment and the 60th Rifles.

On the other flank of the brigade the Black Watch was compelled to tarry in its wild rush, in order to storm a redoubt, the heavy guns of which, in the now breaking morning light, had begun to play heavily on Graham's brigade and our advancing artillery; and thus, it came to pass that, from both flanks of Alison's brigade being delayed, the charge straight to their front of the Gordon and Cameron Highlanders caused them to become the apex of a wedge thrust into the heart of the Egyptian Army.

The best fighting by the troops of the latter took place here, when their First Guard Regiments fell back silently and sullenly before the Highlanders, even while the latter were under a flank fire.

Sir Archibald Alison continued:—

Then occurred a matter which all troops are exposed to in a very severe fight—a portion of our line, reeling under the flank fire, fell back for a moment. Then it was a goodly sight to see how nobly Sir Edward Hamley, my division leader, threw himself into the midst of the men, animating them by voice and example, and amid a storm of shot, led them on to the charge. Here, too, I must do justice to those much-maligned Egyptian soldiers. I never saw men fight more steadily. They were falling back up an inner line of works which we had taken in flank. At every re-entering angle, at every battery and redoubt, they rallied, and renewed the fight. Five or six times we had to close on them with the bayonet, and I saw those poor men fighting hard when their officers were flying before us.

At this time, too, it was a goodly sight to see the Cameron and Gordon Highlanders, mingled together as they were, in the stream of the fight; their young officers leading in front, waving their swords above their heads, their pipes playing, and the men rushing on with that bright light in their eyes, and that proud smile on their lips, which you never see in soldiers except in the moment of successful battle.

Here fell Sergeant-Major McNeill, of the Black Watch, a magnificent soldier, pierced by three bullets, after cutting down six of the enemy with his claymore; and Lieutenant Graham Stirling fell, shot through the head, not far from him.

Quartermaster Elmslie, in his published letter, states that when the Black Watch had reached the crest of the works, but still had numerous guns in front, while the colonel was re-forming them, a battery of artillery swept past on their right, shouting, "Scotland for ever!"

They were one of the batteries of the new Scottish Division, he adds:—

And were scarcely halted, when their shot and shell were tearing along the trenches, and making dreadful havoc among the Egyptians.

In his second and detailed despatch, Sir Garnet Wolseley states that:—

The Highland Brigade had reached the works a few minutes before the 2nd Brigade had done so, and in a dashing manner stormed them at the point of the bayonet, without firing a shot till within the enemy's lines.

Meanwhile, fighting had begun vigorously on the other flank. Dawn was faintly stealing over the Eastern sky, when the crest of a ridge some 500 yards in front of the Egyptian left became covered with moving objects, that told darkly against the pale light It was the brigade of Graham coming on. A single shot from the Egyptian lines rang out, and after that the storm of the battle burst forth.

The Royal Horse Artillery shelled the enemy's extreme left, where the Egyptians are said to have been more prepared than they were for the attack on their right, and for a time held their ground, till the first jets of fire that spirted out in the darkness became one long blaze of musketry over the top of the parapets. Under the guidance of Major Hart, a staff officer, the Royal Irish were sent to turn the enemy's left, and with a wild yell, and all their national and characteristic valour, they went "straight at the works," carried them at the bayonet's point, and completely turned the flank of the position.

Then crowded masses of the Egyptians began to rush across the open, suffering heavily from our fire, which mowed them down in hundreds.

Next to the Royal Irish came the old 87th Royal Irish Fusiliers, and next them the old 94th, now termed the 2nd Battalion of the Connaught Rangers.

These regiments advanced by regular rushes; but it would seem that the rest of the troops in the shadows of the plain had not been perceived, and thus the fire that at first opposed them was of that involuntary kind which tells of want of discipline; but ere long it be-

211

came a steady fringe of fire sparkling out amid the gloom. "Then, with a grand cheer, the tide of British lads was loose, and the blood of the men bounded no less strongly in their veins because their service in the army was to be six years instead of twelve."

Here our troops had been seen fully by the enemy, who poured upon them a hail of bullets. Thick as bees, the Egyptian infantry clustered on the parapets of the redoubts, and were forced down the slopes of these into the deep trenches in front of them. Hundreds of them, lying down, smote the head of the advancing brigade with their fire; but our soldiers deployed with splendid steadiness, and advanced by sections, making, as we have said, rushes that were short and sharp towards the enemy's position, but always under the full control of their officers.

As they drew near the trenches, they gathered themselves in groups, and leaped down into the midst of the enemy; then a hand-to-hand fight ensued with butt-end and bayonet, and the Egyptians fell in scores, our officers having many a personal combat with them; thus, when the second line came on, they found the trenches full of dead and dying Arabs.

The first line of the Egyptian entrenchments, with all the redoubts, was now fully captured, but the stronger lay within, armed with twelve heavy guns, while line after line of shelter-trenches lay beyond.

To have paused for a moment now would, in the opinion of the *Times* correspondent, have been to repeat the dreadful mistake of the Redan in the Crimea. Thus, our troops, cheering with glorious enthusiasm, again went storming up the slopes without the hesitation of a second, won the inner parapets, and bayoneted the gunners before they had time to abandon their cannon.

About twenty minutes after, the first rush on the left and that on the right sufficed to put the carefully-constructed entrenchments and the redoubts, with all their flank-firing and formidable artillery, in the hands of the victorious British troops. Those of the enemy who were able to fly, fled, followed by the withering and searching fire of the victors in the captured positions; and those other redoubts that were yet unattacked, and the shelter-trenches lay beyond; all these availed them not, as the dread of our cavalry and horse artillery sweeping round upon their flank and rear caused the Egyptians suddenly to abandon them.

From the moment that Graham's brigade on the right and the Highlanders on the left were through the inner line of redoubts, the actual resistance of the Egyptians ceased, and the battle was virtually won. Mingled together in bewildered mobs, hurried into wild and disastrous retreat, the Egyptian regiments had no rest given them—no chance of rallying even for one brief moment.

Ere these attacks had been consummated, and while they were in progress, the Indian Contingent and the Bue-Jackets, all under Major-General Sir Herbert Macpherson, had been doing their duty on the extreme left. Sir Garnet Wolseley, in his despatch of the subsequent day, says:—

> They advanced steadily and in silence, the Seaforth Highlanders leading, until an advanced battery of the enemy was reached, when it was gallantly stormed by the Highlanders, supported by the Native Infantry battalions. The squadron of the 6th Bengal Cavalry, attached temporarily to General Macpherson, did good service in pursuing the enemy through the village of Tel el-Kebir. The Indian Contingent scarcely lost a man, which I attribute to the excellent arrangements made by Major-General Macpherson, and to the fact that, starting an hour later than the 1st and 2nd Divisions, the resistance of the enemy was so shaken by the earlier attacks north of the canal that he soon gave way before the impetuous onslaught of the Seaforth Highlanders.

The official report of the operations of the Royal Marine Light Infantry, furnished by Colonel Howard S. Jones, who commanded them, to the Lords of the Admiralty, details them with some spirit. After the march in the dark was achieved, they found themselves, just as dawn was breaking, about 1,200 yards in front of the northern portion of the enemy's lines, after having more than once to make a change of front, owing to the stars being occasionally obscured

While the brigade of which they formed part deployed into line, a continuous fire of shot and shell was poured into it. As soon as the brigade formation was complete, Colonel Jones formed the marines for "attack" by sending forward three companies in fighting line, with three in support and two in reserve; and as the first of these in extended order approached the position, they found themselves destitute of all cover, while under a fire that every moment increased in fury and intensity.

Yet the marines pressed forward up the slope of the glacis, reserving their fire, as ordered, until within about 150 yards of the first ditch, when, fixing bayonets, the fighting line being reinforced by its supports and by the reserves under Lieutenant-Colonel Graham, the whole worked their way by a succession of impetuous rushes, in spite of a terrific fire of cannon and musketry, to the summit of the works, and with loud cheers threw themselves into the ditch, and dashing up the slope of the nine-foot parapet, met the foe in a close hand-to-hand fight with butt and bayonet.

This lasted but a short time, as the Egyptians in that quarter broke and fled in all directions, the report continues:—

> The marines followed them up for a distance of about four miles, until they came to Arabi's headquarter camp at Tel-el-Kebir. This they found standing, but evacuated, it having evidently been left in haste, as everything appeared in order. Here they were ordered to halt and occupy some of the deserted tents.

The casualties among the marines were very severe: amongst them,

> Major Strong, who was shot through the heart while most gallantly leading his fighting line up the glacis, within twenty yards of the enemy; Captain Wardell, one of the most valuable and efficient officers in the battalion, was also killed, being shot through the head close in front of the parapet, while cheering on his men.

The Naval Brigade performed its task as nobly as if the eye of Nelson himself had been fixed on every blue-jacket.

With Macpherson's brigade, they crossed the canal by a pontoon bridge at three a.m., and marched along the opposite bank to the Naval Gatling-gun Battery. These heavy pieces sank, at times, to the axle-trees in the soft sand The men, however, worked with a will, cursing, however, the authorities for giving them such clumsy guns to handle, when, with a little forethought, better machine-made guns could have been supplied to the fleet "Would the battery ever be got to the front in time for action?" was the thought of all.

"Come along, lads!" "Heave her out of the hole!" "There she goes—hurrah!" were the expressions heard ever and *anon*, muttered between their teeth as the gallant Bue-Jackets strained every nerve, and taxed their iron muscles to get their guns forward. The toil was frightful. The morning hours were pitch dark, and the sand to be traversed so soft that the seamen sank into it more than ankle-deep as they struggled along, and when they tallied on at the drag-ropes, it gave freely, affording them no efficient foothold.

Their anxiety to get on was intense; they would scarcely halt to draw breath, lest they might be too late to share in the conflict; and daylight had just begun to dawn at the flat and far horizon when a staff officer came up to inform Captain Fitzroy that he was close to the enemy's position.

Just at that moment the guns in Tel-el-Kebir, on the right of the Naval Brigade, opened fire, and the red flashes in quick succession began to streak the sable sky. The mules were lashed into their best pace. Inspired by the booming of the cannon, the Bue-Jackets strained every muscle, and got their guns on the double, but General Macpherson now ordered Captain Fitzroy to halt and reconnoitre some fields of maize on his left front.

Quickly the Bue-Jackets deployed at a swift double, with cutlasses fixed to their rifles, and swept through the reedy stalks; but nothing was there to meet or oppose them, and their battery resumed its advance. Then almost immediately the enemy's cavalry, looming through the twilight, appeared in their immediate front, and in some strength.

The guns were slewed round, and instantly brought into action. A storm of bullets, that tore up the sand and dust in clouds, swept through the Egyptian horse, and many saddles were emptied, while steed and rider went down, and, completely cowed by the leaden hail, the remainder fled on the spur.

The guns were limbered up, the mules were scourged, hands and shoulders were put to the wheels, and the brigade was soon within easy range of the enemy's works, then all garlanded with fire—there were guns in front, guns on the right and left, flashing and booming out, and a storm of rifle-shot sweeping over all.

"Action, front!" was now the order given and joyously responded to. The Gatlings were whisked round, and the horrible screwing and shrieking sound of their discharge began.

An officer wrote:—

The report of the machine-guns as they rattle away rings out clearly on the morning air. The parapets are swept. The embrasures are literally plugged with bullets. The flashes cease to come from them. The Egyptian fire in that quarter is silenced. With a cheer, the Bue-Jackets double over the dam, and dash at the parapet, only just in time to find the enemy in full retreat

That machine-gun fire was too much for them. Skulking under the parapet, they found a few poor wretches, too frightened to retire, yet willing enough to stab a man if helpless and wounded. But few wounded were found, and not a single casualty occurred among the Naval contingent

Before the grand advance of Graham's brigade, the Egyptians were flying as fast as those on the other flank before the furious rush of the Highlanders. The battle was won and practically over—won in the good old-fashioned British way, by the cold steel chiefly. If new occasions demand novel means, old occasions require the old means, the bayonet and the sword-blade. And now the only danger accruing was from the bullets of our own troops, who were firing in all directions upon the fast-flying enemy, while with loud cheers the whole line advanced in pursuit, the active Highlanders leading.

On former occasions our cavalry and artillery had been mainly conspicuous, but the Battle of Tel-el-Kebir was won by the infantry alone. The defeated foe did not preserve the smallest semblance of order, but fled, a rabble in confusion, at the top of their speed. No chance of rallying—had they been so disposed—was allowed them. The guns in the redoubts were wheeled round upon their former masters, and with amazing swiftness portions of our artillery bounded over intervening ditches and breast-works into the very heart of the position, and tore the accumulated masses of men asunder by their fire of shrapnel shells.

At the railway station two trains were suddenly crammed almost to suffocation with fugitives, and steamed away at a furious rate before our troops could reach them. Another engine, on the point of starting, was blown up by a single shell. Soon after, General Drury Lowe, with his staff, came riding up to Sir Garnet in the position, having cut across the line of retreat, where many were killed by the horse artillery fire; but immense numbers flung away their arms, and delivered themselves up as prisoners of war.

At the canal bridge Sir Garnet Wolseley dictated his orders to Generals Macpherson and Drury Lowe.

The former was to move at once with his Indian Contingent on Zagazig, and the latter, with horse and sabre, was to continue the work of totally dispersing the enemy. As he was speaking, the troops were cheering Alison and Graham, who came riding into the trenches. There it was the former, as he passed the 79th, exclaimed:—

THE HIGHLAND BRIGADE STORMING THE TRENCHES AT TEL-EL-KEBIR.

Well done, the Cameron men! Scotland will be proud of this day's work!

Straight over the battlefield, without losing a moment, went the Indian Contingent and the Seaforth Highlanders, in hot and swift pursuit, and together that afternoon they occupied Zagazig, an important town, said to contain 40,000 inhabitants, and its possession as a railway junction, where many lines converge, was certain to prove of inestimable value to future operations.

The bulk of the Cavalry Division and the Mounted Infantry, having cut through the flying masses, rode southward by the road through the desert upon Belbeis, which they occupied that evening after a brief skirmish, though the guns and heavy cavalry were somewhat delayed by obstacles on the route, and from thence Drury Lowe was to push on to Cairo.

Arabi escaped our cavalry by galloping off alone from the field of battle upon a fleet Arab horse.

After Captain Fitzroy had led the Naval Brigade into the main works of the enemy, the halt was sounded. Then Admiral Beauchamp Seymour, with his staff, came up, and, addressing the officers and men, complimented them on their gallantry, and ordered them to push on to Zagazig. They gave their admiral a hearty cheer, and, after cooking a meal most methodically amid the dying and the dead, started on their march to Zagazig. They bivouacked for the night six miles from that place, which they entered on the 14th of September.

When the Brigade of Guards came in, they joined Alison's Highland regiments, and made themselves comfortable for a few hours in the abandoned tents which had belonged to the Egyptians.

Brigadier General Nugent, R.E., remained during the action in command of the left at Kassassin to cover the rear of the army operations in his immediate front, and to protect that position, with all its stores and depots, from any possible attack made by the enemy's column at Salahieh; and he rejoined the headquarter force in the evening at Tel-el-Kebir, after carrying out the orders he had received.

Sir Garnet, in his despatch on the battle, says:—

In the removal of the wounded on the 13th and 14th instant to Ismailia, the canal boat service, worked by the Royal Navy, under Commander Moore, R.N., did most excellent work, and the army is deeply indebted to that officer, and to those under his command, for the aid he afforded the wounded, and the satisfactory manner in which he moved a large number of them to Ismailia.

The despatches and casualty lists were sent home in charge of Major George FitzGeorge, of the 20th Hussars, a member of Sir Garnet's personal staff. The casualties were most numerous in the Highland regiments, on whom the brunt of the fighting fell, as the following lists attest;—

Staff.—Two officers wounded.

2nd Battalion Grenadier Guards.—One non-commissioned officer and one man killed; one officer and nine men wounded.

2nd Battalion Coldstream Guards.—One officer and seven non-commissioned officers and men wounded.

1st Battalion Scots Guards.—Four non-commissioned officers and men wounded.

2nd Battalion Royal Irish.—One officer, one non-commissioned officer, and one private killed; two officers and seventeen men wounded.

Royal Marine Light Infantry.—Two officers and three non-commissioned officers and men killed; one officer and fifty-three non-commissioned officers and men wounded.

2nd Battalion York and Lancaster.—Twelve non-commissioned officers and men wounded.

1st Battalion Royal Irish Fusiliers.—Two non-commissioned officers and men killed; thirty-four non-commissioned officers and men wounded; three missing.

19th Hussars.—One officer wounded.

Cornwall Regiment—One officer and five non-commissioned officers and men wounded.

Royal Artillery.—Two officers and seventeen non-commissioned officers and men wounded.

Royal Highlanders.—Two officers and seven non-commissioned officers and men killed; thirty-seven non-commissioned officers and men wounded; four missing.

Gordon Highlanders.—One officer and five non-commissioned officers and men killed; one officer and twenty-nine non-commissioned officers and men wounded; four missing.

Cameron Highlanders.—Thirteen non-commissioned officers and men killed; three officers and forty-five non-commissioned officers and men wounded.

Highland Light Infantry.—Three officers and fourteen non-commissioned officers and men killed; fifty-two non-commissioned officers and men wounded; eleven missing.

Royal Rifles.—Twenty non-commissioned officers and men wounded.

Seaforth Highlanders.—One non-commissioned officer and one man killed; three non-commissioned officers and men wounded.

Native Troops.—One non-commissioned officer and one man killed; nine non-commissioned officers and men wounded.

Chaplains.—One wounded.

Total—Nine officers, forty-eight non-commissioned officers and men killed; twenty-seven officers and 353 non-commissioned officers and men wounded; twenty-two missing.

The comparative immunity of the Seaforth Highlanders is explained by the *Times* correspondent thus:—

The leading company was commanded by an ex-musketry instructor, who cautioned his men not to fire, save by word of command, and himself successively named the ranges. The consequence was their fire was so deadly that not an Egyptian dared show his head above the parapet.

The Seaforth Highlanders and the Indian Contingent afterwards considered that the share they took in the victory was not sufficiently recognised, and asserted that 700 dead bodies and thirteen captured guns were actually counted at the point where Sir Herbert Macpherson delivered his attack.

We have never seen the actual losses of the Egyptians stated, but those who have examined the field say that they were very great, and thought it marvellous that so many men could be slain in so short a time. At the bastions stormed by Alison's brigade, the correspondent of the *Standard* says:—

The enemy lay in hundreds, while only here and there a Highlander lay stretched among them, face downwards, as if shot in the act of charging.

But few of these were hit in their rush at the outer trenches; it was after these were stormed that the greater part of the casualties occurred. A few feet in front of one of the bastions he saw six men of the 74th (Highland Light Infantry) all lying in a row, heads and bayonets pointed forward, while immediately in front of these was the body of young Lieutenant Somerville, who had been leading, claymore in hand, when a volley laid them all low.

The Egyptian loss he computes at from 2,500 to 3,000, including those slain by the cavalry and horse artillery, extending over a mile beyond the position. In several places he counted from thirty to fifty lying in heaps, and they lay in long rows, where the Black Watch, getting in flank, enfiladed the lines they held against our front attack.

When advancing into the first line of entrenchments, a soldier of the Scots Guards wrote:—

Such a sight I never wish to see again. All around was strewn with dead. There were some with heads blown off, and others cut in two. It was a ghastly sight. Farther on we found hundreds of rifles, thrown down by the enemy in their flight.

The sufferings of the Egyptian wounded—as many were dying from bayonet stabs and lacerations by exploded shell, that set their cotton clothing on fire—were awful. Their cries for aid and water loaded the morning air, and many were seen to tear off their scarlet tarbooshes, and bury their bare heads frantically in the sand for coolness.

The Scripture-readers with the Highland Brigade stated that they procured water for many of them, also some large baskets of ripe peaches, of which:—

Both English and Arab got a share. As we waved the flies off the latter, we could only pat them kindly, saying, '*Allah.*' They understood our efforts to be kind. . . On the morning of the 14th, we had worship on the field of Tel-el-Kebir; we read the 128th Psalm and sang the 23rd Psalm, and prayed while many of our comrades were on all sides of us. (*Our Highlanders*, by W. Stephen.)

Among our officers who fell we may note the following;—

Major Thomas Colville, of the Highland Light Infantry (late 70th and 74th), an ensign of 1860; Captain C N. Jones, of the 2nd Battalion of the Connaught Rangers (94th), attached to the Royal Irish as a volunteer; Major Harford Strong, of the Portsmouth Division of

Royal Marine Light Infantry; and Captain Wardell, of the same regiment, who had played a considerable part in the capture of two Krupp guns from the enemy in front of Kassassin. Lieutenant Luke, who was the subaltern of his company, avenged this gallant officer's death a few moments after he fell. Watching the Egyptian who shot him, he closed in, and by one stroke he severed his head from his body. Captain Wardell's sword and other relics of him were brought to England for his widow, in custody of his servant.

Lieutenants Graham-Stirling and J. G. MacNeill, who fell in front of the Black Watch, were both very young officers. The former was shot on the summit of the parapet while gallantly leading on his company. The latter had joined his regiment from the militia only on the 29th of the previous July.

Lieutenants D. S. Kays and Louis Somerville, of the Highland Light Infantry, were also mere youths, and in the preceding July the former had been distinguishing himself more peacefully with the West of Scotland Cricket Club. Lieutenant H. G. Brooks, of the Gordon Highlanders, had been gazetted to the service in March of the previous year.

Among those reported wounded, we may note Lieutenant Allen Park (mortally), of the Black Watch, who expired on board the *Carthage*; Lieutenant-General Willis, C.B., Colonel Richardson, of the Cornwall Regiment; Colonels Balfour, of the Grenadier Guards, and Stirling, of the Coldstreams; and Lieutenant Wyatt Rawson, R.N. It was not the first time that Rawson had shed his blood for Queen and country, as he was severely wounded in the Ashantee War of 1874. He was most dangerously wounded at Tel-el-Kebir, while guiding Alison's brigade by the light of the stars. His last words to Sir Garnet Wolseley, to whom he acted as naval *aide-de-camp*, were exultant amid his agony:—

Didn't I lead them straight, general!

He expired on board H.M.S. *Carthage*, and a tablet to his memory in the Royal Garrison Church at Portsmouth bears an inscription stating that it is erected:—

As a token of affection and esteem by Lord Wolseley and the members of his personal staff.

While our troops were at Tel-el-Kebir, reposing after the fatigue and fierce excitement of the preceding night, a body of Bedouins, some thousands strong, came down at three in the afternoon upon the camp at Kassassin, expecting to find it empty, or, at least, easy to pillage. But the 50th Regiment turned speedily out, and poured several volleys into them, on which they fled at full speed, with shrieks and yells. And it was deemed that it would be necessary to take severe and active measures with these ubiquitous and wandering desert warriors, who were hovering in thousands in the vicinity of Ismailia, waiting for chances of plunder and, if possible, to loot the town.

Sir Garnet Wolseley, in his evening despatch of September 13th, estimated the guns taken at Tel-el-Kebir as numbering between fifty and sixty pieces. They eventually proved to be sixty-six, according to the report of Colonel Jones, Royal Marine Light Infantry.

LEONAUR

ALSO FROM LEONAUR
AVAILABLE IN SOFTCOVER OR HARDCOVER WITH DUST JACKET

THE FALL OF THE MOGHUL EMPIRE OF HINDUSTAN *by H. G. Keene*—By the beginning of the nineteenth century, as British and Indian armies under Lake and Wellesley dominated the scene, a little over half a century of conflict brought the Moghul Empire to its knees.

LADY SALE'S AFGHANISTAN *by Florentia Sale*—An Indomitable Victorian Lady's Account of the Retreat from Kabul During the First Afghan War.

THE CAMPAIGN OF MAGENTA AND SOLFERINO 1859 *by Harold Carmichael Wylly*—The Decisive Conflict for the Unification of Italy.

FRENCH'S CAVALRY CAMPAIGN *by J. G. Maydon*—A Special Correspondent's View of British Army Mounted Troops During the Boer War.

CAVALRY AT WATERLOO *by Sir Evelyn Wood*—British Mounted Troops During the Campaign of 1815.

THE SUBALTERN *by George Robert Gleig*—The Experiences of an Officer of the 85th Light Infantry During the Peninsular War.

NAPOLEON AT BAY, 1814 *by F. Loraine Petre*—The Campaigns to the Fall of the First Empire.

NAPOLEON AND THE CAMPAIGN OF 1806 *by Colonel Vachée*—The Napoleonic Method of Organisation and Command to the Battles of Jena & Auerstädt.

THE COMPLETE ADVENTURES IN THE CONNAUGHT RANGERS *by William Grattan*—The 88th Regiment during the Napoleonic Wars by a Serving Officer.

BUGLER AND OFFICER OF THE RIFLES *by William Green & Harry Smith*—With the 95th (Rifles) during the Peninsular & Waterloo Campaigns of the Napoleonic Wars.

NAPOLEONIC WAR STORIES *by Sir Arthur Quiller-Couch*—Tales of soldiers, spies, battles & sieges from the Peninsular & Waterloo campaingns.

CAPTAIN OF THE 95TH (RIFLES) *by Jonathan Leach*—An officer of Wellington's sharpshooters during the Peninsular, South of France and Waterloo campaigns of the Napoleonic wars.

RIFLEMAN COSTELLO *by Edward Costello*—The adventures of a soldier of the 95th (Rifles) in the Peninsular & Waterloo Campaigns of the Napoleonic wars.

LEONAUR

ALSO FROM LEONAUR
AVAILABLE IN SOFTCOVER OR HARDCOVER WITH DUST JACKET

A DIARY FROM DIXIE *by Mary Boykin Chesnut*—A Lady's Account of the Confederacy During the American Civil War

FOLLOWING THE DRUM *by Teresa Griffin Vielé*—A U. S. Infantry Officer's Wife on the Texas frontier in the Early 1850's

FOLLOWING THE GUIDON *by Elizabeth B. Custer*—The Experiences of General Custer's Wife with the U. S. 7th Cavalry.

LADIES OF LUCKNOW *by G. Harris & Adelaide Case*—The Experiences of Two British Women During the Indian Mutiny 1857. A Lady's Diary of the Siege of Lucknow by G. Harris, Day by Day at Lucknow by Adelaide Case

MARIE-LOUISE AND THE INVASION OF 1814 *by Imbert de Saint-Amand*—The Empress and the Fall of the First Empire

SAPPER DOROTHY *by Dorothy Lawrence*—The only English Woman Soldier in the Royal Engineers 51st Division, 79th Tunnelling Co. during the First World War

ARMY LETTERS FROM AN OFFICER'S WIFE 1871-1888 *by Frances M. A. Roe*—Experiences On the Western Frontier With the United States Army

NAPOLEON'S LETTERS TO JOSEPHINE *by Henry Foljambe Hall*—Correspondence of War, Politics, Family and Love 1796-1814

MEMOIRS OF SARAH DUCHESS OF MARLBOROUGH, AND OF THE COURT OF QUEEN ANNE VOLUME 1 by A. T. Thomson

MEMOIRS OF SARAH DUCHESS OF MARLBOROUGH, AND OF THE COURT OF QUEEN ANNE VOLUME 2 by A. T. Thomson

MARY PORTER GAMEWELL AND THE SIEGE OF PEKING *by A. H. Tuttle*—An American Lady's Experiences of the Boxer Uprising, China 1900

VANISHING ARIZONA *by Martha Summerhayes*—A young wife of an officer of the U.S. 8th Infantry in Apacheria during the 1870's

THE RIFLEMAN'S WIFE *by Mrs. Fitz Maurice*—*The Experiences of an Officer's Wife and Chronicles of the Old 95th During the Napoleonic Wars*

THE OATMAN GIRLS *by Royal B. Stratton*—The Capture & Captivity of Two Young American Women in the 1850's by the Apache Indians

www.ingramcontent.com/pod-product-compliance
Lightning Source LLC
Chambersburg PA
CBHW032052080426
42733CB00006B/246